P9-CMA-885

WITHDRAWN

EMORY & HENRY LIBRARY

PROPERTY POWER

BOOKS BY MARY ANNE GUITAR

Property Power:
*How to Keep the Bulldozer,
the Power Line, and the Highwaymen
Away from Your Door*

The Young Marriage

22 Famous Artists

PROPERTY POWER

How to Keep
the Bulldozer, the Power Line,
and the Highwaymen
Away from Your Door

MARY ANNE GUITAR

Doubleday & Company, Inc.
Garden City, New York
1972

For the Town of Redding

Library of Congress Catalog Card Number 71–180079
Copyright © 1972 by Mary Anne Guitar
All Rights Reserved
Printed in the United States of America

The race between education and erosion, between wisdom and waste, has not run its course . . . Each generation must deal anew with the "raiders," with the scramble to use public resources for private profit, and with the tendency to prefer short-run profits to long-run necessities. The nation's battle to preserve the common estate is far from won.

JOHN F. KENNEDY

Each town should have a park, or rather a primitive forest, of 500 or a thousand acres, where a stick should never be cut for fuel, a common possession forever, for instruction and recreation.

HENRY DAVID THOREAU

Trend is not destiny.

LEWIS MUMFORD

QD
205
.68

134320 EMORY & HENRY LIBRARY

ACKNOWLEDGMENTS

I would like to thank the many individuals mentioned in the text who corresponded with me or allowed themselves to be interviewed.

I am particularly grateful to *The New York Times* for covering significant environmental battles from coast to coast. The *Times* has been an invaluable resource.

I am also indebted to publications which specialize in environmental issues: *Audubon, Connecticut Conservation, Conservation Leader, Cry California, Earth Times, Maine Times, National Parks and Conservation Magazine, National Wildlife, Natural History, Nature Conservancy News, Smithsonian Magazine.*

I would like to thank *West* Magazine for permission to quote substantially from an article by Elinor Lenz ("Right On, Lillian") in its July 11, 1971, issue.

Contents

Preface *xi*

1 A Nice Place to Live 1
What Price Progress? . . . Homeowners Have Leverage . . .
Backyard Battles . . . Armed With Expertise . . . Eternal
Vigilance . . . You Can Stop Progress . . . The Public Won't
Be Damned . . . Environmental Equity . . . The Boosters
Recant . . . An Eye on City Hall

2 People Against Progress 32
Arousing Public Opinion . . . The Odd Coalition . . .
Putting Pressure Where It Counts . . . Thwarting "Mr.
Subdivider" . . . The Public Giveaway . . . Forming an
Emergency Committee . . . Bringing Suit . . . Legislative
Double-Cross . . . Is Nothing Sacred?

3 One Town's Triumph 59
A Case in Point . . . "Right Through My House" . . .
Eliminate the Interchange . . . The People Speak . . . The
Constructive Alternative . . . The Million-Dollar Parcel . . .
A Bitter Battle . . . The Industry Threat . . . Citizen Protest
Prevails

4   The Spoilers   87

Man-Made Destruction . . . The Environmental Imperative
. . . The Dwindling Resource . . . The Vulnerable Investment
. . . The Big-Timers in Action . . . Ripe for Development
. . . Big Money in Land . . . Industry and the Suburbs . . .
A Stiffening Resistance

5   Save the Land   111

Enlightened Self-Interest . . . Tax Inducement to Hold Land
. . . Giving an Easement . . . Buying Open Land . . . Gifts
of Land . . . Land Trusts Can Help . . . Starting a Land
Trust . . . The Dollars-and-Cents Message . . . Help for
Trusts . . . Land-Save Programs . . . Financial Facts of Life
. . . Guiding Growth . . . Develop It Properly

6   Positive Protest   148

"We Didn't Want to Alarm People" . . . Sophisticated
Infighting . . . Working for That Better Way . . . The Public
Cross-Examines . . . A Passionate Protest . . . The Basic
Questions . . . Legislative Help . . . Getting Results . . .
Some Lessons . . . Dramatize the Effects . . . Sell the Plus
. . . Touching the Power Base

7   Building Local Safeguards   181

"Who's in Charge Here, Anyway?" . . . Broad Powers . . .
A Land Inventory . . . More Than "Beautification" . . .
Conservation and Development . . . Looking Ahead . . .
Controlling Big Development . . . A Snowballing Effect . . .
People Make Plans Work

8   Getting Outside Help   214

The Missionaries . . . The Conservancy . . . Sierra and FOE
. . . Audubon Takes Action . . . The Academics . . . The
Funders . . . Legal Help . . . The Politicians . . . Public
Protectors . . . The Competent Amateur

9 Some Tough Questions 246

Economic Growth Zero? . . . Who Is to Decide? . . .
Where's the Power Coming From? . . . More Efficient Power
Distribution . . . Ecology or Jobs? . . . Property Tax
Revision . . . Where Will the People Live? . . . Suburbs vs.
the City . . . The High Price of Housing

10 Staying Power 269

The Movement's Future . . . "Bridge-Burning Acts" . . .
Sampling the "Kooks" . . . Toward a Land Ethic . . . Do
We Care Enough?

Appendices 283
Some Models 285
Bibliography: Books That Can Help 310
People Who Can Help 311
Publications That Can Help 312

Index 314

Preface

I probably wouldn't have written this book if I hadn't become intimately involved with my own battle to save a particularly beautiful piece of New England. Like so many other property owners I learned firsthand what it means to fight "progress." I found that getting the mortgage was only one small step toward security. If you wanted to keep your investment what you paid for it, your special corner of the world clean and green, you had to do battle every day.

This book is written *to* the hundreds of thousands of American homeowners whose property is threatened by the onslaught of man-made things. It tells them how they can, literally, keep the bulldozer, the power line, the highway builders away from their door.

It is written *for* the thousands of men and women who are fighting locally for the control of their environment. They are the ones who serve selflessly on town councils, planning and zoning boards, conservation commissions. They are largely self-taught in the ways of land use. They need all the help they can get, exposure to methods which have worked in other communities, strategies which they can borrow to save a green and pleasant land.

Finally, it is written *at* those on the top of the heap, the people who make corporate or governmental decisions to hoist a power line over a secluded valley, to plant industry in an unpolluted corner of the world, to run still another concrete corridor through prime residential land. I hope they get the message. Those who have been long accustomed to designing our world for their own ends no longer have a free hand.

I have dedicated my book to the Town of Redding out of appreciation. If I hadn't had the opportunity to fight as a private citizen in what has become something of a national crusade against the commercialization of the environment I could never have written about it. I know what property owners everywhere are up against because I have been there too. I know what can be done to defeat or deflect the enemy because I have learned firsthand how to fight him. I know what precautions must be taken to preserve the public estate because my town has pioneered many of them.

I think these lessons are worth passing along. That's why I wrote the book and that's why I fervently hope it will be read by everybody who cares about the land—and before it's too late.

Mary Anne Guitar
Redding, Connecticut
January 1972

PROPERTY POWER

1

A Nice Place to Live

When I was growing up in St. Joseph, Missouri, in the thirties, I took for granted its parks and open land. There was Corby Grove, Krug Park, Wyeth Hill, the scenic "boulevard system," lands given to the city by public-spirited citizens. Long before "open space" was an announced public goal, we had it. Even today, with its population of seventy-three thousand, the city has plenty of room for kids to roam, ponds for skating, hills for tobogganing, woods full of wildflowers—a generous acre of open land for every sixty people.

Back then, particularly in the Midwest, land was abundant. Setting it aside involved no great sacrifice, but it did represent the vision of a pleasant and open environment. In those days pollution was virtually nonexistent. The boulevard system was built for leisurely Sunday drives, not bumper-to-bumper traffic. The open land was there to enjoy, not exploit.

Over the years, I learned that what seemed to me to be
the norm was, in fact, something of an exception. As the
bulldozer of the postwar building boom ripped up the landscape, as population multiplied and people crowded in upon
the best land, as affluence generated pollution and waste
problems, living on the land became more nightmare than
dream come true.

You got your acre or two only to find that you sat in
the path of a power line or a superhighway, or you discovered that your neighborhood was slated for demolition
on somebody's master plan. The threat is so common that it
is becoming a national joke. *The New Yorker* ran a cover
not long ago showing a middle-aged knight on white horse,
lance at the ready, tilting against a yawning bulldozer. Man
against the machine; the absurdity of our time.

There is a greeting card—made in California—which looks
like a formal announcement and reads:

> *The Freeway Planning Commission*
> *announces that construction will begin*
> *immediately on an underpass and interchange*
> *right where your house is sitting.*
> *Wishing to avoid imposition to you,*
> *the Commission voted to move*
> *your house to Alberta, Canada,*
> *to avoid placing an off-ramp*
> *through your bathroom.*

Of course, it's no joke to anybody who sits in the way of
progress. If you've just finished an addition to your house
only to discover that the highway department plans to

straighten a curve and take part of your land, putting that new bedroom and bath uncomfortably close to traffic, you don't feel much like laughing. Or, suppose you've built your dream house for retirement in a secluded valley far enough from civilization to make you feel safe. One day a utility company announces that it is going to run a giant power line right across your view. And, to compound the indignity, at right angles to your house as well so you won't be able to miss it. It's no joke when you've sunk your savings in a house which, if the power line goes forward, is going to be worth a lot less than you have invested.

There is ample cause for outrage.

When the spoilers aren't busy destroying natural beauty, they are desecrating it with man-made insults. Nothing is sacred. What's wrong with planting an ugly and potentially dangerous oil depot in the middle of a lovely harbor? Or, stringing a high-tension line on monstrous utility poles across a scenic reservoir? Or, slapping a freeway interchange where the natural folds of the hills create a remarkably pastoral scene?

Looking out on what was once a green and pleasant valley, you can see the gravel miners at work, stripping the landscape with an offensive machine, appropriately named "the pay-loader." The gravel is worth cold cash to them. Never mind what the view had been worth to you and your neighbors. The men who pushed this project through will make a buck off the deal, then move on to attack another piece of land. But, what happens to the value of your property when it perches on the edge of a newly carved-out no man's land?

What Price Progress?

Most of us simply want to live on the land, take care of it and love it. But, we have come to realize that there is another group for whom land is purely and simply a commodity. It is there to be drained, filled, mined, endlessly built upon until not a scrap of green is left. The confrontation betwen the two groups, homeowner and entrepreneur, has become a daily drama in most American communities as land grows scarce and competition for it intensifies. There are few towns left, especially in the more settled areas of this country, which do not lie under the sword of "progress."

People used to take security for granted when they bought property. A place of your own meant you were dug in and nobody could uproot you. No longer. You must fight an incessant delaying action against those who want to turn a profit on your land.

No one is exempt from the threat of a jetport within earshot, from highway tentacles which reach out into once-remote areas, from the rapacious bulldozer eating up the countryside. The horrible examples are there in abundance, but there is a hopeful side to the story. Property owners are striking back. There is a genuine, increasingly successful, homeowner's revolt against raw, crude "progress." No longer are we resigned to the rape of the landscape. No longer are we willing to be mowed down by the machine.

We are discovering that we too have power—property power.

If you own land you are entitled to a say in how your community will develop. That's property power.

You are a part-owner of the block you live on, your neighborhood, your town, and you can use your equity as a lever to influence change.

Being a landowner you are a taxpayer and this carries weight. If you're paying the bills in town surely you have a right to make judgments about the way the common estate is managed. If you don't like the way the money is spent you can band with other taxpayers and vote the budget up or down.

Property power means voting for or against public officials. You can turn the rascals out if they are not sufficiently attuned to the public interest.

Property power is saying no. ("We're the people of Mayfield and we don't want it," is the way one community voiced its objection to a proposed major development scheme.)

Property power is taking your case to court, bringing a citizens' suit when the environment is threatened. Since 1965 the courts have recognized the rights of private citizens to sue when natural resources are endangered. In this short time, dozens of suits have given environmentalists more legal leverage, more tactical advantage in the courts.

Michigan law professor Joseph L. Sax believes that legal action is the most effective way for the average citizen to have a voice in decision-making. His fine book *Defending the Environment* is a lawyer's brief for more environmental suits to stop the raiders in their tracks, block officialdom's shortsighted plans for the public estate.

The lawsuit is an effective weapon. It is being used increasingly by conservationists to block "progress." But, we should be pulling other levers of power long before the courtroom stage is reached.

Sax recognizes this: "Talking about the prospects for environmental litigation makes most people very uncomfortable. 'A lawsuit over every marsh!' they ask. 'We must do better than that.'"

We can do better if we will only use property power where it does the most good—at the local level.

Homeowners Have Leverage

Property power means electing officials who are responsive to the environmental crisis. And riding the old-timers until they do right by the public interest.

It means taxpayer petitions calling for hearings to air policy plans before they become final, referendums to decide such far-reaching questions as buying land for open space.

It means property owners with a respect for the land serving on planning and zoning commissions where the small decisions on land use ultimately add up to a community pattern of decent development.

It means homeowners insisting on ordinances to protect the landscape from gravel mining, dig and fill.

It means taking a firm stand against the exploiters, against the notion that land is money in the bank and that a man has the right to use his land any way he likes for his own profit.

Property power is immensely enhanced when two or more homeowners join together to press their cause. An entire neighborhood united against the interests carries more weight than a single taxpayer. Environmental activists realize this.

There are so many ad hoc groups springing up all over the country—TREE (Toward Restoring Earth's Environment), ACUTE (Active Citizens Urging Transmission Line Ecology), FOE (Friends of Earth)—that we're running out of acronyms.

There is a strong tide running toward decentralization, neighborhood control, people power. James Reston has remarked on "the frontier instinct of concerned citizens at the local level," saying: "There is much more of this personal and community action to deal with the social problems of America than is generally realized." In another column he questions the prevailing image of the helpless American who is numbered and computerized into anonymity and reminds us that there is another American who is taking hold of his life and shaping circumstances to his own design. "Here and there the people are stirring and organizing to regain their sovereignty. Not since the days of the New Deal in America has there been so much insistent questioning of the institutions and purposes of America as there is now, and not without evidence of progress either . . . citizens' groups are forming to protect the environment of their communities, to challenge the assumptions and priorities of their elected officials, to defend the average consumer from the commercial gougers, and to work in many other ways for the improvement of American life."

Reston is commenting on a growing tendency in American life to create new institutions when the old ones fail, to bypass conventional avenues of help. Neighborhood groups, organized for emergency action, find they have more power than they ever did through orthodox political structure. Once they do form a "Concerned Citizens" coalition the politicans will respond. Over a hundred civic organizations rallied to save Breezy Point in New York's Rockaways when the word went out.

The sophisticated environmental infighter knows that he must do more than press legislators to pass laws and write bills. Local enforcement is where the testing comes.

Some time ago John Cole, editor of *Maine Times*, decided that his crusading conversation-minded paper was naïve in thinking that State House action could preserve the environment. He cited several admirable laws which were written to protect wetlands, put controls on the oil industry, mining interests, highwaymen but which have been undercut by the courts or simply ignored by those responsible for enforcing the law. He points out, quite properly, that the average citizen is pleased to hear about progressive lawmaking and, believing that the job is being done, sits back to relax. Says Cole, "the legislature . . . provides the illusion of action when, in actuality, no action has been taken." If the lawmakers had done nothing at least the people would still believe there was a threat.

"Where, then, can those who would save the state carry their battle? On what field, or fields, can the fight for environmental sanity be effectively fought?"

Cole believes "creative citizen action . . . offers the least expensive, most effective area for energy concentration. It involves local harassment (on an innovative, nonviolent level), local ordinances, local protest, and local counter-action. Essentially, it means that instead of looking to the legislators for statewide solutions to the environmental crisis, the communities of Maine are going to have to wrestle with the issues in their own backyard.

"We've been working from the top down when all the time we should have been working from the grass roots up."

Backyard Battles

A vocal grass roots movement for environmental preservation is stirring in communities across the land. Individuals who had once felt powerless to stop the rape of the landscape have gained courage from a string of victories won by organized conservation groups.

We've saved the redwoods and the Grand Canyon, halted jetports and canals and pipelines. The President's Council on Environmental Quality has responded to citizen protest and blown the whistle on projects which would once have slid through unquestioned. At the end of last year the Council demanded proof from the Army Corps of Engineers that the controversial Tocks Island Dam would not have a damaging environmental impact. Plans for construction were halted while the engineers set about proving their case.

Governor Nelson Rockefeller of New York has learned the hard way about "property power." In November 1971 he admitted defeat in his six-year battle to build a Hudson River Expressway. Citizen groups, homeowners, environmentalists had fought the plan with publicity, petitions, and a court case which went all the way to the Supreme Court of the United States. "The people have spoken," Rockefeller said. "I therefore regard the proposed Hudson River Expressway and the five alternative routes as a dead issue. They will not be built."

Earlier that month, Rockefeller had been soundly trounced on a proposed $2.5 billion transportation bond issue. Analysts attributed its defeat to a growing public conviction that highways were overbuilt while mass transit suffered. Rockefeller himself acknowledged that "peoples' priorities are changing." Indeed they are.

At the same time that New Yorkers voted down the transportation bond issue, New Jersey voted in an $80 million Green Acres bond issue. The money would be used to buy up open land. Voters apparently sensed the urgency of the issue, which was spelled out for them by the state's Open Space Policy Commission. The Commission warned that eighty acres of open land disappeared in New Jersey every day and unless something was done the state would "be smeared with a sprawling pattern of housing and industrial and commercial development."

The professional advocates of environmental protection—Ralph Nader, Friends of Earth, Sierra, Audubon, the Environmental Defense Fund—are fighting the big battles every day. But, it will be up to every one of us to look after our own backyard. Perhaps the small skirmishes will matter most in the long run. Winning the interminable everyday battle against the bulldozer, the power line, the highwaymen, community by community, can mean the difference between a country which is green and pleasant and one which has been mined and exploited and chewed to death.

As Congressman John D. Dingell (Michigan) puts it: "The sizzling sixties will be remembered by conservationists for the battles they won and lost over the awe-inspiring great wild places . . . However, a more subtle, perhaps more important, battle is taking shape as we move into the seventies. There is little doubt that this decade will be devoted to the problems of the environment. But, for the first time, the problems of air, water, and land pollution will be placed on everyone's doorstep. It is here, within the environs of our own neighborhoods, that the new fight will occur."

Increasingly, Americans are unwilling to pay the price of a degraded environment for "progress." They want to keep what they've got.

"The most precious thing in America is going to be a nice place to live." That's not a doomsday conservationist speaking but William T. White, who is Commissioner of Commerce for the State of Nevada and who fully appreciates the dollars-and-cents value of an unspoiled landscape. Right now, Nevada is the fastest-growing state in the Union because it can offer new settlers plenty of elbow room. "I've always had the urge to get back to a place where I could take a walk and be by myself," said a refugee from California. Nevada suits him fine. It is still green and open and it has a fair chance of staying that way. Other states are not so lucky.

Once there was land enough to go around, plenty of room to make mistakes. The spoilers moved on when they had had their fill. Now they must work and rework the same territory. Inevitably that means disturbing people and when that happens the people fight back.

The headlines tell the story: "Hudson Expressway Foes Gain Point in High Court"; "800 Swamp Wetland Hearing"; "West Virginians in Land Dispute—Seek to Stop a Power Plant and Army Plan for Dam"; "Norwalk Conservation Association Achieving Its Purpose Island by Island"; "Lumbermen vs. Conservationists in Fight Over Thicket in Texas"; "Opponents of L.I. Nuclear Plant Succeed in Delaying it a Year"; "Judge Halts Building of Coast Freeway"; "Bay Expansion of La Guardia Airport Killed."

I know from firsthand experience what can be done and how to go about doing it. My neighbors and I have fought our battles against a string of threats which would have destroyed our quiet corner of the world and we've won a good share of them. We defeated a state highway proposal to put a major interchange at the foot of our lightly traveled country road and turn it into an east-west traffic monster. We've won out against a coalition of commercial interests that tried to grab the last big tract of land in town for major development. (The town bought it for open space.) We've fought the Connecticut Light and Power Company to a standstill on their proposed power line which would have scarred our lovely countryside.

It has been a long, costly, unremitting battle, but worth it. Our town still looks much as it did when I bought my own piece of land in the mid-fifties.

I picked Redding, Connecticut, because it was unscarred, relatively undeveloped, and off the beaten track. Some sixty miles from New York City, it looked rural, not exurban. The cynics liked to remind us—and still do—that Redding stood smack in the middle of expanding megalopolis, that it would be no time at all before it would be sewered and paved and streetlighted, so, rather apologetically, we changed rural to "semirural." Lately, we've been calling what we have "country atmosphere," recognizing all the while that this sounds a bit synthetic, like one of those come-on real estate ads. In point of fact, we do have the atmosphere because we have preserved the deep country with its open fields, wooded ridges, clear-running brooks. We're the only town around that hasn't been ordered to "abate pollution." We've successfully fought "progress."

Armed With Expertise

This achievement came about because people banded together in a common cause—preserving the environment they knew and loved. We used every trick in the book, becoming quasi-experts on arcane planning and zoning and sanitation techniques. Who, by choice, wants to be trained to build a curtain drain or to estimate the seepage rate on hardpan, or understand the difference between Charlton and Paxton soils? Yet, we found that we had to develop some expertise if only to ask the right questions. One of my power-line pals expressed the exhaustion we have all felt during these lengthy battles when he said, "Last year when we were fighting the zoning change I would wake up in the night repeating *'amicus curiae'* to myself. This year it's the power line and I dream about ozone and corona effect."

We've taken time away from families and jobs to carry on the endless chore of keeping the plunderers off our land. The sacrifice is often financial because you can't carry on a full-time job and a crusade at the same time. "I used to be in photography," said one free-lancer who is working hard to defeat a commercial project which threatens his neighborhood. "Now, I'm in sewer prevention work."

It sometimes seems that there is no time left to enjoy the hard-won open space. Instead of sitting on the lawn in the evening, breathing clean, fresh air, you are closeted in a stuffy hearing room trying to outwit those who have designs on your town. Instead of a day in the garden, you're driving around town filling petitions for a referendum on buying open space.

"A lot of it would make me laugh," says a young property owner I have come to know because of his battle to save a high tract on the Hudson from massive development. "But, you can't laugh when it has to do with land and how the rest of your life is going to be spent."

What keeps us going, keeps us hopeful, and therefore successful is a sense that history is on our side. The "bad guys," with their oil slicks, strip mining, slash cutting, bring home the absurdity of raw, crude progress every time somebody prints a picture of the damage they've done.

The excesses of the past have turned many Americans against a growth philosophy which finds anything and everything expendable—whether it is people, landmarks, landscape. Speaking against a proposed utility line which would be located in a mile-wide corridor ripping its way for seventy miles down the State of Connecticut, endangering the scenic and historic assets of eleven towns in its path, playwright Arthur Miller expressed the doubts many of us have about so-called "progress."

"I am sure," he said, "that the businessmen and engineers of the power industry who have designed this project believe that it represents progress.

"Progress not only for the power business but for the people of this state as well. I am equally sure that none of these men is against beauty. So the question, I think, is how much landscape you are ready to destroy for how much progress . . .

"I think this is the most beautiful part of the world I have seen. And it would take an awful lot of progress to make me believe that what I see ought to be destroyed in order to bring that progress about . . .

"It is bad enough to see the ruin of beauty when the life of the people make it necessary. But, it is unpardonable when it is done because not enough time and money and passion went into its avoidance."

What Miller was suggesting, and millions of property owners would agree with him, was that nobody has the right to rip through a natural community resource without examining every possible alternative.

Eternal Vigilance

Property owners are learning the hard way that they must be eternally vigilant, nosy about official plans, irreverent and critical when it comes to accepting professional judgments on "need." They can never afford to turn their back, leave the fort unmanned because any agency bent on appropriating land keeps its strategy secret until the groundwork is laid for the "take."

No one is more vulnerable to attack than the absentee owner of the second home, and his numbers increase every year. Bought for vacation living now and possible retirement later, second homes number a million and a half and are steadily multiplying. The owner shows up in summer or for ski weekends, but he cannot fly in for town meetings or special decision-making sessions. His interests are left unprotected when he isn't there. He has to trust local government and a friend or two among the year-rounders to alert him when a vote is coming up.

Thanks to a sharp-eyed Maine property owner a tiny legal notice buried in the December 5, 1970, edition of the Biddeford-Saco (Maine) *Journal* did not slip by unnoticed. It announced that the Saco Planning Board would consider rezoning for commercial purposes a lovely stretch of residentially zoned beach front. A sleepy summer colony could, if the rezoning were approved, be wide open for motels, high-rises, hotdog stands.

Summer residents were alerted to come for the hearing by the various associations which had formed some years ago to protect beach property. The Kinney Shores Association, Ferry Beach Association, Bay View Association engaged lawyers to represent them and the confrontation was on.

Some hundred and fifty furious property owners turned up at the hearing. They brought tape recorders and secretaries armed with pads and pencils so the record would be clear.

One lawyer who owns three lots on the beach voiced the views of the crowd: "It's too bad people can't buy property and then be able to depend on existing zoning codes. Who is behind this deal? I think the board should know. And I think the people should be advised of the planning board's decision or recommendation instead of giving it to the council in secret."

Saco's mayor, who is also a residential, commercial, and industrial real estate broker, later told the *Maine Times* that it was "no special program and nobody had pushed for it." Next, he told the paper the plan had been decided verbally at a meeting between the City Council and Planning Board. Finally, he credited the proposed change to a 1967 comprehensive municipal development plan prepared by a consultant.

When the consultant was asked about the rezoning, he sent *Maine Times* a copy of his comprehensive plan, which showed no such change, "absolutely no provision for commercial development." The consultant added, "I feel these recommendations would be hard to misinterpret . . . Since the city officials of Saco seem to be misinformed, we thought you might be able to set the record straight."

The hundred and fifty part-time residents who attended the hearing were outspokenly against the rezoning and even more outraged at the mystery surrounding the proposal. A hand vote showed that not one person was in favor of the change. Even the mayor conceded, "from what I hear of the public meeting the other night, the council will be against it."

One wonders what might have happened if somebody hadn't seen the legal notice, if the summer people hadn't turned up in force, hadn't protested. Would a change sanctioned by no official body of the town, one which went against the town's own plan of development, have slipped through?

Property owners everywhere, whether they are on the scene or not, must know that they can't take an unchanging landscape for granted. Someone has designs on it. This is particularly true in the cities, where planners and profiteers are forever reworking a meager supply of space for their own benefit.

You Can Stop Progress

Ten years ago, even five, nobody would have given odds on our power to stop the giants in their tracks as they strode across the countryside taking what they wanted. Everybody "knew" that you couldn't stop progress, that growth was good, that that's the way it is, somebody always has to get hurt. Today a genuine alarm at the national drift toward environmental disaster has put man in the driver's seat and the machine has been stalled—at least temporarily—while we stop to consider what we're giving up in the name of progress.

The citizen activists are having success because they are speaking up, frequently loud and clear, against losing precious open land, against those who would foul the water and air. No longer can the giants operate discreetly in the back room. Their trespasses are likely to land them on the front page when their victims sense what's going on.

In the late spring of 1971, New Yorkers began to hear rumors that the highwaymen were going to tear down the scenic West Side Drive and replace it with an eight-lane truck and car corridor. Sections of Riverside Park would be taken for the project. With the encouragement of Governor Nelson Rockefeller, bills to make the rebuilding possible were slipped into the legislature in its closing sessions. There was little publicity until the West Side erupted in protest. An ad taken by a group calling itself "Save Riverside Park" expressed the outrage residents of the area felt when plans for the park take were finally discovered. The ad was an open letter "To the Governor and Legislators of the State of New York and To the Mayor of the City of New York" and is a splendid example of the kind of outrage the environmentalists are capable of mustering:

**NO,
DAMMIT.
YOU MUST NOT DESTROY
RIVERSIDE PARK FOR
AN 8-LANE HIGHWAY.**

What madness is this?

This week the State Legislature will vote on an unannounced bill which will create a monstrous flow of vehicles from Canal Street to the George Washington Bridge. Great for trucks. But do the people want it? No, Damn it.

You say you will recreate parts of Riverside Park after the highway is completed. But how many years will that be? The children who play in our park today will be all grown up. The old men who rest in our park today will be dead. And no matter how talented, can anyone recreate an eighty-year-old tree or glacial rock? No, Damn it.

We need less noise and air pollution in this city, not more highways. We need fewer cars in this city, not more highways. We need green moments in this city, not highways. We need to think of people, not highways.

Progress that diminishes people is not progress.

The ad was planned for Monday, the day the legislature would consider the transportation bond issue and decide on the bill to rebuild the West Side Highway. Opponents of the project held a rally over the weekend and made sure their legislators were there. Assemblyman Albert H. Blumenthal responded admirably, announcing at the rally his opposition to the project. "If to build a highway you have to destroy the park then let the highway fall down. Don't believe people who tell you they will put back the park. Don't let them take a blade of grass because once they do, your kids and mine will never use the park."

Blumenthal himself had heard about the park take only

two weeks earlier. At that time he told some of the young community activists of the danger. One of them, Bob Goodman, a lawyer and president of a West Side political club, lost no time in alerting the community. "That night we started our mimeograph machines rolling! We called all our contacts in buildings on the West Side, and we passed out leaflets for an emergency meeting to be held Wednesday night at the club."

Some hundred and fifty people turned up at the meeting. "The response was phenomenal," says Goodman. They had little more than a week to plan the rally, a week to circulate petitions against the bill, raise money for the ad, ring doorbells, and pressure legislators. By the weekend they had more than sixteen thousand signatures opposing the park take. And, the rally was a conspicuous success.

Goodman explains why: "The park is really an emotional issue. It's right there in front of you. It's not like the government is doing something in Southeast Asia. The park is right outside your window."

Another resident of the area volunteered, "They couldn't have picked a worse time to start talking about destroying the park. It's so beautiful now and people are really starting to use it in the spring."

Even before the rally ended, rumors flew that the bill had already been amended to avoid defeat. Sure enough, the Tuesday *New York Times* reported that the legislators had substantially altered the plan "to rebuild the West Side Highway into an eight-lane road with truck traffic." Riverside Park would not be touched and the bill ordered the study of an alternate truck route to run on the other side of the river.

The Public Won't Be Damned

In New York City, governmental agencies seem bent on competing with one another in their drive to destroy the parks by erosion and theft. Precious scraps of green are viewed only as vacant land by elected officials, who have no qualms about utilizing them for subways, loading areas, or buildings. The City Planning Department recently proposed dipping into Crotona Park's 148 acres for land to accommodate new housing and the Board of Education asked permission to put a high school in the northern section of the park. Nobody was surprised at the attempted land grab, but what did surprise those who tried it was the immediate and vocal outrage expressed by citizens of the area.

Herschel Post, writing in *New York* Magazine, reported that residents of the area suggested "that tactics more commonly associated with housing, school or welfare disputes might soon be employed in defense—of all things—of a park. After all, park encroachment has traditionally been a 'white shoe' issue, an intellectual tilting match where venom alternated with wit, but wounds never seemed to bleed."

True, any incursion into park land was once viewed with alarm only by those cherished little old ladies in tennis shoes. But, that was before land became scarce and scraps of green so precious. We recognize, at long last, that an open environment protects and enhances property values. We know now that we will have to fight a long and exhausting battle with "the interests" if the great majority of people are to have any elbow room at all.

The issue is simply this. Do the residents, the property

owners, the shareholders in the community stock have a voice in how their common lands will be used? The answer must be yes. And, that answer is being hurled at the spoilers from coast to coast as beleaguered property owners band together to fight for their personal stake in the land. They are winning, too. Citizens, plain, ordinary men and women, have defeated those who sought to ram their projects through and the public be damned.

In a landmark decision New York State Supreme Court Justice Joseph P. Hawkins ruled against a builders' petition to overturn a local zoning ordinance. The builder had sued the town of Wappinger's building inspector and zoning administrator because he would not issue building permits for 342 apartment units in an area which was zoned for one-family residential use.

Joseph E. Ludewig, the building inspector, had denied the permits because he said the apartments would put a burden on the area's water and sewage capabilities.

In ruling against the builder Justice Hawkins took note of the environmental impact of the proposed apartments: "Respecting ecology as a new factor, it appears that the time has come—if, indeed, it has not already irretrievably passed—for the courts, as it were, to take 'ecological notice' in zoning matters . . . The definition of public health, safety, and welfare surely must now be broadened to include and to provide for these belated recognized threats and hazards to the public weal. The town's decision to forego what undoubtedly would be substantial additional tax revenue would appear to constitute a recognition that it as well as an owner must subordinate immediate to long-term interest."

Citizen groups have found that they have assumed far more responsibility than they bargained for when they set out to be stewards of the environment. The Southbury (Connecticut) Clean Water Task Force, to take just one example, had its hands full one month when a bulldozer was pushing silt into the Pomperaug River, raw sewage was being pumped into the Housatonic River and there were reports that trash was being used to "beautify" a state boat-launching ramp on Lake Zoar.

Still, participatory democracy has its attractions, not the least of which is some kind of control over your own air, water, and land use.

Politicians who might like to put people into the planning for a little democratic window dressing have learned that once people do get into the driver's seat they want to drive.

New York City has sixty-two "community planning boards," panels made up of citizens appointed by their borough presidents to review actions affecting their neighborhoods. They were established as long ago as 1963, but their power dramatically surged in 1970. At that time the City Council passed a law which required the City Planning Commission to notify local boards before making decisions on matters affecting them.

The community boards have power in direct ratio to the influence and tenacity and professional capabilities of their members. When they succeed in directing the decision-makers they feel a sense of power that leads to more victories. The Brooklyn Community Board 13 fought a six-month battle in 1970 to save several blocks of private houses slated to be scrapped in favor of an industrial park. The compromise they suggested, to leave the residential area alone and put industry in an area already used for that purpose, was accepted. Seems obvious, doesn't it? At least to anyone who is also a homeowner with sympathy for his fellow citizen/taxpayer. But to planners who view projects from on high and move building blocks around at will without thinking of the humans who inhabit them, this would have been no consideration.

Community Board 8 serves New York's Upper East Side and its members are sophisticated in the ways of bureaucracy and adept at blocking projects which offend them. *The New York Times* describes them as "well-connected with the city's political and administratve apparatus."

Their chairman, William J. Diamond, is not only a skilled lawyer, but, as a former city official, is practiced in the ways of City Hall. Not long ago the Planning Commission presented plans for a giant shopping complex which would drastically alter Diamond's neighborhood. It would, in his words, develop "another crosstown canyon of high-rise buildings. We want to maintain the present mixture of residences with small neighborhood retail outlets."

Board 8 is working hard to preserve the ethnic mix of the neighborhood and keep it from being high-pressured into a sterile high-rise building boom. They have pushed the Planning Commission into limiting high-rise construction to the north-south avenues, thereby saving the quiet streets from invasion.

The fight to keep neighborhoods clean and green is being waged in the city as well as the country, in crowded urban centers and out in the deep country where you might suppose no threat could possibly exist. When property values are jeopardized, people mobilize for action, even those who commonly sit back and let others do their fighting for them.

Environmental Equity

To take nothing away from the crusade, it must be said that it is fueled by economic necessity as much as by moral fervor. After all, when you've scraped together a down payment, mortgaged yourself for most of your life, you have a selfish interest in what happens to your property values. Anyone who buys a piece of land is buying a piece of the community as well. He has an undivided interest in the whole. This is his environmental equity. No wonder he cares when common green space disappears, smoke and noise fill the air, and traffic pounds down country roads or clogs his street. What goes down the drain is not just a lovely little scene, but his own investment. He's not being sentimental about the landscape, but hard-boiled about his own self-interest.

Arthur Miller made this point when he reminded the Connecticut Light and Power Company that they were, in fact, taking money from the pockets of hundreds of property owners by reducing the value of their property with a proposed power line which would be visible for miles.

"We do not mine coal in Connecticut, or gold or silver; one of our realest and most valuable resources is that intangible feeling of well-being as we look out on an undefiled woodland or forest unmarked by steel girders.

"There are scores of towns along the pathway of this project whose basic resource is purely and simply the view, townships populated by families who have paid their good money for a piece of land where they can walk with a bit of beauty.

"Those towns are going to have to pay a price for this surgical scar across their landscape, a price in lowered land values. So a wider viewpoint is not merely a poetic idea but a question of dollars and cents, and it doesn't affect merely the privileged rich, but everyone who owns a piece of ground, or hopes to."

The battle has been joined by those who cry "you can't stop progress" and those who mean to because they prefer a livable environment to what passes for progress these days. Increasingly, property owners are claiming rights that were always theirs, but went by default. They want to have a say in the decision-making. They are discovering when they speak up they do have influence. No one has more of it than the suburbanite. His numbers are growing at an astounding rate as Americans move out of the city in search of the good life. The suburbanite represents the largest single group in America, outnumbering both rural and urban dwellers. He is a considerable political force, one to be reckoned with not only by office-seekers, but by entrenched interests on all levels. If his community is endangered, he can use property power to block or reverse decisions made by special-interest groups.

He is not the stereotype suburbanite—gray-flanneled, martini-drinking, uncommitted mobile man. A Lou Harris poll taken recently for *Time* Magazine uncovered a sturdier breed in the suburbs. More than half have lived more than ten years in their community and take pride in it. Said *Time:* "the Harris survey points to a high incidence of civic concern . . . Suburbia may never re-create the New England town meeting, but it could be the locus of a new localism that will succeed in allowing its citizens to reassert some control over their lives, and their governments, to create a fresh sense of community and roots across the land."

This is more than a pious hope. The mood of the country has changed in the last few years, swinging from frustration and apathy to the hopefulness expressed in Earth Day celebrations. We have had it with destruction. An environmental conscience is developing and this, of course, makes it easier to fight those who want to muck up the landscape for personal profit.

The Boosters Recant

One hopeful sign is a new awareness that growth in and of itself is not always a blessing. Most states have a Department of Economic Development whose job it is to boost growth and create more building, more commerce and industry. But there are signs of a welcome change. Oregon's Department of Economic Development recently revised the name of its publication *Grow With Oregon* to *Oregon Quality*. The change is significant. Oregon's Governor Tom McCall tells people, "Come and visit us again and again. But for heaven's sake, don't come here to live."

Delaware recently passed a law which puts its 125-mile ocean, bay, and river coastline off limits to heavy industry. Governor Russell W. Peterson was told by federal officials, "You are interfering with the prosperity and security of America." His answer is that the unregulated cycle of industrialization must be broken. He fears both the pollution that industry might bring and an increased population.

Florida, long known for its trumpeting boosterism, is going

through what might be called antigrowth pains, trying to balance resources against people. Last spring State Senate President Jerry Thomas said, "Florida no longer desires to be known as the fastest-growing state in the union. We have our hands full taking care of over 6.8 million permanent residents without encouraging more."

In California the Los Angeles Planning Commission proposed drastically revising its zoning laws—upwards—to cut the future population to five million people instead of a projected ten million.

Commenting on these and other examples of altered attitude, *The New York Times* commented:

"These developments could indicate the beginning of a new trend toward public officials and planners. In small, but growing numbers, they are challenging the gospel of unlimited, uncontrolled expansion. Bigger, they are saying, is not always better . . .

"On a deeper level, the trend reflects a questioning of some basic values. In the past, progress has always been defined as growth. As one political scientist said, 'America always has to be the biggest, the best, the tallest, the fastest.'

"But several months ago, a writer in the San Jose *Mercury News* could say, 'In our times, progress could mean a step backward, a pause to find a straighter path.'"

Economically depressed areas have been considered fair game for new development, even the environmentally suspect project, if it brought jobs. Yet, when Governor Nelson Rockefeller proposed putting a jetport in sleepy little Newburgh, New York, there was an instant outcry. It came not just from the preservationists and homeowners whom would be directly affected but from legislators and businessmen. Even the president of the Newburgh Chamber of Commerce denounced the plan. "We can see through all of this nonsense about the jetport providing jobs," he said. "For years, we have been seeking quality jobs in this area. But this won't provide them. Some of our residents will get jobs as baggage handlers and custard stand waiters, I suppose. But the professional jobs— the pilots, the traffic controllers—these will be filled by qualified people who will come up from New York."

You might expect the builders in the area to welcome construction the jetport would surely create. But, one woman whose husband's plumbing business would doubtless boom wasn't sure she wanted it. "What good is it? What about the quality of life? My boy keeps asking me what my generation is doing to his and I don't know what to tell him. I don't see why we can't keep some beauty for the future."

Even the director of the Chamber of Commerce held back. "A jetport here is like the Trojan horse. It looks great till you get inside."

The real horrors of instant growth can be seen all over California, which was a land grabber's paradise. Consider the grisly case of San Jose.

Twenty years ago San Jose had a population of 95,000. Today, it is bursting at the seams with 436,000 which makes it, according to *Newsweek,* "perhaps the country's fastest growing boom town." It is plagued with double sessions in the schools, has virtually no parkland or open space. Residents trace their problems to the misguided "vision" of their city manager and a group of contractors, developers, and real estate men who became known as the "Book-of-the-Month-Club" because they met regularly to talk acquisitions.

The city has had grave second thoughts about the ad-

vantages of "growth for growth's sake." A new breed of local
officials more concerned with the environment has been
elected. "We've got to start thinking about preserving the
natural qualities that make this area so desirable," says one.
There isn't much left to save in San Jose, but its history
should serve as an object lesson. The city's planning director says, sadly, "They thought they could have the best of
both worlds. But they had to destroy one to build the other."

An Eye on City Hall

The lesson, taught here and elsewhere, is pretty obvious.
If you want to live in a decent environment you're going to
have to pay a price. You must put restraints on growth. You
must involve yourself in local politics and planning. You
can't depend upon the guys at City Hall to know best. You
must assume that the nicest of them have more than one iron
in the fire.

It is customary for local politicians to own or run businesses
which have a direct relationship to growth. Perhaps it's a
gravel or trucking outfit, or a real estate firm. Many are
contractors or suppliers, or they sell insurance or work at the
bank. They are pushng growth all the time because they
want to sell more, service more, trade more. Many of their
decisions, made on the governmental level, reflect quite spon-
taneously their naïve belief that growth is good.

The real enemy is a mentality rooted in an earlier experience. It's an American article of faith, passed down from
rough pioneer days, that man has a right to make as much
off his land as he can. The people who still think this way
have never been exposed to another point of view.

Another conviction, shared unhappily by a good many public officials, is that they know best. Once they are in the establishment, set off from the populace, they feel immune to criticism. They don't have to answer for the deals they choose to make with the entrepreneurs. Many are of an older generation (Consciousness I) which sincerely believes that big deals and influence automatically go hand in hand. If you've made it big, you hold all the cards and have all the rights. The big developer, the big gravel operator enjoy special privilege as a result.

The new wave of consumerism, protest, citizen action seems radical and somehow un-American to the old-time official. He is accustomed to granting favors but very unaccustomed to sharing his decision-making function.

However, we are gaining on them. Even the generally gloomy Ada Louise Huxtable, *New York Times* environmental critic, sounds a note of hope: "For every bulldozer disaster, there is a concerted and frequently successful effort being made somewhere else to keep something of value against a considerable procedural and economic odds. The world may be coming to an end in our cities through forces too large to control but fewer people are willing to help the progress along." In reporting a successful fight to stall the Charleston (S.C.) bridge, she suggests that we are developing a new "consciousness." "Environmental Consciousness I operated on the assumed virtues of bulldozer cleanup and relentlessly poured concrete. Environmental Consciousness III may ultimately discover the relationship of the city to the spirit of man." Meantime, we may be living through Environmental Consciousness II, which seeks to stop progress *per se* while we buy time to study new solutions.

2

People Against Progress

Ever since *Silent Spring* the preservationists have been called "bird watchers" with just a trace of contempt. The implication was that they were sentimental, unrealistic, dead-set against change, unwilling to look at the hard facts, and too soft to trade off a few hazards against money saved and efficiency multiplied. They weren't tough enough, worldly enough, experienced enough to become a force.

Nothing could be further from the truth.

Those in the vanguard of the movement to preserve property are professionals in their working life, educated, sophisticated, and plenty tough. Lawyers, engineers, architects, writers, artists, advertising and public relations men, scientists, and teachers bring expertise to the battle. They know how to counter the rape of landscape because, sad to say, they may have participated in helping the clients they serve at work do in somebody else's property in another part of the land.

One citizen action group heard, with mixed emotions, the advice of a local public relations man who was telling them how to lick a proposed highway program: "What you have to do is sit down with the political bosses, get them in on the deal, make them see what you could do to them if they don't support you." He went on to describe how his company had successfully beaten down opposition to a giant housing development by using some of the techniques he was advocating. "Thank God, he's on our side," one observer whispered.

When Hilton Head (S.C.), an environmentally conscious retirement resort, was threatened by the advent of a German chemical company (BASF) which planned to build a complex of plants a few miles above this coastal paradise, Hilton's colony of "pastured industrialists" began to attack with practiced aim. Said one: "I've lived in Chicago, Cleveland, Detroit. I know the price of industrialization. The threat of pollution is so much easier to prove after the fact than before."

The irony of the situation was not lost on reporters who covered the developing story. As one writer put it, the industrialists, in their new passion for ecology, found themselves on the sunny side of a national issue, "uncannily on the side of righteousness for a change."

William F. Kenney, retired vice-president and general counsel of Shell Oil, spoke for his fellows when he said: "Most of us on Hilton Head moved here to get away from industry and pollution." Kenney also admitted that he had had considerable success in fighting conservationists from his corporate perch. "I have never lost a case." But, this expertise only gave him an edge in a battle to save his personal environment from industry. To preserve and protect his place in the sun, Kenney joined the Hilton Head Island Community Association and threw all his legal skills—honed by twenty-nine years of fighting the battles of his corporate clients—into the war against BASF.

Arousing Public Opinion

Kenney figured that legal tactics might delay construction of the chemical complex, but a permanent win was possible only if public opinion could be changed.

"We must never lose sight of the fact that our opponents are the public officials, not BASF. As long as the public officials want the firm, there is almost no chance of stopping it. On the other hand, if the public officials changed their minds and decided they did not want the plant the company would not build, even if it had the legal right to do so. No company will move into a state where the government is hostile to it. The only way to change the opinion of the government is to arouse enough public opinion against the plant. Legal action may give us the time we need to reach the public."

Kenney's estimate of the situation proved to be correct. Newspapers and magazines carried columns of indignant comment on the conservation crisis in the Carolinas. The press visited Hilton Head and got a royal welcome from its developers, who were now championing nonprogress. The story made good copy—Germans invade a prized national resource. The cast of characters was improbably colorful. Writing in *Harper's* Marshall Frady described them: "an eclectic assortment of housewives, professional men, retirees of both opulent and modest circumstances, black fishermen, tense lank-haired rumpled young circuit riders from the Audubon Society and Friends of the Earth . . ." They had mobilized to fight for their territory and challenge the presumed benefits of industry.

Ranged against them were the state and county development directors, who, having hooked BASF, were not about to let the opportunity for a big-time plant slip away. Frady explains why: "In the South, the land of Canaan consists of a horizon of smokestacks. Industrialization—the devout acquisition of factories—has been a kind of second religion there; the secular fundamentalism." Frady calls it neo-Babbittry, peculiar to "those eager, sharp-eyed, checker-coated, rawly barbered, ruthlessly enthusiastic young men in the Jaycee chapters of all dowdy little Southern towns, with faint sniffs of wilt along their quiet main streets, which pursue with a poignant indefatigability their own factory as a sort of golden fleece, a Holy Grail, a deus-ex-machina deliverance from impending exhaustion and extinction. In this desperation, they seem willing to suffer the loss of any elegancy." Governor George Wallace once called pollution the sweet smell of prosperity.

The strange coalition which had formed itself to fight BASF was clearly on the side of the angels. The Germans were once more the "bad guys." Yards of publicity making BASF look like a villain and Carolina public officials just plain stupid finally did the trick. As William Kenney knew they would, BASF called off the deal. Marshall Frady could see the handwriting on the wall when he interviewed the Germans some months before the decision was made.

"They had proceeded in all innocence on the natural as-

sumption that the old mystique still prevailed, the old com-
binations were still viable; all the proprieties and mechanics
had been attended to. 'I was led to believe everyone had
accepted the idea,' said Dr. Lautenschlager recently. 'It is
always good to be welcomed all over, but I don't understand
this. It is completely under control. I mean, everyone we
talked to seemed to accept the idea.' According to one of
the firm's public relations figures, a hulking, robust, blond,
apple-cheeked Berliner named Dietrich Rogala, it is all simply
a question of 'Facts! If everybody would just keep to the
facts, there would be no trouble. Facts. But all this emotion
— My God! What can you do.'"

What they did was move on to Savannah, a lovely old
city whose waters are already so polluted it seems hopeless to
try to fight against more commercial disasters. They learned
that the defenders of the land include people from all areas
of American life and that they possess a spirit and a com-
petence which helps them fight for their land—and win.

The Odd Coalition

The big guy and the little guy are in the movement together. Both have a stake in clean air and water, room to
move about, the view over the next hill. One may be fighting
for a thousand-acre spread; another for a fifty-foot lot and
privacy. The landed gentry of Bedford, New York, who
waged an expensive and losing battle against Nelson Rockefeller's I-684 Highway which cut through their green estates
have much in common with the homeowners of Corona,
Queens, desperately trying to hang on to their neighborhood
threatened by a school playground.

It is a curious crew, an odd coalition. Radicals and conservatives have joined forces. Young and old are fighting side by side. The movement crosses party lines and often breeds a new political force which can invigorate a community.

In one small town a starchy corporation lawyer, whose political views might be expected to be establishmentarism, urged his neighbors to band together to fight down a proposed highway project by reassuring them that "citizen action is as old as the American Revolution, as new as the Black Panthers."

Those who fight must expect to be attacked, vilified, and even sued by those they oppose. One group of homeowners up the Hudson River was sued "for conspiracy" because they successfully blocked a developer's plan for a supercity which, in their view, would have wrecked the beauty of the surrounding area.

The preservationists also have legal power and they are using it when attempts at persuasion fail.

Just in time for Christmas 1970 the Suffolk County Defenders of the Environment presented Suffolk County, Long Island, with a suit which would bring all development— residential, industrial, commercial—to a halt. This case represents a major challenge to zoning practices which are, according to Victor J. Yannacone, Jr., lawyer for the citizens' group, "ecologically unsophisticated, environmentally irresponsible, socially irrelevant and politically naïve." The suit, against ten towns and twenty-nine incorporated villages, would have blocked development until "ecologically sophisticated, environmentally responsible criteria for such development have been established."

A month later the town board of Huntington, Long Island, unanimously backed a pilot program suggested by the citizens' group which would develop a zoning code based largely on ecological principles.

This represents a radical change in attitude. Instead of looking at land as a marketable commodity and zoning up or down according to a potential price tag, you zone with an eye toward preservation, not sales.

The preservationists have taken many of their tactics from those who fought for civil rights and against the war. They know how to lead marches, wave provocative and embarrassing placards, write ads, get publicity, and organize sit-ins.

One freezing December day in 1970 over a hundred Exeter (N.H.) protesters gathered in front of Dudley House, a splendid example of Federalist architecture, which was slated for destruction. The Rockingham National Bank wanted the space for a new building. To the protesters, led by an English teacher at Phillips Exeter Academy, this was unthinkable. A movement to declare Dudley House and the remaining buildings on Front Street a historic district was in the works, but the bank jumped the gun. "We thought," said the bank's president, "we should announce our plans before they decided to declare the site for preservation. Even so, we just never expected the reaction we got."

Robert H. Bates, the Exeter English teacher, expressed the mood of the crowd when he stated: "We are protesting the way organizations, which the citizens of this town cannot reach, go around changing the whole character of the town." Another Exeter teacher, Henry Bragdon, added, "You cannot destroy symbols without doing violence to the values they represent—craftmanship, hard work, trust in one's neighbors, a sense of proportion, putting public good ahead of private gain."

Another got to the heart of the conflict: "If progress means hot-topping one more residential parcel of land and removing a handsome and historic house from the heart of town I am against that progress."

The bank offered to move the building and preserve it, but this compromise was not accepted. The protesters offered to pay for a planner who would find an alternative site for the bank. The bank refused the offer. This matter is currently at a stand-off but one important gain has been realized. The people of the town have exerted some measure of influence over the way their community should develop.

They are not particularly sanguine about the outcome because as one woman put it, "I am afraid we all just took Exeter's beauty for granted too long." She predicts "the bulldozers will begin again and the town will discover how much of its center will be given over to asphalt paving and drive-in, drive-out banking." Others believe that the rebellion over the bank will spur a concerted effort to save what's left.

Putting Pressure Where It Counts

To the surprise, and consternation, of town officials everywhere, preservationists know how to fight a rear-guard action and they have the tenacity to do so. They know where the power lies in small communities and how to apply pressure that gets results.

Take Miss Laura Flewellyn, an eighty-nine-year-old of Mount Kisco (N.Y.), who outfoxed the town fathers. They have long yearned to put a parking lot on Miss Flewellyn's one and a quarter acres in the heart of town and finally resigned themselves to doing it over her dead body. She has resisted alluring financial offers, veiled threats, the suggestion of condemnation because, she believes, "the town needs a little open space, in what will become a congested area."

Every time the movement to take her land has surfaced, Miss Flewellyn, a schoolteacher in the area for sixty-two years, signaled her former students to assemble and petition on her behalf. One former mayor admitted that no board "would have the intestinal fortitude to condemn property owned by Miss Flewellyn, who has taught our children, our uncles and our aunts and even our mothers."

Miss Flewellyn, who says the battle has "made my life utterly miserable for eighteen years," is not reassured. "They're thinking of appointing a committee that can take any property, without leave or license. I have an immense following, but I don't know whether we could ward off a group like that."

With the help of local conservationists Miss Flewellyn worked out a plan to insure preservation of her piece of green—forever. She has written a will which leaves the land to the town for a park. If the town refuses the gift the property will then go to the Bedford Open Space Society. If the town does succeed in condemning the property for commercial use it would have to pay a considerable sum in compensation and this amount would go to the Nature Conservancy. Miss Flewellyn believes the town fathers would think twice about destroying the land when its dollar value is so high, and they would have to pay cold cash to get it.

Is her determined battle merely a last willful act? A gesture of defiance? Pure obstructionistic revenge? Not at all. When the Flewellyns came to Mount Kisco in the early years of the century, Miss Laura remembers the town as "a charming village with trees along Main Street." There was "the loveliest little meandering stream, and it had a waterfall that ran so fast they said it could have provided enough power to light my house." But the town decided to cut off the brook and run it through a culvert, thereby initiating the first in a series of man-made "improvements."

Miss Flewellyn's battle has a long history and, one would now expect, a hopeful conclusion. She says, with characteristic understatement, "It doesn't look as if I've accomplished much, but there wouldn't be one stone on another if I hadn't stayed."

Thwarting "Mr. Subdivider"

All the way across the country, in California, another doughty lady has fought the forces of commerce to a standstill. Anna Laura Myers, age seventy-nine, helped defeat a developer's plan to cut 1535 homesites out of the 3638-acre El Capitan Ranch which lies twenty miles west of Santa Barbara. The ranch, with its spectacular site on the Pacific, was zoned "agricultural" until Jules Berman persuaded the County Board of Supervisors to rezone it for "residential and recreational use." When this was announced conservationists sprang into action and quickly gathered more than eleven thousand signatures on petitions calling for a public referendum to decide the land's use.

They learned that elected officials cannot be counted on to support a taxpayers' protest against radically revising what was conceded to be a General Plan for the area, one which would protect natural areas and homeowners against a massive development.

Says Mrs. Myers, "The vote here on opposition to Berman's project was a resounding 46,861 'no' to 33,822 'yes.' All of this in spite of the fact that two members of the Santa Barbara County Board of Supervisors and the state assemblymen openly endorsed the development and the one supervisor who had to run in November was beaten by his challenger who had endorsed a 'no' vote. Berman appeared both stunned and very angered by the election results. He had spent large sums to campaign for the measure but has found no loophole through which to accomplish his original plan."

She says, with considerable satisfaction, "Mr. Subdivider has been thwarted and the master plan still stands.

"This piece of zoning of agricultural land with ocean frontage epitomizes the entire coastal crisis, and stopping the rezoning of El Capitan was the finger in the dike until some kind of meaningful state legislation can be hammered out, hopefully in this session, or it will be too late.

"Out of it, I believe, there has been an aroused awareness in our area of the issues at stake. That what has been termed 'progress' has been a dangerous and costly trap for the citizens with our space devoured, higher taxes incurred, and the profit ending in the pocket of the land developer.

"Because California has had so much open space and a salubrious climate we have been the center of the 'Recreational subdivision' syndrome with its attendant evils.

"I fervently hope that we are not going to be too little and too late in our rescue efforts."

Mrs. Myers and another petition collector, Selma Rubin,

were indicted on three felony counts because they altered or added addresses or dates on signed referendum petitions. Their lawyer maintained that they were merely correcting inaccuracies. Eventually the charges were dismissed, but not without much expense to the accused and to the county taxpayers. Mrs. Myers is full of righteous indignation as she tells what happened. "After some thirteen or fourteen court appearances (which throw a shocking light on the antediluvian judicial system in our country) the result was as follows:

"September 17, felony charges filed against Mrs. Rubin and me. I'm sure this occurred because the forces who favored the zoning fully expected to win in November. February 19 the Superior Judge ruled an 'acquittal' for us—after some thirteen or fourteen court appearances—and we assumed the vicious and ridiculous case was ended. Not so. The District Attorney promptly appealed the decision to the District Court of Appeals where he was told the case was 'not appealable.' Then, nothing daunted, he appealed to the State Supreme Court where he was again told 'appeal denied.' So the case is ended after much expense both to us and the county taxpayers—but the Santa Barbara County Master Plan still stands."

Mrs. Myers won the battle but she knows the war will go on interminably. And, her opponents may have scared off other protesters with their case against her and Mrs. Rubin. It could have "a chilling effect," say conservation leaders, on petition circulators and signers to come.

The Public Giveaway

What Mrs. Myers and others have come to appreciate is the tremendous effort they must make to block those who would give away the natural and historic resources of an area. Instead of protecting the public interest, the common estate, elected officials are often more responsive to special pleadings. They tend to identify with the business community more than they do with the homeowners who put them in office.

It is not the wholly corrupt who make decisions which could change the character of a town irrevocably and depress property values. They aren't getting money under the table, necessarily. Or, even some business on the side. They may be well intentioned and feel that their decisions are in the best interests of the community. They are, simply, thinking of business first. "You can't take a man's property away from him," they reply when challenged on their decisions to rezone or permit dig or fill. Clearly, they will have to be challenged again and again, taken to court, voted out of office if the public will to preserve the environment is to prevail.

A few cases chosen at random illustrate just what the citizen activist is up against when he elects to fight the powers-that-be.

The Main Street of Greenwich, New Jersey, was named "Ye Greate Street" in Colonial America. Laid out in 1683, it ran from the Cohansey River on the south to Piney Mount Run on the north. A mile and a half in length, it is said to be the oldest traveled street in Cumberland County, New Jersey. And, because Greenwich (pronounced *Green*-wich, not Gren-itch as its posh Connecticut namesake calls itself) is off the beaten track, it still looks much as it did in Colonial days with pre-Revolutionary houses occupied by some of the same families who built them.

Greenwich was, along with its twin-town Salem, the first

permanent English-speaking settlement on the Delaware River. As a seaport, it antedated Philadelphia and for many years competed with it successfully for commerce.

In December 1774 British tea was burned in Greenwich as New Jersey citizens declared their independence from the Crown. The churchyard at "the Head of Greenwich" on Main Street holds the remains of these patriots and rebels, later to be revered as the Founding Fathers of the Republic.

Today, Main Street is the scene of another territorial battle. This time Americans are challenging other Americans. Some citizens of Greenwich are resolved to resist the encroachment of industry in the person of Atlantic City Electric Company while others are more than eager to sell to the highest bidder, cash in their land and, to their way of thinking, bring "progress" to Greenwich.

In 1967, Ye Greate Street—and the several spurs running from it—was zoned as "The Historic Village" to protect it from trailers, gas stations, commercial and industrial development. At issue today is a new zoning law which has reduced the Village to two fifths of its area and removed much of the protection it had against pollution and commercial intrusion.

Some time before 1966 an outfit called Overland Realty began picking up parcels of land from old Greenwich families. Option agreements, signed by ninety different owners, bound the seller "as part of the consideration to join with the buyer in the buyer's efforts to procure the land to be zoned in such a way as to make it vendable for 'General Industrial Purposes.' "

Greenwich is sparsely populated, with 966 people and only 494 registered voters. Those who sold their land, and their right to protest any rezoning, represent some 20 per cent of

the voters. Overland Realty, operating for Atlantic City
Electric, managed to buy up a third of the town and effectively silence one fifth of its people.

In 1968, Atlantic City Electric came before the Greenwich
Planning Board and requested a change in zoning. By then it
had assembled forty-five hundred acres of meadow and marshland which were being assessed at the low rate accorded farmland by the Farm Land Assessment Act of the State of New
Jersey and protected against development. The Planning
Board granted their request in September 1968, thereby re-
leasing some forty-five hundred acres for residential and commercial development.

Efforts made by preservationists to persuade the town that
they were taking a fatal step down the road to pollution and
environmental disaster were futile. They were met with
hostility every time they tried to intervene. Historian J. Meade
Landis says, "I was literally expelled from one Planning
Board meeting just as an Atlantic City Electric man arrived."
On another occasion Landis and interested taxpayers were
barred from a Township Committee meeting by a uniformed
guard who told him he was stationed at the door "to keep
people out."

Forming an Emergency Committee

The preservationists banded together to form "The Greenwich Emergency Committee" to protect and preserve the environment of the town. Some of the committee represented
old settlers determined to keep the town's history and heritage
intact. Others were newcomers who had been drawn to
Greenwich because it was unspoiled and, thanks to the His-

toric Village, would remain so. Roberts Roemer, director of the Wheaton (Glass) Historical Association in nearby Millville, decided to buy his farm overlooking the Cohansey River because he felt it would always be protected.

In one statement the committee expressed its concern over the "seeming decay of the political process in Greenwich. We are dismayed by the multi-interests of certain of our local officials and the possible effect of these upon decisions, now or soon to be made, affecting zoning and the granting of variance. We are fearfully occupied with the upcoming problems related to pollution of our environment—radiation, wastes, smoke, dirt, noise, and glare; also with the many problems and higher taxes we will have with the establishment of trailer parks."

The trailer park reference was to another proposed rezoning, this time offered by the town fathers in 1970. They wanted to reduce the size of the Historic Village and permit commercial use. The Emergency Committee worked diligently throughout 1970 to persuade the Planning Board that the town would be opening the door to every kind of nuisance, as well as destroying its most precious natural and historic resource if it adopted the new zoning ordinance.

The question of rezoning of the Historic Village came to a head on September 14, 1970, at a public hearing before the Greenwich Township Committee. Roemer, Landis, members of the Emergency Committee, the county soil conservationist, the director of the New Jersey Historical Society, and others spoke against the rezoning. Even the town's paid planning consultants were on record as being against the changes. The Emergency Committee had found thirty-three errors in the new ordinance and asked that it be rejected on this ground alone.

Over a hundred persons attended the meeting and the great majority were against the change. Not one voice was raised in favor. When Mayor Robert Thomas told them that historical zoning "was restricting land use for farmers and the farmers don't like it" he was roared down by the crowd.

No sooner was the public hearing officially closed than the Township Committee voted unanimously to adopt the new ordinance. The audience shuddered in disbelief. "How could they do it when everybody is against it?" asked one woman.

Even after the decision was announced the Emergency Committee kept on trying. They appealed to the town fathers on their own terms, equating historical preservation with profit to the town. "One single historic building brings revenue to a community equal to that of one industry with a $100,000 payroll. Greenwich, of course, offers not just one historic building but an entire village with the potential income of a Williamsburg or Sturbridge—and with added advantage that it is, along with Old Salem, a genuine, occupied, original village and not a reconstruction—albeit carefully researched—such as these other two presently better known and financially successful resorts. How many industries with a payroll of $100,000 or more does each member of the Greenwich Township Committee anticipate seeing erected overlooking Greate Street? In this case REDUCTION IS DESTRUCTION.

"It is plainly obvious that the authenticity of Greenwich has a two-part base—the pristine condition of its buildings PLUS the original setting of those buildings with their gardens and fields as a backdrop. Real estate values alone provide proof—boosted above neighboring area because of the Historic Zone guaranteed environmental protection. Destroy these open areas beyond Greate Street and you destroy the entire atmosphere of the Village.

"Change Greenwich in the way you propose and you will change it irretrievably, irreversibly. Reverse the decision on the Historic Zone and you will WIN. It is not too late . . . yet."

There was no response from the town fathers, only irritation that their judgment was being questioned.

Bringing Suit

On October 21, 1970, The Greenwich Emergency Committee sued the Township of Greenwich. They specifically cited the reduction in property values under the new zoning: "Now a large part of the protected or reserved area being stripped away by the new ordinance complained of, they are liable to and indeed will lose a large part of their investment, all made with full faith and dependence upon a local government of stability and so incapable of arbitrary and capricious acts."

They asked the court to set aside the new ordinance.

Commenting on the expense of taking their case to court, Roemer said, "We regret having to pay double, as both defenders and prosecutors. (That is, as townspeople they were also defendants in the case and their tax money would be spent to fight their own case brought by the Emergency Committee.) But we are willing to do it."

The Emergency Committee was trying to, in Ada Louise Huxtable's words, "keep the there *there*." Their efforts did not go unnoticed or unappreciated outside of Greenwich. The State Historical Commission cited them approvingly for their preservation efforts and they were invited to a state dinner in June 1971, at which time officials heaped honors on their cause.

Roemer and others believe that this publicity will help them win through in the effort to save the Historic Village. The state had already designated the Historic Village as an area worth saving and this, of course, would strengthen the hand of the Emergency Committee in court.

Getting some kind of historic designation for an endangered area is one way to fight the destroyers. Miss Carolyn Pitts, who had fought long and hard to preserve Cape May, New Jersey, quietly went about getting her very special Victorian seaside resort on the National Register. Without whispering a word to anyone she simply applied to state authorities for the designation. As Ada Louise Huxtable tells the story, nobody knew what she had done until the whole town found itself on the National Register.

"The Mayor nearly died. The City Council swooned. Real estate men had fits . . . 'I'm sorry it had to be that way,' said Miss Pitts politely in the Trenton *Evening Times,* explaining that she had despaired of ever getting anything on the Register at all. The city is now bargaining for revised boundaries and the preservationists are negotiating from strength. Excelsior."

Unhappily for the cause, even well-recognized historic sites are not immune to the pressures of progress.

Mystic, Connecticut, is a lovingly restored old whaling village which has retained its residential charm despite the summer influx of tourists. In the closing days of the 1969 session state legislators approved a million-dollar 1.2-mile connector from Mystic to the Connecticut Turnpike, a project which has been energetically attacked ever since by a determined bank of Mystic preservationists.

Known as the "Allyn Street Connector" the road would go through the last remaining large parcel of woods and meadow land in the Mystic area. This, according to those who have steadfastly fought the project, is precisely why it was located there. "It would open the woods to commercial use, making preservation prohibitively expensive. The state's million-dollar road is a bonanza for private developers."

Opponents of the Allyn Street Connector have a talent for dramatizing the impact of the road if constructed. One of their mailings leaves nothing to the imagination. "Visitors to the historic Mystic Seaport look across the river at the hillside panorama of church spires, predominantly old homes and trees: a 19th century village. This proposed 40-foot-wide road would slice along the crest of that hill to join Route 1, and then proceed along West Mystic Avenue a tree-lined avenue of ship captains' homes. The road would Eliminate its Destination, and create a throughway to nowhere. The Dept. of Transportation has no plan to handle the traffic this corridor would attract once it reaches Route 1.

"America spends millions of dollars planning ideal communities; we *have* such a community already, and the Dept. of Transportation's plan would destroy it.

"We are on the edge of an era which will value stewardship of resources, *natural* and *historical,* above over-development and *exploitation.* Please help save Mystic as an historically beautiful destination, not only for those of us who live here, but for all Americans who visit and go home with a memory of this very special village."

Legislative Double-Cross

Since 1969 a group called T.R.E.E.S. (To Reassess Ecology-Environment Safety) has been fighting to rescind legislative authorization for the project. Their first act was to tie red streamers on the trees which would be cut down in construction. A sign read, "See 96 trees soon to be destroyed by the State." Many were a venerable age, as much as seventy-five years old.

Mrs. Kathleen O'Beirne who has been coordinator and spokesman for TREES recently reviewed the ups and downs of their efforts. They called their state representative, Lillian Erb, as soon as the organized opposition surfaced. Mrs. Erb agreed to ask the State Highway Department to review the project.

The protesters asked Mystic's mayor to intervene and managed to get a Town Council vote against the project— 5 to 4—after an earlier vote went against them. The council decided to ask for a more modest road but not abandon the project completely. This strategy seemed most workable at the time. The state canceled bids on the Allyn Street Connector and promised to "review and consider a new design that will satisfy the desires of town officials and the people, and provide a safe highway, and be compatible with the environment of the area."

TREES' optimism was short-lived. On January 1971 the Department of Transportation came back with its new offer.

It would remove the sidewalks from its original design, but not budge on the location or the forty-foot width.

TREES then asked State Representative Erb to put in a bill to rescind the authorization to build. She flatly refused, telling Mrs. O'Beirne, that they would have to prove she had to do it legally. This, says Mrs. O'Beirne, "is a rather outrageous act when our fourteen-hundred (petition) signers constitute about one third of the votes cast in the fall election."

They then asked George Crafts, their new state senator, to put in the bill. He said he would do so and indeed he did introduce it for two days, then took it out without telling anyone. Explained Crafts later, "It has become a political football and I don't want to be involved in the scrimmage." In an editorial called "The Arts of Crafts" the *New London Day* observed: "Crafts should have thought about scrimmaging before he got into politics. It happens to be too late now to decide he doesn't want to play the game because he doesn't like the rules or the way the ball is bouncing . . . Privately, Crafts is said to be blaming pressure from high Republicans for his actions."

Mrs. O'Beirne is convinced that "the pressure comes from those who stand to gain from the road. The only possible motive can be profit—the woods (one mile of them) will be opened up by the road. They are inaccessible now." She is well aware of who is doing the pressuring and who stands to gain. But, "he has fired up a small group to push locally for his position so that he can avoid the limelight."

Says Mrs. O'Beirne, who has not given up the fight and still hopes that through legislative maneuver she will get the bill killed, "In a very real way, this particular project has become symbolic of the fight of the environmentalists vs.

profit-progress powers, with proper representation in government as a side issue."

Many a state legislator has learned to his dismay that the
old-time interests cannot be served if they conflict with the
goals of environmentalists. Deals made in backrooms will
surely embarrass any public official when they come to light.
There is no fury like that of a conservationist scorned. One
state senator who had not anticipated the rage stirred up in
his constituency by a proposed utility line received so many
phone calls and telegrams urging him to fight the utility
and the PUC that he cried out in anguish, "Get those
damned housewives off my back. I've got a law practice to
run."

Local boards and commissions which ignore conservation
sentiment discover that they have ignited community rebellion
and generated fierce opposition to their projects. Where once
upon a time citizens took for granted the good sense and
judgment of their elected officials they now scrutinize
decisions which seem shortsighted or expedient. We are much
more aware than we once were of the need to plan for the
long haul and impatient with those who settle for the quick
and easy route.

Is Nothing Sacred?

The Stevens-Coolidge Place, a historic house and eighty-
nine acres of open land, was left to the Massachusetts Trustees
of the Reservation in 1962. It represents the only open space
left in the developed portion of North Andover, Massachusetts, and would, you might think, be off limits to builders.

In 1969, however, the North Andover School Building

Committee elected to put the new high school on the site. They knew this would require a special act of the legislature since the property had been formally designated as a historic site. Yet, they apparently felt that popular support would be with them. They had no fear of conservationists "favoring blades of waving grass over the town's school children."

They couldn't have been more insensitive to changing public attitudes. Writing in *Connecticut Conservation* Magazine, September 1970, Donald N. Keirstead of North Andover told how a multipronged campaign by townspeople defeated the plan.

Keirstead was a member of the Town Planning Board and he drafted a statement which summed up their position and served notice on the Building Committee:

"The best possible use of this land would be to preserve it in its natural state, as a green belt of open space, in an otherwise increasingly congested and developed area.

"Furthermore, to take land that has been left as a legacy for future generations by a former public-spirited resident of this town would be a breach of faith. Such land-taking, at this time, would discourage other residents from similar generous acts, so necessary to the preservation of the open character of our town. The town must act to encourage open space preservation, wherever practical and desirable.

"The Planning Board feels that long range considerations of land use and other factors should take precedence over the expediency of selecting a site in time for March Town Meeting action."

When the statement was presented to the School Board Committee the chairman at first declined to read it. When he was persuaded to do so members of the Committee made disparaging remarks, claiming that the action of the Planning Board was "frivolous."

"It will be an easy matter to get this action reversed," said one gentleman whose son was a member of the Planning Board. (Mr. Keirstead remarks, "These turned out to be prophetic words.") The Building Committee went so far as to take a vote "not to accept the letter" and returned it to Keirstead.

Other town officials supported the Building Committee and when the Planning Board met again the Building Committee won that round. Significantly, the votes cast in favor of taking the property came from the son of one member of the Building Committee, a former employee of another member of the Building Committee, and a realtor. However, by this time public opinion was beginning to stir against the take.

The Conservation Commission quite naturally wanted to save the Stevens-Coolidge Place pointing out that it was shown on the Town's Open Space Plan.

But it was the work of a single interested citizen which made the difference in strategy and results, according to Keirstead. Mrs. Sally Webster took it upon herself to photograph the natural area. She then obtained equal time to show her slides whenever the Building Committee met in open session. Says Keirstead: "Her slides of the beautiful Stevens-Coolidge Place, contrasted with slides of children playing in the streets of congested cities, together with her soft-sell presentation, probably were the rallying point that began interesting regular citizens in our campaign. Sally was widely quoted in the newspaper and obtained 'equal time' on WCCM, a local radio station."

Other citizens began to do their own research into the costs of acquiring the property and using it for a school. Their figures indicated that the Building Committee was far off in its estimates. A local builder did his own site examination and began to ask questions about the underlying ledge on the property.

Predictably, opposition came from people who wanted to add on to the existing schools and, hopefully, cut costs. There was also an outcry from property owners in the neighborhood who opposed the location of any school "in their backyard."

The core of the opposition developed in a group Keirstead characterizes as "conservationists that paid a substantial premium for property in close proximity to this conservation land because of their love of the amenities."

As the March town meeting drew close another interested citizen came up with a brain storm. Mrs. Lynn McCarthy organized an off-season open house. She persuaded a group of volunteers to give the place a spring cleaning and serve as hostesses. They put ads in the paper announcing the tour. An astonishing eight hundred visitors came through that Sunday before the town meeting.

If the Building Committee could get a two-thirds vote at the meeting they could proceed with their plan to take the property. Instead, the vote went just exactly the other way. Only 154 were in favor of the proposal and 772 were opposed.

Summing up the victory, Keirstead says, "This should serve as a clear indication to future well-meaning public officials that the Town of North Andover prefers to keep the Stevens-Coolidge Place in its natural state. At least we hope it will. None of us is anxious to repeat this struggle."

Different people, different problems, different parts of the country—but there is a common thread.

It's not simply people against progress, but people pushing their elected officials to do something. It's the property owner standing alone at first against those who mean to take away his assets, then banding with others to fight the interests. It is a growing awareness that cupidity and greed work behind the scenes to influence planning and zoning decisions. But, along with that comes increased knowledgeability about turning the issue to public advantage, and a resolve to fight to the finish.

The once cozy coalition of commercial interests, local officials, and political parties has been fractured by citizens who join in common cause, motivated by their own pocketbooks to stand firm. The theft of public land is no longer so easily tolerated. In the first place land is getting scarce. When you raid the public purse you inevitably hurt the entire community. Property owners are far more sensitive in these environmentally conscious days of the importance of preserving open space around their private domain.

Where there is indifference to historic or scenic values the people will take up arms in the preservationist cause. No longer can they assume their public officials will do the right thing. If they want to save the land and its landmarks they now know that the people will have to do it.

3

One Town's Triumph

It takes only one significant incursion into the landscape to change everything. The far-reaching impact of a highway, power line, sizable development, new industry, or shopping center cannot be overestimated. As soon as a force for change is introduced it will, inevitably, affect the equilibrium of the entire community. Being able to anticipate the impact, forestall it, or, failing that, minimize its effect, has to be the citizen's job. He must ask the questions, demand the facts, insist that his public officials project future change. If he doesn't search out the pro's and con's of change he won't be able to make a balanced judgment. The proponents of any sizable project are too anxious to promote its benefits, and only too happy to minimize any negative side effects.

When the new Route Seven, to run north and south, through densely populated suburban Connecticut, from Long

Island Sound to the Berkshires, was first announced there
was general rejoicing. No one could dispute the need for
the road. Old Seven was choked with traffic. Commuters
inched their way to the trains or to small factories which
were beginning to burgeon in suburbia. ("Designed enterprise" was the name given to this quasi-industrial development, a name designed to create a pleasing image of discreetly landscaped, low-slung buildings which would employ
the pick of the white-collar labor force.)

Speculators jumped in to buy land along the projected
corridor. They saw splendid sites for designed enterprise,
corporate headquarters, shopping centers, gas stations. Homeowners in the path of the highway resigned themselves to
eventual condemnation and made plans to move. Caught in
the middle were the homeowners whose property lines
wouldn't change with the route, but whose lives certainly
would.

The highway meant traffic streaming in over the hills,
through narrow side roads, churning through sleepy, once-
safe neighborhoods. There would be pressure to rezone residential areas for industry and business.

In the light of the big money to be made on designed
enterprise or industry located near a major highway, any
use that left great chunks of green open would be deemed
"inappropriate." Entrepreneurs would apply for excavation
permits, persuading their local zoning boards that they might
as well take the gravel out since the lands would be con-
demned for the new road. Never mind that the state would
then have to buy the gravel back in order to make a bed
for the road. A battalion of bulldozers, backhoes, draglines
stood at the ready, just waiting to hear the word "go"

before descending upon the Route Seven corridor and its environs.

But one little town along the route had another army dug in behind the hills, working out a counterattack, ready to prove that you can fight "progress" and win. For four years a coalition of energetic citizens worked to keep one community from being destroyed by the new highway. It took every ounce of energy they had, untold man-hours of work, and an unquenchable optimism that they could prevail.

When Redding, Connecticut, celebrated its bicentennial in 1967, new Route Seven was on the drawing boards and plans to exploit it were well formulated by the builders and contractors and real estaters and bankers who would share in the spoils.

The town had never looked so green and pleasant as it did that summer of 1967. The local notables—Edward Steichen, Elmo Roper, Stuart Chase—headed up a bicentennial committee. The town congratulated itself upon preserving a special corner of Connecticut, one which still offered plenty of open space to refugees from New York City and the overpopulated Connecticut suburbs which are closer to metropolitan areas.

Mark Twain, too, had been looking for "elbow room" when he came to Redding shortly after the turn of the century. "This place seemed at its best when all around was burning with the autumn splendors; and now once more it seems at its best, with the trees naked and the ground a painter's palette . . . How beautiful it all is! I did not think it could be as beautiful as this."

Redding is still beautiful, almost as unspoiled as it was in Twain's day and this despite the flow of families into the

town. There are more schools than there were when Twain
came, more blacktop, and more houses, but there is plenty
of open space as well, carefully preserved and cherished by
townspeople.

Twain was not the first city fellow to spot the charms of
outlying, unspoiled towns like Redding, and he most certainly
was not the last. Ever since World War II, the green acres
which rim urban centers have been invaded by families seeking elbow room. As they crowd in upon the land the very
thing which attracted them, that "country atmosphere," be-
gins to disappear.

A Case in Point

Redding is a case in point. It has kept its blessings, but
not without fighting for them, planning for them, and
stalwartly refusing to go with the trend. What is happening
in this one small town is being duplicated across America.
Some communities are winning the battle; others have sur-
rendered. In Redding the fight goes on—with more success
than otherwise. The story of how it is being waged is told
here with an eye to helping others go and do likewise.

World War II and the years which followed it marked a
watershed here and across the country as far as building
practices and land-use patterns went. After World War II
people no longer took the green and open landscape of
America for granted. A whole generation had to be housed.
The pent-up demand for a split-level and lot of your own
broke as soon as the war was over. Suburbia exploded. When
the price of land and housing soared young families moved

farther out searching for a bargain. They came to towns like Redding.

The new people meant new schools, town services, recreation apparatus. This cost money and the old-timers hurt every time a town meeting appropriated more dollars for something "those people want." With their demands the new people were an expense, but ultimately they would be the town's salvation. They valued what they were buying and were determined to help the town keep its country atmosphere. They would be strong advocates of open space preservation.

A 1960 poll made it clear that "the overwhelming majority of the people of Redding wished the Town to retain its present open, rural character."

In 1963 a sample taken by Redding resident Elmo Roper confirmed this same attitude. The most recent poll, run in the summer of 1970, demonstrated that Redding valued its "country atmosphere" and wanted to protect it by buying open land, holding residential zoning at two-acre density, giving preferential tax treatment to owners of large tracts. Most people appreciated the obvious fact that they lived in a beautiful, but fragile, environment. To protect it from erosion and pollution they would have to institute and maintain certain land-use controls.

Redding was blessed—or cursed, depending upon your point of view—with a boulder-strewn terrain, steep slopes, copious wetlands and ridges running north and south, making east-west travel difficult. It looked beautiful, but it was a developer's nightmare. The land could accommodate only limited development. The town couldn't be sewered, not with that soil and slope. Each house would have to have its own well and septic system, and two acres were needed to make each household self-sufficient. The more rugged parts of town were slated for four-acre zoning on the 1960 master plan, but this never went through. Instead, a soils map was used to guide development, and, hopefully, help the Planning Commission put "impossible" sites off limits for builders.

The town had established zoning in 1950. In 1956, residents voted in a Planning Commission charged with regulating subdivisions and preparing a master plan to guide development. In 1964 the town approved the appointment of a Conservation Commission to watch over natural resources. The commission became, to the surprise of some who thought of conservation only as a harmless kind of nature-watching, the most aggressive force for land acquisition in town. When it was formed the town owned virtually no open space, except for school sites, office grounds, and the dump. Five years later the town owned 750 acres outright and many hundreds more were protected by acts initiated by the Conservation Commission and its determined chairman, Samuel Hill.

Despite a careful program to preserve the look and character of the town, Redding was not fully prepared for the impact of forces unleashed by the prospect of a new Route Seven. Shortly after the bicentennial celebration in 1967, the roof began to fall in. Redding was to learn that its first two hundred years had been the easiest.

"Right Through My House"

The first inkling of what the road would mean came at a Planning Commission meeting in the fall of '67 to consider a new circulation plan for the town. The commission's consultant—Technical Planning Associates of New Haven—unveiled a map which showed a big, black line running east and west from a proposed Route Seven interchange on the western border all the way across town to the eastern line. It chewed through much of the most scenic and historic areas. The grading of this "major connector," to carry as many as three thousand cars a day, following the torturous path of existing country roads, would involve monumental cuts and fills. The landscape would be torn up, the small, intimate scale of the countryside irrevocably destroyed with this concrete monster and the attendant horrors it would bring. The mapmakers had, apparently, no sense of the historic sites they were obliterating nor any awareness of the public outcry this plan could set off.

"My God, it's going right through my house," said one resident who just happened by the planning meeting that night. The word went out that houses in the path were to be jettisoned, that some of the town's most precious artifacts—cemeteries, pre-Revolutionary buildings, churches, the Library—were in danger. The Planning Commission realized it had a hot potato on its hands and asked for a revised map. For the moment the town relaxed.

The reprieve was short-lived. Residents on the western border learned one day that the Zoning Board of Appeals had come close to granting a rezoning, for business, to the owner of property lying near the proposed interchange. Had it not been for Victor Lazzarro, an alert member of the board who protested that nobody knew enough about the design and location of the new road to make such a judgment, the deal might have gone through.

Clearly the heat was on. A group of concerned citizens

formed a Citizens Action Council to establish a counter-pressure group to block those special interests which wanted to change the character of the town and fatten their own pocketbooks.

In its first town-wide mailing CAC spelled out its purpose: "Today, Redding stands at an important crossroads. As one of the last towns in the area still enjoying an abundance of undeveloped countryside, it can, if it chooses, continue to retain this open, unspoiled character. Or, it can easily go the way of such towns which have permitted ever-larger portions of their land to be given over to the expediently conceived man-made enterprises.

"Citizens Action Council, an organization of concerned Redding residents, has been formed to give all the town's citizens an option, a choice between ugly, unbridled urbanization, or a planned, orderly, imaginative pattern of growth that is compatible with the future welfare of the town at large."

At their first meeting, held in November 1968, CAC organizers showed maps of four superhighways, proposed by four regional agencies, all, as the *Redding Pilot* reported, "cutting carefree swaths from west to east through the southern half of the town—one putatively planned to cross the Aspetuck Reservoir on pilings." You did not have to be a professional planner to see that the big black east-west line, which had been considered by the Planning Commision in fall '67 and, according to one member "gone up the chimney," could be tied into such a master plan for an east-west New York State to New Haven road.

At a December meeting a CAC director reminded the audience that no money had yet been appropriated for this stretch of Route Seven. The plans "are only lines projected on a map. The legislators are not bound by secret vows to lay out the road on a certain plan." He told about a successful campaign to eliminate two interchanges along the Merritt Parkway when that was built: "This was not an accident. It was because the people demanded that there be no interchanges at these points."

A month later the Planning Commission held a formal hearing on the controversial and presumably revised circulation plan. There was the big black line still running mercilessly through the town. CAC members and others asked why. Because the state had located an interchange on the border between Redding and nearby Ridgefield. Technical Planning Associates expected this to generate traffic through Redding. Humbert Sacco of TPA told them that the biggest spurt in a town's growth usually occurs when a highway comes through and the biggest spurt of all occurs around an interchange.

Three interchanges were planned for a 4.5-mile strip along the Ridgefield-Redding line even though highway standards usually dictate that interchanges be no closer than four miles. Someone asked why so many and Sacco answered, "Undoubtedly the commercial interests on Route Seven have had a lot to do with that interchange," adding, "There will be pressure from gas stations and other commercial interests such as industries looking for prestige sites and good access." Also: "If the plans are too unpalatable and you are able to do something about them, it will change everything."

Eliminate the Interchange

The chicken-and-the-egg argument went on. The east-west road was there because of the interchange. Get rid of the interchange and Redding could be spared this ghastly corridor. Sacco, himself, suggested this approach, telling the group that "until they get a shovel into the ground it is never too late. I suggest you get Ridgefield into it and get it endorsed by the chief executives of both towns."

The Ridgefield selectman was for the interchange, emphasizing its value in attracting industry to the corridor. But, his planning and zoning commissions and conservation commission were against it.

Ridgefield residents who lived near the proposed interchange set about mustering public opinion. They circulated petitions and had success in getting some three hundred signatures of residents opposing the interchange. Although Ridgefield was not faced with a major road fanning off the interchange, any such project would surely increase traffic on their already-crowded country roads.

Early in February, four Redding and Ridgefield citizens drove to Hartford to meet with Highway Department officials.

Clearly impressed by the enterprise and fervor of the group, Lembit Vahur, who was the designer for this stretch of the road, volunteered, "If the local people don't want it, we won't put it in." He added that it was quite unusual for the people of a locality to come to him requesting the removal of an interchange. Usually it was the other way around: "they" wanted one put in. By "they" he doubtless meant commercial interests.

State Senator Clark Hull and Representative Herb Camp also attended the meeting. Hull, who had long pushed for "Route Seven Now," seemed torn between his responsibilities to constituents, saying, "Although those opposed to the interchange gave a strong presentation, it did not appear they made much of an impression on the planners, who made it clear that they felt the residential growth and industrial potential was there to make it good highway planning."

Opponents of the interchange later learned that towns up the line wanted this short cut through Redding and, of course, commercial interests saw the possibilities of intensive development around the interchange and were pushing for it. One selectman, also in the construction business, wanted it because he said, quite honestly, "I'll have to admit it would make it easier for my trucks to get through."

In March, Redding and Ridgefield selectmen met in Hartford with CAC reps and state legislators to discuss the interchange with the State Highway Department. This time the Ridgefield selectmen took the initiative and announced they were for the interchange. The members of the Ridgefield Planning Commission were late in getting to the meeting and the force of their opposition was somewhat diluted. The meeting was "disastrous," according to the CAC president. But, the Redding selectmen did agree to call a town meeting in April to get a reading on public opinion before committing themselves.

Citizens in both towns had been working diligently to make the public aware of the potential effects of both the interchange and the east-west road. CAC directors had held meetings with local officials and political leaders, explaining the case against the interchange. They secured reams of publicity describing the damaging impact of the road. They disputed traffic projections offered by both TPA and the State Highway Department and pointed out that the planners and the state did not agree on what would happen once the

road was built, nor could they demonstrate a clear need for
the interchange. The campaign to make local residents appreciate the threat to their town and their property values
paid off.

The People Speak

The night of the town meeting hundreds of cars poured
into the school parking lot. The overflow crowd was humming
with outrage and the mood of the meeting was clearly opposed to the interchange.

Highway planner Lembit Vahur had been invited to present the case for the state. He began by saying that he was
surprised at the number of people present. "I expected a
question-and-answer session with twenty or thirty people,"
he said.

Speaker after speaker followed him to the microphone to
express objections. They reminded the highwaymen again
and again of Vahur's statement: "If the people of Redding
and Ridgefield don't want the interchange, they don't have to
have it, but we would like to hear from the people."

When Vahur attempted "to eliminate your fear of increased traffic through Redding, I assure you it will not
happen" he was greeted with laughter. Other speakers asked
him why the interchange would be needed, then, if there was
to be no increase in traffic.

Loren Becker, president of CAC, was cheered when he
concluded, "I hope we will hear from many speakers tonight,
so that the Highway Department will realize we are not just
a little band speaking against this, but the whole town, and

that through our democratic process we can change this highway plan."

State Representative Herbert V. Camp summed it up when he said, "If the crosstown traffic count is low, the interchange is unnecessary. If it is high, it is dangerous for these town roads."

The crowd applauded every resounding speech made against the interchange and expressed its hatred of the idea by voting 335 to 3 against it.

The three who voted for it all owned property which would appreciate in value if the interchange went in.

One CAC director took note of this in a letter to the *Pilot* shortly after the meeting. Bob Knapp wrote:

"Who wants the interchange? You know who oppose the interchange. We have stated our names and our reasons. We have stood up and spoken out publicly. Why don't those who want the interchange make their names and their reasons known to their fellow townspeople? Along the Redding section of the present Route Seven there are just seven or eight places of retail business. It is hard to see how any of these can be harmed in any way as a business by the elimination of the Old Redding Road interchange. If those who really favor this proposed interchange were to come forward, I wonder if it would be found that they are not actually concerned about business in the area of the interchange, but interested purely and simply in the skyrocketing land values that would unquestionably follow interchange building. I wonder if what they want is not a windfall at the expense of the vast majority of the town. I do not object to a fair profit on rising land values, but I object most vigorously when that

type of profit is collected by land values forced up through
injury to the rest of the town.

"We'd like to hear from those who want the interchange,
every one of them. We'd like them to tell us who they are
and why they want it. We know what it will do to us. We
want to know what it will do for them."

Following the decisive town meeting CAC officials wrote
to Governor John Dempsey, reminding him of Vahur's earlier
comment—"If the local people don't want it, we won't
put it in." This, they said, was "in the best tradition of our
State and its long record of working democracy." But, more
in sorrow than anger, they reported how Mr. Vahur had be-
haved at the town meeting.

"Speaking in an authoritarian tone and manner that left
no doubt of his intent, Mr. Vahur told the people of Redding
that any decision they might make at their town meeting
would not be 'binding on the highway commissioner.' As you
can imagine, this caused a great stir in the audience.

"What we would like to ask, Governor Dempsey, most re-
spectfully, is whether Mr. Vahur is expressing your views and
the views of your administration, when he says that the
State Highway Department puts in million-dollar interchanges where it pleases without regard to the wishes of the
people of the locality?"

The governor never answered the question, but he did
acknowledge the letter and passed it along to Highway Commissioner Ives.

A month later Redding and Ridgefield citizens who had
led the fight and Representative Camp were invited back to
Hartford to "restudy the plan." A new traffic study was announced which would determine whether the interchange was

needed. CAC members reported that the meeting was harmonious and that the highwaymen were "very sensitive to the
feelings of the town."

In June a Ridgefield town meeting voted 188 to 1 to oppose the interchange. "I hope this will be the final nail in
the coffin of the plan," one speaker observed.

Near the end of 1969, town officials received word that
the interchange had been dropped. The transportation commissioner left the door open for future consideration by
saying it "will be deferred until the need is clearly evident."
The state planned to buy the land to "preclude the development of presently vacant land and to preserve the feasibility
of operational integrity of the future interchange."

Representative Camp congratulated CAC for its efforts to
stop the interchange. Where he once had called them "Citizens'
Re-Action Committee," he now seemed completely sold on
the idea that they had as much right to fight for their
concept of good land use as did the entrepreneurs.

The Constructive Alternative

All effective protesters know that you can't just be against
something, you have to be for something else. Otherwise you
will be labeled obstructionistic and negative.

The people who had fought the interchange were for keeping this western section of the town unspoiled. How to do
it? Two opportunities presented themselves as the interchange
battle drew to a close.

At a membership meeting in June 1969, CAC leaders
explored the possibility of designing a green belt along New
Route Seven which would buffer the road from neighboring

houses and provide a natural look for the highway. "A Merritt Parkway look, not a freeway horror," one explained. The idea had been discussed in Wilton, to the south of Redding, and in Brookfield, to the north. CAC asked Richard Carpenter, planning director for the Southwestern Regional Agency, to show his suggestions for acquiring permanent open space along the route. The idea was received with enthusiasm by those who attended the meeting and a Route Seven Green Belt went onto CAC's action agenda.

Within a year, an intertown committee, headed by energetic Gert Kaufman from Ridgefield, would be formed to push the idea. Four out of the seven towns along the highway would contribute funds for a feasibility study of what came to be called "The Northwestern Connecticut Linear Park," and the Environment Committee of the legislature would approve bills establishing it.

Here was a competing use for the land along the corridor. Instead of pushing against gas stations, neon, and motels, the citizens of the area were going to push for a park which would run along the road, linking open space and recreation areas, providing biking, hiking, and riding trails. The land which the state said it was going to buy on the site of the defeated interchange could be used as a rest area and, hopefully, this use would keep any interchange from being built for many years to come.

The new highway also ran close to the spectacular wild tract of 412 acres owned by photographer Edward J. Steichen. It had been identified as a possible town recreation area in the 1960 Plan of Development, and the Conservation Commission had put it on the 1966 Open Space Map as land worth acquiring for town use.

If this immensely valuable tract, because of its access to the highway, were developed, the floodgates would be open. It was the anchor to the west, and, if it could be saved and kept open, the town would guard against the rush of developers sure to move in on the highway's perimeter.

The Million-Dollar Parcel

In the fall of 1969, the Conservation Commission asked the ninety-one-year-old Steichen if he would consider selling to the town. He would, and named a price—one million, one hundred thousand dollars. This figured out to $2500.00 an acre, an exorbitant figure to those who fought the proposition, a reasonable price to those who were for it. The Conservation Commission proposed applying for state and federal open space grants, and, if these were forthcoming, the price would be reduced to a quarter million.

The figures flew as both sides sought to establish an economic argument for their position.

The proponents marshaled statistics to show that if the land were bought by a developer 150 new houses would mean 300 school-age children. And Redding taxpayers, according to economist Stuart Chase, "will be out of pocket about $150,000.00 year after year . . . It is the old story of saving at the spigot and leaving the bunghole wide open; the old story of penny-wise and pound-foolish. The price of land will never again be so low as it is now."

The opponents calling themselves "Concerned Taxpayers Group" hammered away at the million-dollar price tag. They played on fears of those who opposed government funding by implying that the town would be overrun with

blacks and "people from Bridgeport" if the land were bought
with state and federal aid. The leaders of the opposition
were those who had wanted the interchange earlier and
who were strong advocates of industry. Some of them also
owned property along the route or were in the development
business.

Once more outraged citizens protested against the coalition
of profiteers who sought to mold the development of the
Route Seven corridor to their own advantage. One wrote
the *Pilot:* "It is interesting to note that the hue and cry
against the purchase of the Steichen property is being generated chiefly by those who have the most to gain personally
by its defeat. This is that alliance of the special interests
whose stock in trade is land exploitation for personal profit
. . . Through anonymous handbills, and through a telephone and whispering campaign that equates this purchase
with that of the Brooklyn Bridge or a cartload of counterfeit
three-dollar bills, these 'Concerned Citizens' betray their self-
interest every time they are heard. Wouldn't it be the crown-
ing irony if their campaign to defeat the Steichen purchase
resulted in their, or their allies, ultimately buying and developing this same property, with you and I—the taxpayers
—picking up the tab in increased taxes?"

CAC and other civic groups which had fought the interchange now mobilized to win the Steichen battle. They got
out mailings, took ads, made speeches, held coffee hours, and
tried to counter last-minute charges, and as the town referendum drew near admitted to themselves that they were
afraid they had lost. Not so. On January 31, 1970, the
town approved purchase by a vote of 919 to 724. And,
the town also approved seeking state and federal funding.

Time elapsed while the Conservation Commission tried for the funding, which had been relatively easy to secure on the other open space purchases. However, an evolving recession, a new federal administration policy on giving HUD money to the inner city and not the suburbs, slowed—and eventually defeated—their efforts. As the negotiations dragged on, the opposition got wind of what was happening and called for a second referendum, claiming that the town was not going to get the money and should, therefore, vote once more on buying the tract.

A Bitter Battle

This time around the mud really flew—charges and countercharges on the price, the quality of the water ("a mudhole in August," said the opposition), the proponents ("certain people posing as public servants about to sell you down the river"). This time around the battle lines were firmly drawn —by the opponents—between what they liked to call "the cocktail party set" and "the little guy."

Once more ads were taken, fliers mailed, and a telephone brigade summoned to get out the vote. But this time the opposition won; by a vote of 965 to 838, the town decided to rescind the first decision.

Some admitted later that they had been torn, but voted against it because of the credibility gap carved by opponents. "I didn't know who to believe."

There was plenty of bitterness expressed in the pages of the *Pilot*. One letter written by school board members Mary Erlanger and Barbara Roll said it all:

"Both of us are veterans of a number of Redding battles—

hard-fought campaigns for schools, budgets, open space, town planning. We've won some and lost some—have more than once been on different sides—but always felt when the vote was taken that the town had spoken. Never before, in our experience, have the issues been so distorted by personal attacks and misleading propaganda.

"Saturday's 'victory' by opponents of the purchase, based on innuendo, aspersions on the integrity of town officials and outright misstatement of facts, is one that any resident of Redding, whatever his views on the Steichen acquisition, had little reason to celebrate.

"What was indeed achieved was the polarization of the town, with a serious attempt to undermine the confidence of its citizens in the integrity of its officials. Those same officials have labored for long years and with great dedication to make Redding the attractive, well-governed community that made many of our new residents seek it out . . . We hope that the tactics used to win this vote will be rejected by thoughtful citizens in future confrontations, whatever the issue."

In August the local papers visited the site to see if it was indeed "a mudhole." On the contrary, Steichen lake was full of water, in sharp contrast to other wetlands severely depleted by the year's drought. Pictures of the brimming lake brought furious letters of protest from the old opponents of the purchase.

Perhaps they could see the handwriting on the wall. The Steichen issue was not dead. It would come back to haunt them. And it did. Exactly a year to the day of the first referendum, the third was held. And, on January 31, 1971, the town voted to buy, with its own money, 270 acres of the Steichen tract.

All through the summer of 1970, small groups of people met to try to work out a way of salvaging it. A band of young families kept the project alive by insisting that they would work themselves to death to bring it to another vote, and this time bring out the facts about the property. They lived near it. They knew its beauty and that it was not a mudhole. Said one, publicly, "Many of us became extremely aware of the facts concerning the Steichen purchase—unfortunately at the eleventh hour—when the only thing left to do was wring our hands, speak loudly and desperately to our neighbors, and close our eyes to see that simply beautiful lake slipping away. I hope we never forget this bitter lesson."

Analyzing the defeat, proponents decided that the million-dollar price tag—without any hopes of government funding—was the crucial factor. But, now that the funding was out, so was the threat of outsiders using the property. The town would have to buy it with its own funds but it would then have complete control. The problem revolved around price. How could it be brought down?

Jim Edwards, chairman of the Board of Finance, tried for a solution. ROLI, Redding Open Lands, Inc., a group of Redding citizens who were willing to bankroll worth-while land projects and develop them for low density, was approached. Would they take part of the land so that the town could buy only the major section around the lake? This negotiation took months of effort and exploration with ROLI and with national conservation groups. Finally, ROLI agreed to buy 117 acres from Steichen so that the town's share

of the property could be reduced to 270 acres and the price
tag reduced to $675,000.00 This did it. When the issue came
to a third referendum, the price, the issue of town control,
and the pictures taken in August settled it once and for
all. The Steichen tract was safe.

The Industry Threat

Just as this battle came to a successful conclusion, another
threat to the sanctity of the western corridor surfaced. A
syndicate owning some 147 acres in the northwest corner
of town applied for rezoning, from residential to industrial.

The northwest corner of Redding is the interface between
"progress" and the good life. Old Route Seven runs close
to the Redding/Ridgefield/Danbury town lines which meet at
this point. The Danbury Airport is only a few miles away.
Industrial Danbury has developed around the airport and
is inching southward. IBM recently bought a large tract in
Ridgefield for corporate headquarters. Not only would the
Danbury Airport put its executives in touch with the world,
but new Route Seven would give them access to New York
City and the Metropolitan business community spreading
into the suburbs. A projected Route Seven interchange at
the Danbury/Ridgefield/Redding lines would create a com-
mercial-industrial hub and make commercial land values
soar, but depress residential property.

Danbury and Ridgefield have sought industry, preferably
the clean, corporate, name-brand variety. Some Redding residents have longed, too, for an IBM. Sold on the well-
advertised theory that "bedroom towns" cannot support
schools and services, they wanted some business/industry to

"broaden the tax base." According to another persuasive argument, you might as well accept industry because you'll be educating IBM's children or Barden's or Perkin-Elmer's. "They get the taxes, and we get the kids."

Some are not so sure. They reason that if Redding had an IBM they'd get those kids as well, plus the cost of providing services to industry. Narrow, inadequate, country roads couldn't handle industrial traffic. A town without public water or sewage systems is hardly geared to the demands an industrial park would make.

Basically the dispute over industry raged between those who would get nothing out of it except a doubtful tax bene-fit—probably canceled out by the improvements and services the town would provide—and those who stood to gain from more of industry's service-generating capacity. Open land doesn't provide a market for builders, salesmen, suppliers. The Chamber of Commerce wants growth; so do small-town boosters everywhere. Growth means money changing hands.

For the owners of the tract in northwest Redding a change in zone from residential to industry would mean tripling the value of their land—even if they did nothing more with it. When the highway came through, they would get three times its residential valuation if it were zoned industrial.

The tract had been partially mined; gravel taken out in the guise of "improvement." Some thought that the owners had long since recouped their investment by selling off the land, literally.

One homeowner who lived within sight of the tract appealed to the Zoning Commission: "We are increasingly concerned by the seemingly endless gravel operation across from us. Excavations are now so deep one can hardly see the tops of the huge bulldozers from the road. Our concern is not only the very real damage and detriment to property for living—indeed greatly downgrading a desirable residential area—but more seriously for us there is actual and grave danger that such extensive and deep excavation will change the very nature of our land, draining off its excellent natural moisture, making it arid, and seriously affecting the pond which we consider a valuable part of the property."

Having destroyed the environment to the point where the place looked like the craters of the moon and neighbors worried about the water table, the syndicate now wanted it rezoned. It was no good for anything else, they said. Who would want to live on it, or even near it, particularly when Route Seven slashed through.

Who indeed? Just the people who already lived in the area.

They mobilized for action, and CAC helped them organize their protest. The local paper, weary perhaps of activists, observed: "CAC Against Light Industry—What Else Is New?"

A town-wide mailing made six points against the proposal:

1. It was premature because the Town Plan of Development had not yet been aired in a public hearing.

2. Land costs to the state, and taxpayer, would triple if the property were rezoned.

3. The Linear Park study was not complete and some of this area would be taken by the park.

4. New Route Seven would not be built for five years and the State Department of Transportation had asked that the "status quo be preserved until the highway goes forward."

5. TPA had projected a possible sewer line in the northwest corner, but this would not be needed if there were no industry. The town should weigh the cost of providing this service against tax income.

6. What about the economic-environmental-social impact of industry? It would surely stimulate population growth as well, with attendant school costs and town services.

The mailer concluded by urging citizens to attend the Zoning Commission Hearing on the proposal in December 1970. "Not only is a radical change in zoning at stake, but a radical change in the unique and irreplaceable character of our town."

The Zoning Commission also planned to unveil new regulations for industry at the scheduled hearing. A preview of these led CAC members to conclude that they were more permissive than existing ones. Not only was there a clear danger that the northwest corner would be industrialized, but if the plan went through, companies which settled there would have more freedom than in the past.

Five buildings could be put on a ten-acre site instead of the old rule of two. Building setbacks had been reduced. The two architects who reviewed them for CAC concluded that the new regulations would be harder to enforce and provide more loopholes than "the simpler and more general" regulations then in force.

TPA, the consultants who drew the new regulations, defended them by saying that the increased density was intentional because of the small area of town zoned for industry. This would seem to be self-defeating, at best, and, at worst, would lead to what one observer called "creeping industry." If you let down the standards it will be no time before another group will want in on the same terms.

Citizen Protest Prevails

In reporting the hearing on the proposal, the Danbury *News-Times* said: "If there are strong supporters of light industry in Redding, they did not make themselves heard at the public zoning hearing on the subject Friday night."

Speaker after speaker assailed the proposal. A petition signed by residents of the area was introduced in opposition. Clearly, industrialization in their neighborhood would depress residential property values. One of their number predicted that industry "would open the door to down-zoning all of Redding." Another speaker, a corporation lawyer with wide experience in industrial zoning, reminded the audience that "having industry doesn't mean getting something for nothing, and many towns have had sad experiences. Once industry is in, you have a new town. They say these regulations are too stringent. Change them or we will take ourselves off your tax rolls."

The Zoning Commission later turned down the request for industry in the northwest corner but accepted the new regulations. The victory was mixed.

Opponents still had to fight the Planning Commission, which, it was rumored, would identify the northwest corner as a potential industry site on the new plan of development.

Sure enough. The Planning Commission held an information meeting on the town plan in May 1970 and the chairman of an Industry Study Committee announced that his group was for industry in the northwest corner. Residents were stunned. One said, "If my voice quivers it's because I'm upset. You are totally disregarding the voice of the citizenry at the hearing in December." Another said, the recommendation was "incredible" given the situation in the area. "It is densely populated, with lots of children. It can't be screened effectively, the area is swampy and much of the land has been gouged out by some landowners removing gravel for profit."

Several speakers attacked TPA for their consistent advocacy of more industry. "They're making the town fit their plan, not the plan fit our town," said a critic.

The tone of the meeting was decisively anti-industry, but those present had no firm hope that the Planning Commission would heed their sentiments. They girded themselves for the formal hearing on the town plan to be held later in the summer.

However, the Planning Commission did not recommend the northwest corner for industry. Whether they were responding to public opinion, or simply avoiding a bitter confrontation mattered little to those who had fought the project. Industry was not shown on the map. The Zoning Commission had denied the application and at least the town was safe for a few years until the highway was actually under construction.

For four long years, 1967 to 1971, the town was under siege by those who wanted to exploit the new Route Seven. Ranged against them were townspeople who reminded their elected officials and planners again and again that they wanted to keep Redding a beautiful and unpolluted place. A Citizens Action Council had to do their own research

being unwilling to trust town boards and commissions to do
it. Residents were obliged to goad their officials into meeting
with state decision-makers to protect the interests of the
taxpayers.

Not only did townspeople have to do much of the work,
display all the fire and passion, but they were accused of
being troublemakers, noisy, and obstructionistic. The establishment ignored the very real question of lowered property
values for those who stood in the way of progress.

Tom Bergeron, who had fought hard for the Steichen
acquisition and just as hard against industry in the northwest corner, reminded the Planning Commission that Redding
had "pure water, clean air," and asked them why the town
should give up its priceless natural resources. "This would be
a giant step backward," he concluded in a fiery speech
against the proposed industrial zone. Bergeron, who describes
himself as a "little guy," knows only too well that his own
property on the western side of town would have depreciated
in value if the interchange had gone in, the Steichen property gone into development, the northwest corner been industrialized. More than that, the entire town would have
changed character. Restraints on growth would have been
loosened and before long Redding itself would be just another
town, and not the clean, green oasis its people have fought
to preserve.

4

The Spoilers

Anyone who doubts that the battle for land is fought all over America every day—including Sunday when the real estate men are showing their wares—has only to visit his local town hall. Right-of-way men from the Highway Department, realtors, lawyers, money men representing supermarkets, gas stations, developers, utility companies are searching land records. They look up deeds, check aerial surveys, pore over the assessor's maps as they interrogate him on the latest sales records and property taxes.

Lately, another crew has been using the records. They are the preservationists. They too take land inventories, but to see how much is left. They too search titles so they can visit the holders of large tracts and perhaps persuade them to give some or all of their property for open space or to sell to the town at a reasonable price.

They are laying their plans to convince town fathers of the virtues of open-space preservation as a growth-control technique. They want to buy strategic parcels now. They would put wetlands and other environmentally sensitive areas off limits for building by means of conservation easements and zoning restrictions. They know, too, that there is no time to lose. If a community wants to preserve its character and natural resources, it must move fast.

A formidable array of "interests" is after the land. These include small-time developers looking for cheap land—usually the most desirable conservation acreage because it is wet and rocky and steep—as well as big-time operators looking for prime land—near a highway, near good water, near population. Giant companies are searching for a spot to locate their suburban/exurban offices and plants. Resort developers are planning vast new vacation complexes. "New towns" and retirement villages are on the drawing boards. The only problem is finding a place to put them.

The government is in the land business as well. It needs acreage for highways, defense projects, bridges, buildings. State housing agencies like New York's Urban Development Corporation (UDC) want to buy up sizable tracts on which to locate mass housing. The Federal Government owns millions of acres of open land which it leases to agriculture and mining outlets. This is the public estate, but private interests would like to get their hands on it.

Land is a best buy because, as anyone knows, it is in limited or short supply. One real estate operator wears a tie clip with the letters TDMTSA. It stands for "They Don't Make That Stuff Any More." People multiply, but land is a fixed quantity. When the good land runs out, the entrepreneurs then set about "improving" what's left.

Property owners everywhere are uncomfortably aware that the landscape they love is slowly disappearing, shifting, and imperceptibly changing for the worse. Before their eyes, the rolling hills and ridges, deep valleys which harbor wildlife and vegetation, the marshes and streams so vital to water storage and filtering are being replaced by a bleak, neuterized scene.

Man-Made Destruction

In the seventies, wherever you look, from coast to coast, you can find these disasters common to the American landscape. I have seen them within a few miles of my own house.

There will be a stream, winding its way from the uplands down to a lake or sound or river. Long before it finds safe harbor, if ever, it will be a target for enterprising contractors who add fill to the banks and thereby acquire an extra building lot. They not only change the course of the stream, they add to pollution and make flood control less workable.

At one point, a stream spreads out into marshland covered with swamp maples. What a temptation—to cut down the trees, then channel the water to the rear. Top the muck with gravel and you have a dandy commercial site. The water table in the area is sure to be lowered; wells will have to pump harder and possibly run dry. The storage capacity of the marsh, so vital in time of flood, had been destroyed. The plant and animal life which once flourished here will, of course, disappear. And what will be the gain, besides the developer's profit? Another filling station will go on the reclaimed site, another station pouring its oil and waste into the channeled stream.

A handsome cliff, distinguished by ferns, mountain laurel, and wildflowers, is slowly but surely being cut down. A bulldozer is taking great bites out of its lower reaches. The prospects for erosion are promising. A search for gravel has led the payloader to this spot. After the precious stone has been mined, the cleared site will be sold for another supermarket location. What will happen to the gravel? It will be used to build still another highway. The highway itself will consume more land as it crisscrosses pastures, tears past landmark houses and historic sites—often uprooting them in the name of eminent domain—bringing noise and pollution as it rips along.

How can we fight the spoilers?

By calling attention to the disasters and embarrassing those who perpetrate them. By complaining endlessly to the proper authorities and, if need be, embarrassing them if they fail to act.

It is going to be a continuing struggle, this battle over proper land use. Property owners will have to form their own organizations to combat the well-financed and strongly motivated forces which are bent on extracting a profit from the land. They will have to show up at hearings and town meetings to protest the rape of the landscape. They will have to get out endless mailings of their own to alert the public to what is happening, make telephone calls by the hundreds, circulate petitions. They will have to press for new laws to control the spoilers.

The Environmental Imperative

Put in its simplest and most shocking terms, the preservation of land is linked inextricably to life itself: unless we save enough land to provide a vital balance of nature, we will perish.

Lamont C. Cole, professor of ecology at Cornell, has explained what has happened to the environment as land has disappeared:

"The amount of carbon dioxide put into the atmosphere is rising at an ever-increasing rate. [The Boeing 707s, to name just one group of polluters of the atmosphere, discharge over thirty-six million tons of carbon dioxide annually.] At the same time, we are removing vast tracts of land from the cycle of photosynthetic production—in this country alone, nearly a million acres of green plants are paved under each year. The loss of these plants is drastically reducing the rate at which oxygen enters the atmosphere. And, we do not even know to what extent we are inhibiting photosynthesis through pollution of fresh-water and marine environments.

"The carbon-oxygen balance is tipping. When, and if, we reach the point at which the rate of combustion exceeds the rate of photosynthesis we shall start running out of oxygen. If this occurred gradually, its effect would be approximately the same as moving everyone to a mountaintop—a change that might help alleviate the population crisis by raising death rates."

Summing up, Dr. Cole says, "Man, in the process of seeking 'a better way of life,' is destroying the natural environment that is essential to any kind of life at all."

The average homeowner may or may not appreciate the awesome consequences of our traditional and grossly destructive land-use pattern. But, certainly, he knows the environment is getting worse, not better.

What property owners the world over want is to keep their personal environment, their homestead, clean and green and worth what they paid for it. To that end they will take on the developers, the big corporations, or anyone who tries to wreck the landscape for personal gain. Sometimes, they must take on their neighbors and fellow townspeople.

Any restraint on land use is bound to stir opposition from landowners who can see commercial possibilities in their own acreage. To them it's real estate, land to be exploited, not land to be conserved and managed for its intrinsic natural value.

When a town decides to put in zoning, the screams can be heard from outraged farmers and large landowners who are contemplating the profits to be made when they eventually sell out.

Overnight they develop a social conscience and wonder piously about the young couples who won't be able to build modest houses if land is zoned for large lots. There is little concern for the people who paid their own hard cash for a place they thought would be decently preserved.

Towns that have let gravel miners get away with murder discover that regulation is not easy. The gravel men complain that they are being zoned out of business. In one New England town a proposed ordinance to slow the mining by putting limits on the amount to be taken out every three months was challenged by an operator who said the commission did not tell the grocery store how many cans of peas to sell and therefore should not tell the gravel operator how much gravel to take. One commissioner tried to explain, "Gravel is a natural resource. Are we permitted to deplete it?"

This question gets to the heart of the matter. How much of a community's natural resources—its earth, water, sky— belong to the community and how much to the individual who bought land with an eye to exploitation?

One property owner who had listened through a public hearing on an application to take forty thousand cubic yards of material out of a residential lot so it could be made commercially attractive protested that the discussion hinged on the wrong issue. "I hear statistics. I hear about land, but not about human beings. You have a conflict between profit and human environment and enjoyability of life. This should be considered philosophically."

The Dwindling Resource

Not only are we destroying the land we have and over- loading its capacity as a buffering agent, but, as population increases, we are going to demand even more from the land.

The need for nonagricultural uses of land is accelerating faster than our need for food production. By the year 2000 we can expect the following rise in demand for land re- sources:

Land for recreation—up 300%;
Land for homes, schools, factories—up 215%;
Land for transportation—up 125%;
Land for wildlife refuges—up 133%;
Land for reservoirs—up 180%.
Land needs in the year 2000 for a population expected

to expand from our present 203 million to more than 300 million will mount to a total of far more than our full land area.

Within the twentieth century the number of people occupying the same number of square miles will have tripled.

Consider, too, that people tend to congregate where land is scarce. Right now 70 per cent of Americans live on 10 per cent of its land. By the year 2000 an estimated 90 per cent will live in or around congested areas.

Pick up any magazine or newspaper and you will find the land speculators advertising. They may be selling lots in Florida, Arizona, California or up in the northeast ski country, appealing to the hunger many have for a second home. Or, the ad may be an invitation to join the raiders and go into the land business not just for fun, but for profit.

A giant publishing company (Prentice-Hall) advertises a "Special 12-Page Report on Raw Land: How to Find, Finance & Develop It."

The prospects—so glowingly described—for a fast buck are indeed enticing.

"America is on the verge of its greatest of all real estate booms—a giant boom in raw land—a boom so large it dwarfs anything that has gone before . . .

"You get 6 tested angles that help you line up the most desirable land and rake in top profits from it . . .

"Here is the country's last great real estate frontier—the small investor's last great opportunity for the land to make him rich."

The "Special 12-Page Report" does indeed give practical advice on circumventing local taxes and development restrictions. It supplies juicy case histories of undaunted speculators who turned impossible sites into desirable tracts simply by spotting a salable angle. One New York real estate agent picked up ninety-one acres of woodland at a country sale. He had observed its proximity to a new thruway and a proposed local highway. Just before he contracted to sell off the timber to get back his purchase price, he walked through the woods and noted fresh deer tracks. "The caption 'Hunter's Paradise' flashed through my mind immediately. I ran an ad. It produced 200 phone calls, 4 offers and a buyer within 10 days."

The urge to buy a place of your own, out where the air is fresh and landscape green, has created a bonanza for the land salesmen. On a recent January morning when the temperature was eighteen below zero some 250 men and women arrived at a "Free Real Estate Seminar" held over a hundred miles from New York City near the Massachusetts border. "It's either getting a place in the country or leaving the country," said one exhausted New Yorker as he explained why he had come.

Irving Price, president of one of the largest real estate firms in upstate New York, thought up the seminar and ran it. He says that his prospective customers have changed over the years. No longer does he get well-heeled, mature couples looking for "a manicured estate." His average buyers are "looking for an abandoned farm that'll cost them ten dollars an acre." He smiles at their innocence—"as if the world had stood still here"—but he sympathizes: "They come wanting some privacy and the joys of country living and the satisfaction of owning a share in the United States. I feel we have to cater to them."

Price breaks the bad news about the high cost of even worn-out farmland, telling his audience that values have tripled in the last fifteen years. Then, he warns them against forces they may not be able to control, which will have a powerful effect on their property if they do buy some. "Even if land values in general are bound to keep going up, that doesn't mean every parcel of land will double or triple in value. Nothing to prevent a trailer park or an auto junkyard right across the road from you. Then what happens to the value of your property?"

The Vulnerable Investment

He might also have described the threat of massive development which hangs over every unspoiled valley, every wooded mountain, every uncontaminated brook or lake.

Let's say you love skiing and you put up an A frame on twenty acres, more or less, of Vermont green. Your tax bill is less than two hundred dollars a year. The old-timers are friendly in a live-and-let-live spirit. You ask nothing from them and vice versa. You assume some kind of zoning exists to protect the ground water supply. Your own well and septic systems were put in by local contractors who assured you that they met specifications. There are only a couple of hundred voters in your town because part-time residents don't qualify. You have to count on the good intentions of local officials to protect your investment. All of a sudden a lumber company which, as it turns out, owns thousands of acres surrounding your little oasis decides to sell to a mass-merchandising developer. Before long your uncrowded, unpolluted paradise will be overwhelmed with three thousand new households. Town officials couldn't begin to cope with the police, garbage, traffic, sewer, water problems it will bring; but, they usually don't see the danger or take steps to prevent it until it's too late.

When a big-time developer moves in he spares no effort in bringing local influence to bear on his side. When Stratton, Vermont, was threatened by an instant vacation-home complex, its Planning Commission reported that the giant paper company which masterminded the deal hired all the lawyers from miles around and even offered to put the town's selectmen on its payroll.

Environmental experts can help small communities assess the impact of massive incursion, but too often small towns jealously guard their right to home rule. They are wary of regional planning, reluctant to adopt zoning codes which, they think, take a man's right to exploit his property away from him. Unable to comprehend the horrors of the giant development bearing down on them, they cling to old-fashioned laissez-faire. They don't have the technical expertise, they haven't been out in the great world, and they are snowed and impressed by a battery of experts—engineers, lawyers, salesmen—the companies bring along. Dazzled by the prospect of growth, they ignore the schools they'll be building, the roads they will have to put in and plow and repair.

The Big-Timers in Action

Suppose you want to move in on a community. What do you do first? You approach the local banks, the local politicians, the local power structure. You talk about the jobs you'll be creating—somebody has to haul the gravel, work the bulldozer, sell the insurance, loan the money. And, when you've finished developing, you point out that new construction has added dollars to the tax rolls, conveniently forgetting the children you've just added to the schools.

The individual who buys a single summer cottage doesn't create severe problems, but multiply him by hundreds and you put a heavy load on sewers and water supply. This is, however, nothing compared to what happens when a huge development sets its sights on virgin land.

Not long ago Boise Cascade bought 5200 acres next to the White Mountains National Forest and laid plans to build 3768 houses, 177 condominiums, 166 town houses. The plan was sweetened with some land use concessions—a golf course to provide open space, lake facilities, hiking trails. There were no local zoning controls to regulate sanitation plans. "If we hadn't stepped in they would have been dumping the refuse from that development into the lakes," Mary Louise Hancock, New Hampshire state planning director, told *The New York Times* which reported the affair. Using what Miss Hancock called "an inadequate and limited tool—a State shoreline protection law," the state was able to hold off development until the corporation came up with an approved sewage disposal plan.

"Without better statewide land use control," says Miss Hancock, "we're just not going to be able to control such massive developments. Projections indicate our population will triple in the next fifty years. As it is now, a developer can go into a revenue-starved community and, in many cases, build any way he pleases with no control over the sanitation, land use, or construction."

One of the favorite strategies employed by the spoilers is to spend money before they have received permission to build. Site preparation work, architectural fees, money that is tied up by bank loans—these represent an investment by the developer. He then asks for special dispensation because of hardship.

A running battle in Maine over the development of an oil distribution and storage center on Long Island in beautiful Casco Bay suggests the way this strategy can be used.

King Resources, Inc., purchased a U. S. Navy fuel depot on Long Island in 1969. The depot was created during World War II to meet an emergency.

At issue was the question of whether or not the King Resources project was subject to the controls established by the Maine Site Law. These read in part:

"The Legislature finds and declares that the highest and best uses of the seacoast of the State are as a source of public and private recreation and solace from the pressures of an industrialized society and as a source of public use and private commerce in fishing, lobstering, and gathering other marine life . . .

"The Legislature further finds and declares that the transfer of oil, petroleum products and their byproducts between vessels and vessels and onshore facilities and vessels within the jurisdiction of the State and State waters is a hazardous undertaking . . . that such hazards have frequently occurred in the past, are occurring now and present future threats of potentially catastrophic proportions . . ."

The Court held that King Resources was exempt from the Site Law because the depot was in "existence" before the law came into force. They further ruled that because King

134320

ÉMORY & HENRY LIBRARY

had spent certain sums on the project the Court was unwilling to, according to Orlando E. Delogu of the University of Maine Law School, "allow these investments to be lost or the benefit from them to be further delayed by holding King amenable to the Site Law." Mr. Delogu points out: "The Court fails to recognize that King need not have expended these sums prior to gaining all of the necessary permits and approvals. What a novel and mischievous doctrine the Court sanctions—King Resources voluntarily placed itself in a position of hardship and then argued its hardship as a reason for the Court to exempt it from the Site Law and the Court unmindful of legislative intent and the public interest in having the Site Law applied protects the private investment."

Mr. Delogu sees this decision as a damaging victory for the exploiter. He faults the court for siding "with large property interests rather than protect(ing) the public's interest. They have ignored (avoiding applying) the single most important piece of environmental control legislation on the statutes, they have allowed the single most dangerous environmental activity (oil handling) to operate in a new and very strategic location in Casco Bay."

Ripe for Development

States like Maine, Vermont, and New Hampshire with their enormous recreation potential are ripe for exploitation and state officials know it. When superhighways crisscross once inaccessible lands and bring vacationers in by the thousands, not the hundreds, then you get trouble.

Half the population of New Hampshire, a meager seven hundred thousand, is made up of vacation homeowners.

The New York Times recently estimated that "140 developers are pumping untold millions of dollars into seasonal and year-round recreational developments. And there are realtors who have standing orders from New York and Boston clients to buy any large parcel of land that comes on the market."

New Hampshire governor Walter Peterson understands only too well:

"When all is said and done the central problem of New Hampshire in the foreseeable future is growth. Growth produces enormous benefits and new opportunities, but it also contains the seeds of disaster. Growth puts houses where there were open spaces. It puts pollutants into streams, it requires new schools for which the property taxes of the newcomers do not fully pay, it discourages rather than encourages the tourists who come for elbow room and clean air, it puts demands on state services above and beyond what the average citizen pays in."

Indeed, an entire region may have to cope with problems created by unbridled development in one or two states. And the homeowner will foot the bill for pollution control.

Christopher Percy, executive director of the Connecticut River Watershed Council, has reason to fear the impact of large-scale building in Vermont and New Hampshire. The pollution created by careless development upriver will surely affect the purity of the water in the states below which receive this contaminated flow.

The rate of development in Vermont and New Hampshire has accelerated to the point where Percy worries about a regional pollution problem of real consequence.

He explains that "these are not just any ordinary subdivision developers. These are the corporate giants such as

International Paper, Boise Cascade—and the Mafia, which we may include because of its financial power. These entities are developing at rates of fifteen hundred and two thousand acre slugs of land—and they own thousands of acres . . .

"Boise Cascade is only one of a number of companies which are raping our landscape for profit while making problems for our environment . . .

"All these companies have headquarters outside the valley, so development decisions are being made by people living outside the region. Consequently, it appears that they will have little feeling for the valley environment, or the impact their decisions will have on us. It seems the profit motive is their guiding force and light."

Big Money in Land

The paper companies have long been giant landowners because they use forest products in manufacturing. But other corporations are now looking at land as a prime investment and their plans include development. A headline in *The New York Times* reads: "Companies Now Prospecting for Dollars in Land." The story lists a string of blue-chip companies who "are becoming increasingly involved in land development and other construction activities."

They include: Union Camp, Ogden, American-Standard, Humble Oil and Refining, General Electric, Alcoa, International Telephone and Telegraph, Weyerhaeuser, Transamerica, City Investing, Gulf Oil, Boise Cascade, Chrysler, Gulf and Western Industries, and Westinghouse Electric.

W. D. Eberle, president of American-Standard, told the

Times that real estate development "is a good business and it meets our economic criteria for profits and growth."

There is no question about the money to be made on land. *House & Home* has stated that "since World War II land speculation has created more millionaires than any other form of business investment."

In recent years the leisure market, the boom in second homes and rise of vacation-retirement communities, has made companies interested in exploiting this market go after land.

They may claim that they are meeting a need, providing housing for thousands of mobile Americans who want a place in the sun or on the ski slopes, but the damage they are capable of doing, the impact on the environment when they move in, cannot be overrated.

It will take enormous public will to stop the invaders, those who are determined to make not just a buck off the land but a million bucks. When land is scarce, when it brings a high price, those who buy it feel completely justified in wringing the last ounce of profit from their investment.

Richard Babcock, a Chicago attorney, described for the American Society of Planning Officials just what we may expect as the big-time operators move out for a land grab.

"Private development in the '70s will increasingly be carried on by organizations that treat land development as only one of a variety of investments. Major industrial organizations will be investing heavily in real estate. The reasons are readily apparent. Land has traditionally been a hedge against inflationary periods. More importantly, many concerns manufacturing consumer products see land development as a synergistic operation which will help to merchandise other goods or services provided by the industry . . . What can be expected (is) a major invasion of the real estate field by companies who ten years ago had no interest at all . . .

"These organizations have vast resources. Unlike many smaller developers, they can sweat out the customary delays put forward by municipal bodies to discourage development they do not favor. Secondly, these developers will usually be talking about very large tracts of land and very significant developments. They will be interested in special concessions and will, in effect, want regulations to be cut to favor the pattern of their development."

One of the most significant factors in land use is the way one invasion triggers another. When you have many different pressure groups pushing for a slice of the land you inevitably open the door to more than you bargain for when you give a little. You upset the holding pattern.

Industry and the Suburbs

Industry and business look for cheap land and lots of it when they think of moving out of the city. Once they stake a claim in suburbia and ask for rezoning they invite other land-use changes. Business and commercial interests want to service the industry and ask rezoning for store and office space. Civil rights advocates, egged on by developers who would dearly love to eradicate zoning, come in their wake, demanding land to house the workers who will serve the plant which has moved to the suburbs to cut its overhead.

The town which thought it could have the best of both worlds, large-lot zoning and some clean industry to help pay the tax bills, finds that it has opened the door to problems it would just as soon ignore.

Every town would like to have an industry assessed at three million dollars, which builds its plant underground and has three employees. But what it gets is a plant with people—people who need to be housed and schooled and transported.

If the town is not prepared to carry what civil rights leaders call "social costs" by building low-cost housing, then they claim the town should not profit by taxes levied on the assets of the corporation.

It is not as easy as it once was to invade a residential community and build a plant or corporate headquarters. There was a time when big business was looked upon as the answer to a community's tax problems. No longer. Even nice, clean businesses—and everybody wants those—can go broke and there is no guarantee that the next tenant will be as desirable. Pressure from civil rights groups has forced town officials to acknowledge an obligation to provide housing for low-income groups who may work for the new industry, but who cannot afford to live in a town where zoning makes land high-priced and housing scarce. There are drawbacks as well as advantages when industry moves into open country. Despite the promise of strict zoning laws to control pollution there is always the possibility that such laws will be diluted under pressure from the industry once it is established. There will be the plea to relax them a bit, or the industry will have to move out and there go the taxes.

Big companies are all too aware of the public relations problems they face when they upset the residential pattern of outlying areas.

Not long ago Uris Buildings Corporation and First National City Bank of New York advertised a proposed industrial park with a full page in *The New York Times*.

They had anticipated the problems most companies encounter when they try to move to the suburbs and tried to reassure prospective tenants of the park.

Located on the New York–New Jersey line, Blue Hill is "a reliable 35 minutes from midtown Manhattan." It "provides a happy compromise between convenient executive access and the ready availability of support labor." In other words it is convenient to Connecticut, New York, and New Jersey suburbs where the bosses live, but is located in a low-income area where the "support labor"—that is, poor and blacks—can afford to live. "Its population is predominantly young marrieds and lower-middle management personnel families from which the largest yield of quality clerical applicants is typically drawn."

Blue Hill's developers claimed they had won "the enthusiastic support of local authorities and citizens" for their complex. Any company which came in would, therefore, be spared "potentially serious public relations problems." They must have worked hard indeed because their plans involved building 131,000 square feet of store and commercial space to give workers in the office complete service and stimulate the "variety and excitement of 'downtown.'"

Large-scale builders try to minimize the impact their designs will make on residential areas. A favorite euphemism is "campus style." At Blue Hill the "total project consists of low-rise buildings closely grouped around a 20-story tower. Architecturally, the tower building is conceived as a focal point for the entire development, similar to a bell tower at a university campus."

This type of cautious advertising, stressing the amenities to be preserved rather than simply the cold profits to be realized, shows that the conservation activists are having an impact. In the year between the first Earth Day and the second, they demonstrated enough power to slow, and in some cases halt, the juggernaut of development.

A Stiffening Resistance

Earth Times bemoaned the "Big Boise Rip-Off" on Earth Day I, 1970. A report on Boise Cascade's plans for the Lake Tahoe region castigated the company and government officials cooperating with it. "At Incline Village, for example, county officials have been willing to give Boise Cascade whatever it wanted, without regard for protecting the rights of the public interest, or the ecology of the Tahoe basin . . . What Boise does is run rampant over the land, damaging and exploiting natural environments, for the benefit of a wealthy few and to the detriment of the general public."

Boise was planning at the time to build a recreational development of thirteen hundred lots—called "Sunny Meadows"—on Lake Edson which is near Tahoe. The Public Utilities District wanted a sewage treatment plant built to take care of the sanitation problem. Boise held out for individual septic tanks. Citizens of the area could just imagine the problems this would bring. They were particularly concerned about the fate of their drinking water, which came from Lake Edson. One wrote the local paper: "Boise Cascade wants septic tanks, with future problems and expenses left to a 'homeowners association' with themselves long gone, laughing all the way to the bank."

Earth Times confidently assumed that "Boise will win and that their policy of pollute and rape the land and move on will be followed at Sunny Meadows." Their prediction under-estimated the degree of public outrage over indiscriminate development and the passion for reform sparked by Earth Day.

By year's end, Boise had abandoned the project, taking a half-million-dollar loss in options and planning studies. According to the *Wall Street Journal,* citizens of the area, "led by a woman librarian, mounted a public campaign, and defeated the project. Boise was embarrassed by the outcry— and discouraged by the added cost of a sewage system."

The *Wall Street Journal* counted this as only one defeat suffered by Boise in 1970.

"Earlier this year, Boise dropped plans for a project in Vermont. A consulting ecologist, considering the likely re-action of residents of the area, advised against the plan . . . In other projects, agreements (some voluntary, some forced) with local and state authorities to preserve environmental features have boosted expenses sharply. To compensate for the ecological effects of a project near Seattle, Boise agreed to spend more than $200,000 to build fish spawning beds. At its huge project in Hawaii, Boise has agreed with an archaeological museum to preserve certain ancient Hawaiian artifacts on the property . . .

"Because of such problems, Boise says it has decided to stay out of 'ecologically sensitive' areas. For instance, it has flatly stated it won't develop the valuable coastal property in Northern California's Mendocino County. Area conserva-tionists have been jumpy ever since Boise obtained the land in the acquisition several years ago."

Development costs on Incline Village at Lake Tahoe have risen to more than half of the project's market value, instead of the usual one third because of demands for environmental safeguards. No wonder Boise lost $11 million that year, as it met increasing, and effective, opposition to pollution-prone projects.

The mood of the country has changed. Property owners have learned to anticipate the damage which could follow in the wake of big-time development and they will fight the project to a halt until they are assured that every precaution has been taken against environmental disaster.

Chet Huntley's Big Sky project in Montana is a case in point. This 10,647-acre, $20 million recreational complex could be, in Huntley's words, "the greatest thing that ever happened to Montana." Or, to quote those who oppose it, "it could be something else."

Montana is wide open to speculators at the moment. Dorothy Bradley, a twenty-three-year-old member of the State House of Representatives, says: "Out-of-state developers are buying land all over the state and there are no restrictions as to what they can do with it. Without zoning and planning they can build outhouses over the streams." Miss Bradley won her election with the slogan "Dorothy is for the birds and the elk and the bears and the flowers and for Montana." Her victory reflects the ever-increasing concern for the land. "The people were ready for a strong environmental pitch." Like many others in the state, she is wary of massive development without safeguards and is worried about projects like Big Sky. She knows that what we need is a radical change in consciousness as well as legal and legislative protection for the environment.

Dorothy Bradley's assessment of the situation is more optimistic than otherwise, but she recognizes that we have a long way to go. "My hope is that the 'frontier conviction' of the right to do anything to one's own land will diminish as people realize that they have no more right to abuse their land than to abuse their own children. This may take time, but surely it is coming."

5

Save the Land

One sure-fire way to beat the spoilers is to take the land off the market and put it into public trust. The best defense is often a strong offense. Citizens are forming land trusts to accept and preserve open land. Communities are buying up open space and instituting zoning to protect conservation acreage from exploitation. In some towns enterprising citizens have set up nonprofit development corporations to compete with commercial interests. Once they secure the land, they develop it at low density and set aside large tracts of green for public use.

The Nature Conservancy, Audubon, and other national land-save organizations are having singular success in attracting gifts of prime conservation land. There now seem to be as many nondevelopers around as developers and the prospects for preserving a significant slice of our national heritage are indeed promising.

For those who view the environmentalists as "fundamentally negative" this record of preservation should be reassuring. They aren't simply keeping people off the land. They are preserving land so that the people will have somewhere to go —for recreation and renewal.

There are five major ways to save the land. Every device, strategy, technique used by the landsavers will fit nicely into one or more of these categories.

Get someone to hold it.

Get someone to give it.

Get someone to buy it.

Get someone to control its use.

Get someone to develop it properly.

Success in applying these methods is absolutely dependent upon a community conviction that keeping land open is in the public interest and should be encouraged. If most people believe that all land should be developed, that the highest and best use of a piece of land is its site potential for housing or commerce, then these methods will fail.

In most towns there is an established body of opinion which believes that land is only a commodity. Unhappily, a good many town officials are of this persuasion. There is also, by now, in most towns, a strong movement away from the commodity concept. People have learned to protest when the landscape and familiar landmarks are threatened. And, they no longer feel quite so powerless to stop progress.

They are determined to save the land they love and, fortunately, there is more than one way for them to achieve this goal. Some towns use all the methods described here;

other communities are experimenting with one or two. The town which employs every means of saving land is, naturally, the town which stands a better chance of preserving its environment.

The key to making the methods work lies in a realistic appraisal of human nature. What inspires people to put out good money for land which may never produce a traditional "return" on their investment, land which is preserved solely for "open space?" What makes a man give his land freely without putting a conventional price tag on it? Why would someone hold on to prime land when he could get a handsome price if he would only turn the old farm into house lots?

Enlightened Self-Interest

Self-interest is the key. And under self-interest we can list local pride, the very human desire to return something to a community you love, a sense that future generations will thank the person who put his land in trust for them.

These are the genuine motives, the good ones. But, if landowners are to realize their philanthropic ambitions we must make it economically feasible for them to do so. This usually means providing the mechanism for a tax break. However, there are landowners who have so little real wealth that the taxes they might save through a gift are insignificant. They give because they want to save the birds and the bees and the trees. They may feel that they can't contribute much to posterity, but at least they can leave their land. Usually, they are getting on in years, have no heirs and the land is their whole estate.

Willie Browne is just such a person.

On November 15, 1969, he transferred 361 acres, worth a million dollars, to the Nature Conservancy. This land, along the St. Johns River near Jacksonville, Florida, was Willie Browne's entire estate. He had lived a hermit's life on the property his father left him in the early years of the century with the admonition "Look after it and don't let the hunters in."

Willie Browne kept the tract free of hunters, but open to nature lovers. As he turned eighty, he began to wonder how he could make sure the land would remain in its pristine condition after he was gone. He had never married, had no heirs to consider, and could give the land to anyone who would promise to keep it out of development.

Neither the Federal nor Florida State Government would accept the restrictions he wanted to put on his land, so he turned to the Nature Conservancy, a national organization set up to take land and preserve it. They agreed to his conditions enthusiastically, took the land, and made it possible for him to live in his little house on the property, taking care of the tract until he dies.

Willie Browne is remarkable, but he is not unique. The records of the Nature Conservancy tell the stories of philanthropists on all income levels, men and women who have given a bit of cherished land to the public estate. Some are more than able to give away thousands of acres, for others the gift represents a real sacrifice.

What will motivate, say, a family which owns a hundred acres, all developable, to give at least a portion of this for open space? How, in fact, could they afford to do so? Can they hold off the developers for long when property taxes escalate and the offers to buy and build are irresistible?

How can towns afford to buy up all the open space they need, and want? According to federal experts who are fond of postulating across-the-board standards, a town should have 25 per cent of its land in open space. What town could afford to lay out cash for a real estate investment on this order of magnitude?

Clearly, communities which see the need for open space and who are fearful that prized natural resources will soon be bulldozed out of existence must use every land-save device at their disposal to preserve what's left.

Those who care passionately about what is happening to the landscape must be the modern Paul Reveres rousing their neighbors to action. If they are to get results, actually accomplish miracles in saving the land, they must know why it is to the town's advantage. They must be able to show that it will pay off in the long run and, even in the short run, not break the bank. Just as important, they must prove to individual landowners that it is in their own self-interest to hold the land or give it or allow it to be controlled for the public good.

Only the very rich can afford to hold large tracts of land when property taxes soar through the ceiling. And land values have risen in the last decade to the point where "vacant land," as it is depreciatingly called by assessors, is taxed as much as buildings. Assessors who believe, shortsightedly, that their mission is to raise as much revenue as possible for a town and never mind the impact on the way the town looks or develops, contend that they are obliged to tax on fair market value.

An unholy coalition between town assessors, town fathers, and real estate interests can lead to revaluation of land as a marketable commodity. What-you-could-get-for-it-if-you-sold-it becomes the lever to raise taxes. You may never want to sell. You may envision your ten or twenty or fifty acres as a wilderness area which you, personally, will manage and pass along to your children and grandchildren. Never mind. You could sell it for XXX dollars, couldn't you? Yes. Admittedly, yes. Well, then, we're going to tax you at your potential profit and not take into account what you're doing with it right now.

This is known as "driving land onto the market" by those who resent the tactic and who feel, whether or not they are personally victimized, that it is a shortsighted way to raise revenues. For, they explain, if the land is sold because taxes are too high, then it will soon blossom with houses, inhabited by children who will need new schools, and homeowners who will demand town services.

Assessors like to quote their own professional guidelines which state that land must be assessed at "its highest and best use."

The question then turns on what is the highest and best use. In other times that could be answered quite simply: to produce goods and services. Today, we would offer another alternative: to produce a quality environment.

Tax Inducement to Hold Land

In an effort to combat conventional assessment approach, and make it possible to hold acreage by paying reasonable taxes, several states have instituted preferential tax treatment for farmers and other large landowners. California, Pennsylvania, Maryland, New Jersey, Hawaii, Texas, and Connecticut have tried it.

In Connecticut, Public Act 490 establishes a "use value" rather than a "fair market value." The Act was originally written to help farmers stay on the land because their acreage was being taxed at what it could bring for development. In some communities, 490 is being used to slow development and prevent—in the language of the Act—"the forced conversion of farm land, forest land and open space land to more intensive uses as the result of economic pressures caused by the assessment thereof for purposes of property taxation at values incompatible with their preservation as such."

Undeveloped land can be valued for as little as ten dollars an acre under the "use value" concept. The "fair market value" of that same acre might amount to thousands of dollars.

Toward the end of the '60s, when many towns in Connecticut went through a re-evaluation of property, assessments soared because they reflected the high cost of land. Anyone owning land in excess of his building lot suddenly found himself holding onto some very expensive green space. Could he afford to keep it?

The town of Lyme, Connecticut, considered applying the 490 use value concept to all lands over three acres in an attempt to minimize the impact of revaluation. Open land cost the town nothing in services, but if it were forced onto the market because of high taxes and sold for development, town services and school costs would escalate. A Study Committee concluded that it was in the public interest to protect open land through preferential tax treatment.

Redding is another town which has adopted 490 across the

board, giving a tax break to anything over four acres. True, homeowners will have to pay more property tax because "the burden has been shifted from land to houses," but those same homeowners will be protected against forced land sales which could bring major developers into the town.

Not everybody agrees that tax abatement on open land is an unqualified success. William H. ("Holly") Whyte, who helped write Connecticut's 490, believes that shrewd developers can take advantage of preferential tax laws, hold land while paying low taxes on it until the time is ripe for a sellout. He would like to see some kind of recapture clause which would oblige those who benefit from 490 to hold the land for a specified period of time, or pay back taxes if they sell out before the time is up. There have been several proposals for a recapture clause, and it seems likely that the State Legislature will vote for one. The point of 490 is to help landowners hold their land. They, in turn, should be willing to pay a graduated tax if they sell out.

Giving an Easement

Another means of holding land is the "easement." You trade what Holly Whyte has called "your right to louse it up" for lowered taxes. You sign an agreement—with the local government or land trust or national conservation group —giving the recipient an easement. It can be a positive easement. You might, as was the case in New York, help the state recreation department establish a system of fishing streams open to the public. You are letting people on your land for a worthy purpose. You are, therefore, entitled to compensation by way of reduced taxes.

There is also the negative easement. You agree not to build on a particular piece or property which is highly valued, let's say, for its scenic potential. Or, you agree not to fill in a river or dig gravel or do anything which would change the landscape. You give up "your right to louse it up" and you get a tax break in return.

Many open space preservationists are sold on the easement method, but just as many prefer an outright gift. The transfer of land, in fee simple, is a clean-cut way of saving property. The new owner doesn't have to bother with any prior claims on the land. He can manage it as he likes.

Who has the means to give away land? Those who have what Ned Smith of the Open Space Institute calls "philanthropic capability." By that he means they are rich and they have no heirs. Certainly they are ideal donors. But many others have the ability to give land because they have the will to do so. They are strongly motivated to set aside some or all of their property for open space because they want to see it preserved in its natural state—forever.

Who can afford to make such a gift? A surprising number of middle-income people have decided that they are better off giving at least some of their land than they are selling it to the highest bidder. One such donor worked out an arrangement with his local land trust which enabled him to preserve the open meadow which was his view, conserve the wildflowers and wildlife habitat which gave him enormous pleasure, and at the same time get relief from heavy property taxes and make a modest return on his dollar investment.

He had one hundred acres which had been in his family for generations. Local tax revaluation drove property taxes sharply skyward and forced him to make a decision on disposing of it. His lawyer suggested that he sell fifty acres of the best building land, an old orchard with a spectacular view, for the going rate. He realized a healthy profit on land which was pre-eminently suited for development. It had good soil for buildings, was tucked away for privacy and near town roads. The other fifty acres was a conservationist's paradise.

An old wood road led down into a mysterious rock-bound gorge. The place was loaded with mountain laurel and wild-flowers. Deer bounded over the trails, pheasants could be flushed at will. A small stream ended in a mini-waterfall and beyond that was total wilderness. The tract abounded in wildlife and specimen trees. It was worth saving without any question. He could afford to give because he had sold the old tract and could now use a charitable contribution to set against his profit. He gave the fifty acres of wilderness to the local land trust to keep forever wild.

This donor came out ahead on his hundred acres. He was paid a fair price for the whole hundred if you average it out, counting the tax advantage he realized on the gift. But he benefited in more than one way. He was ahead not just economically, but environmentally as well. He continues to live within sight of the nature preserve he gave the land trust. His personal world has been enhanced by this fifty acres of wilderness. And, of course, he can take pleasure in the school children who roam its trails and enjoy the freedom in nature that he had had as a child.

Buying Open Land

As communities see more and more prize land slip into development, they may come to the conclusion that they are going to have to compete with the developers and buy open land with tax dollars if they hope to keep some balance of nature.

Every town should have an open space plan which establishes priorities for acquisition. Which lands must be kept open and unscarred at all costs? Perhaps it is the river which gives the town its character. Or, the mountain which provides the view. Or, marshes vital to the water supply. Or, a beach or lake which could give pleasure for generations to come.

Towns which have conservation commissions charge them with drawing up such a plan. If the town wants funding for open-space purchases from the state and/or the Federal Government, it must be able to demonstrate that it has worked out a rational program for acquisition.

State and federal funding of open space projects can be generous or stingy depending upon who is in charge politically and what the state of the economy happens to be at the moment. But, no town should let the opportunity for financial help go by default. Fill out the papers, process the forms, apply for aid to every government agency that will listen.

There are communities which deplore government aid. They stanchly wish to go it alone. They don't want anyone from the outside meddling in their affairs. They fear the invasion of visitors entitled to use the town's open space because it was purchased with government money. Some opponents of open space acquisition have played on these fears and suggested that government aid is simply a tool to be used, eventually, to resettle thousands of the disadvantaged on open space bought with federal money.

In point of fact, funding does carry a few strings. The most significant is that the land cannot be used for any purpose not consonant with open space. No development, road-building, or improvement is allowed. That would seem to discredit the charge that these open lands are going to be used for giant low-cost housing projects.

This very restriction which means that open land must stay open is, according to conservationists, a big selling point for government funding. If a town buys land with its own money, it may not be willing to restrict use for generations to come.

With monotonous regularity, federal, regional, and state planners trumpet the urgency of an ambitious land-acquisition program. In September 1970 the president of the Regional Plan Association warned that it would take 350 years to acquire the open space his association believes is necessary to take care of the seventy million people who will be living in the Boston-to-Washington megalopolis by the year 2000. If, that is, the current rate of acquisition is maintained.

Some towns are more willing than others to spend money for open space. They may be the ones who are the most pressured by growth, who can see neighboring communities cave in to the demands of developers. Some of these towns have written remarkable records in land preservation. They show what can be done when an aggressive conservation commission takes the lead and explores all avenues of funding to secure open space.

Redding, Connecticut, now owns 750 acres of land, some 500 of which was purchased with state and federal grants bringing the cost per acre down to around $300 an acre. The last big buy—270 acres of the Steichen property at $2500 an acre—was bought with the town's own money on a twenty-year bond issue.

Gifts of Land

Even the most ambitious conservation commission realizes that the public purse cannot afford all the desirable open land which is going on the market. Town purchase must be supplemented with gifts of land. If a town has a local land trust, it has the mechanism to accept these gifts and to help the donor realize a tax advantage.

Land trusts are particularly strong in New England, although they are springing up across the country. Some private landholding groups, like the Newtown (Conn.) Forest Association, have been in operation for decades, but the modern land trust came into being in the 1960s.

Put simply, a land trust is a private, nonprofit corporation which is legally empowered to accept and manage land. Because it is nonprofit and dedicated to the public interest, it is tax exempt. Because it does scientific, educational, and charitable work, and has invited a broad-based general membership, donations to it are tax deductible.

Under the prevailing laws, gifts to a publicly supported trust can represent as much as 50 per cent deducted from the donor's adjusted gross income.

There are people in every community who would like to dedicate all or a portion of their property to open space. If property taxes in their community have escalated, as they have in most, they wonder how long they can continue to hold the land open. They may offer it to the town to be used for open space, only to learn that there is no interest in such a gift. Not all town fathers are so shortsighted, but an unforgivable number shy away from the responsibility of taking what they like to call "little bits and pieces of land." They complain, too, that such land will go off the tax rolls and since it cannot be used for pure recreation—ball parks and playing fields—they wonder aloud just how valuable it is to the town. In the eyes of conservationists it is immensely valuable, of course.

Towns should—in their own self-interest—be ready and willing and eager to accept any land that comes their way and be obliging when the donor establishes controls on it which insure that it will remain open forever. When a town is reluctant to take land, and the donor does not want to turn to a national organization, which might insist upon an endowment to pay for management over the years, a local land trust can provide the means to save the acreage.

A land trust can work out flexible arrangements with donors negotiating in a spirit of "What can we do for you?" Town negotiators are likely to be all too conscious of what the donor should do for the town, an attitude which has more than once discouraged, or even enraged, a potential philanthropist.

When a municipality does accept land, it wants it to come with no strings attached. Justifiably or not, some donors feel that if they don't write restrictions into the deed, the town might decide in years to come to use the open space for other municipal needs—a town dump, gravel dig, parking lot. When the gift is made to the trust, the land is off the market forever, and the donor's restrictions on its management are strictly observed.

There have been cases where a town was perfectly willing to accept a gift, but the Town Council could not be satisfied that the deed was clear. A land trust can be more of a risk-taker. Trusts are willing to accept any parcel, large or small, as long as it has conservation value. A town may feel that it must be able to visualize public use in the here and now, along recreation lines, to warrant acceptance. A land trust looks ahead and works to preserve acreage which can become the town's heritage of a green and open future.

Land Trusts Can Help

Although trusts are set up to meet the needs of private donors, they can be useful in implementing a town's open space program. Communities which are conservation-oriented know that trusts can complement the work of conservation commissions and other agencies involved in land use.

Some towns have an open space provision in their subdivision regulations and can ask developers to donate a portion of the land to conservation use. The question then arises: Who will accept and manage this public land? The trust can, and often does, volunteer to do so.

A private trust can act quickly when property is about to go on the market. Suppose a town has long wanted to acquire a choice natural area. Before it can act, it may have to cut through a considerable amount of red tape, secure funding, and, of course, bring the prospective purchase before the town for a vote. While this procedure is necessary, it is also time-consuming. The property owner may not want to wait while the town decides whether to buy or not. The land trust could take an option on the property, holding it until the town is able to act.

Trusts also work with planning, zoning, and conservation commissions and with town government to implement new and innovative methods for saving the landscape. (See page 303 for a model easement.)

When the Glendinning Company proposed building its headquarters on a forty-acre tract in Westport, Connecticut, neighboring homeowners protested that the area was zoned two-acre residential. Westport has a discretionary zoning law called "Design Development District." If an applicant for industrial and commercial development can demonstrate that his project will not spoil a residential area, and if he will agree not to use more than 15 per cent of the site for the building, he may be granted permission to construct. Those protesting the Glendinning project were openly worried that the twenty-five-acre green buffer zone would not always stay untouched. What if zoning regulations were to change in the future? What protection would neighboring landowners have?

Their fears dissolved when Glendinning proposed giving the twenty-five-acre tract to the Aspetuck Land Trust to be preserved as open space in perpetuity.

In other communities, trusts have worked out arrangements with developers to preserve crucial natural areas, either by outright gift or through an easement.

Often a trust can initiate a land-save program, later pass along the property it has acquired with a reverter clause to a public group. If this approach is used, the donor can give land to the trust with certain stipulated uses spelled out. Then, when the trust passes along the land to a town or county, the restrictions ride with the deed. If those who have been given the land in trust violate any of the restrictions, the property reverts to the trust.

Private trusts have shown that they can work very effectively with governmental agencies. In some cases they have been the spark that stimulated elected officials to get on with a much-needed job of preservation or control.

The saving of the Nissitissit River which flows from New Hampshire to Massachusetts is a case in point.

The Nissitissit is a wild river, rich in wood duck, blacks and teal. It is clean and pure, full of trout, abundant wildflowers grow along the banks. In 1957 the Massachusetts Department of Natural Resources gave the river a high priority for acquisition. But it took the work of hundreds of concerned citizens to save it. The leader of the effort, Mrs. Annette Cottrell, helped incorporate the Nissitissit Land Trust in 1968, believing that the trust could save the river by picking up land or easements along the river for a crucial 4.7-mile section. When these properties have been acquired, they will be turned over to a local conservation commission or the appropriate agencies. Realizing that donation of land would be slow in coming, the trust began a drive to raise $9000 to buy more land. Contributions ranging from $1 to $2000 poured in, and the New Hampshire section of the river has now been saved.

Starting a Land Trust

If your state has laws which permit private groups to organize as nonprofit corporations, you can start a land trust. First, of course, you must seek the help of a friendly, conservation-minded lawyer who will check the statutes for you. And, if he is a true conservationist, he may not charge you for the service.

After you get a legal go-ahead, you can invite a group of

like-minded, community leaders to discuss forming a trust. You need incorporators to make your land trust a legal entity, capable of receiving and managing land. Any resident of the town can be an incorporator.

Your friendly lawyer will, hopefully, draw up bylaws and apply for tax exempt status and guide you through any red tape required by your state or town. See page 307 for a model.

Once you are legally incorporated, you call a meeting of interested citizens to hear just what a land trust can do for a town. One newly formed trust sent out a letter to everybody in town, inviting them to an organizational meeting:

"We, the incorporators listed below, invite you to help conserve the natural beauty still in Redding before it is too late. Join the Redding Land Trust and help maintain rolling hills, wildflower bogs, bird sanctuaries, streams and ponds. Support the land trust and help keep the unusual range of animal and plant life presently enriching our town.

"Town officials are agreed that open space is an urgent need, not only from a conservationist point of view, but as a means of keeping open and residential lands in reasonable proportion.

"The Trust offers conservation-minded citizens an opportunity to donate land in the assurance that it will be retained in its natural state *permanently*. We have been empowered by the State of Connecticut to accept lands suitable for educational, scientific and conservation purposes. The Trust will manage these properties to make the most of their natural assets for the benefit of all Redding residents. We will also purchase lands when possible."

Trustees should represent a broad spectrum of citizenry, people concerned with conservation, of course, but others who can help the Trust professionally. You might want to include an ecology teacher, a garden club member, a Scout leader. You also need professionals to provide special services for the Trust. It helps to have a lawyer on the board, a banker or insurance man, and a public relations or advertising expert. Some trusts have found real estate men and women extremely helpful. They always know when land is going on the market and what it is worth.

Many trusts send out town-wide mailings to publicize their accomplishments and their programs for land acquisition. They address themselves to problems landowners have in common, and suggest solutions.

Southeast Open Spaces, Inc., (SOS) serving New York's Putnam and Westchester areas invited all residents "to participate in a challenging new venture dedicated to the preservation of the natural beauty that is characteristic of your area . . . Southeast Open Spaces, Inc., has a program that with your participation can have important tax advantages for you, for all residents faced with increasing taxes, and for your town faced with increasing demands to serve newly developing areas."

The Guilford (Conn.) Trust asked in its mailing: "Can Guilford be different? Or, is it going to be like towns whose residents have sacrificed their natural assets. Many of us have moved to Guilford because it represents what we have always known and loved. Others of us have come because we saw here what we have always dreamed of but never had. All of us have been attracted by its old New England charm, friendly people, and its shores, hills and marshes.

"Guilford is a place to enjoy life as it used to be, when

the pace wasn't so fast, the highways so crowded, and the pressure so great.

"So, whether we have grown up in Guilford or have come here more recently, all of us realize that we have something in Guilford that's rare these days. And most of us want to keep as much of it as we can, while we move steadily, intelligently into tomorrow.

"That's why the Guilford Land Conservation Trust was started—to help us retain the past, make the most of our present and plan for the future.

"The Trust's primary objective is to preserve and protect Guilford's heritage of natural resources—to be sure that the reasons we like Guilford shall endure in the years to come. The Trust seeks to set aside, forever, the open spaces of their recreational, esthetic, and educational values."

The Dollars-and-Cents Message

The Redding Land Trust was fortunate in having a number of publishing and advertising professionals in its group. Shortly after the incorporation meeting, the trustees decided to put out a brochure which would describe the potential of the trust and, hopefully, attract donations of land and money.

Gordon Page, a retired advertising copywriter, created an editorial message which would appeal to civic pride as well as every homeowner's desire to improve the worth of his property.

"How the Redding Land Trust, Inc. Can Help You Protect Your Home and Town Investment." This was the headline of a handsomely executed mailing piece, designed and illustrated by artist, Arthur Shilstone. The goal of the Trust was spelled out:

"To conserve natural resources with pockets of open land so that the Redding of the future will retain as much as possible of its attractive character. Open land accomplishes two desirable purposes: First, it helps to preserve the rural aspect of our town. Second, and at the same time, open land contributes to orderly and attractive town growth. The Redding Land Trust was organized to help the landholder and the taxpayer accomplish desirable open space practices, many of which become available and practical for the first time. The Redding Land Trust makes it possible for you to serve the finest goals of conservation through tax-deductible gifts of either land or money.

"Some people think that giving land for conservation results in added tax burden for the rest of the town. Actually the opposite is true.

"Redding faces problems of spectacular growth and the question of conservation takes on new urgency. Experience has shown that land set aside as permanent open space has a restraining influence on your future tax rate. This is because the new homes which might have replaced the open space would tend to be an added tax expense—needing more in new town services than they pay in town taxes."

The mailing served its purpose very effectively. Not only did the Trust begin to receive inquiries—and land—from prospective donors, but many other Trusts copied the brochure and they reported increased interest and activity.

The Branford (Conn.) Land Trust produced an excellent small brochure which makes three strong points in favor of land preservation and shows how the Trust can help.

"Let us assume that 10 acres are owned by Mr. and Mrs. A. About 4 acres are cleared, with house and buildings to suit the resident owners. The entire property is assessed at over $30,000—of which about $6000 is unimproved open land. With retirement less than 10 years away, they are planning for the future. They would like to preserve the natural beauty of the property they love for the long-term benefit of the town.

"The solution is to separate house and lot from the unimproved land and deed the rough open space to the Branford Land Trust as a wildlife preserve. A stipulation gives Mr. and Mrs. A. sole use of the deeded land as long as they live.

"The gift is made in such a way that their income tax is reduced by over $1000 every year until retirement. Property taxes are lowered in proportion to the land gift. In addition, no estate or inheritance taxes can be levied on the donated land. And the value of their home will always be enhanced by the open spaces around it which they can enjoy."

A second case described the way four families preserved a wetlands area abutting their properties by deeding their joint acreage to the Land Trust. Not only did they preserve a vital natural resource, but they reduced their property taxes and "got a welcome deduction from current federal income taxes."

A third example involved a developer who was persuaded to build on the high, good land and donate nine acres of low, poorly drained acreage to the Trust. "The town gained a more attractive group of new homes with permanent open space nearby. The investor was spared the expense of filling or draining land for building purposes and made a fair return on his investment."

Help for Trusts

These cases were drawn from *Stewardship,* published by the Open Space Institute, a most valuable book which has become something of a bible to land trusts. *Stewardship* author Charles Little stresses enlightened self-interest: "Open space, whether a park, a nature sanctuary, a scout reservation or a buffer strip adds to the value of private properties that touch its perimeters and increases the net value of an entire community as well." Land trusts like to underline this thought by pointing out that "every piece of land set aside for conservation becomes an island of wilderness, meadow, or woodland, helping to preserve the charm of our town. Land acquired will be retained in its natural state, making conservation of wildlife, beauty, and natural resources both practical and economically atrractive to the town."

Stewardship was widely used by land trusts in the late '6os and many land trust mailings utilized the approach suggested by Little. It was, perhaps, inevitable that the Open Space Institute would publish a "Monograph on Land Trusts," prepared by Linda A. Murray in 1968. This recites the history of the Redding Land Trust, which has been discussed here, and provides some very helpful information on setting up trusts. It is still available from the Open Space Institute, 145 East 52 Street, New York, New York, 10022 ($2 per copy with bulk rates available).

The New Canaan Land Trust not only produced a well-designed brochure modeled after the Redding mailing, but it has distributed another publication called "The New Canaan Experience." Jack Gunther, president of the Trust, is also chairman of the Association of Conservation Commissions of Connecticut. He believes wholeheartedly in the cooperation between commissions and trusts and his goal in putting New Canaan's experience between soft covers was to stimulate the formation of more trusts.

Perhaps the most useful material in the New Canaan Experience is the discussion of the Tax Reform Act of 1969 and how it affects land trusts. "What is a publicly supported status and how can a land trust qualify for same, thereby assuring its donors of maximum tax benefits?" These and other questions are spelled out and answered by Gunther, who knows from firsthand experience what steps must be taken to achieve this enviable tax status.

"New Hampshire Tomorrow," a foundation-supported conservation-education group published a comprehensive "How-to-Do-It Book on the Formation of Land Trusts and Watershed Associations" in 1970. It contains model bylaws, legal advice, and a summary of the steps necessary to establish either a trust or an association. It costs 35¢ and is available from The Society for the Protection of New Hampshire Forests, 5 South State Street, Concord, New Hampshire, 03301.

Land trusts must do a certain amount of fund-raising because they need contributions to pay for surveys, legal fees, land management, and conservation-education programs. But they depend upon donors for their principal asset—the land. This represents a substantial return on the investment of time and energy made by members. Those who manage local trusts are volunteers and they receive no financial reward. Their compensation lies in the satisfaction they feel when land is saved.

Land-Save Programs

Redding is not the only town which has awakened to the need for open space preservation. All across the country, citizens are banding together in a conservation movement that, at last, recognizes that land can be saved if we will only act now.

The little town of Lunenburg, Massachusetts, (pop. 7400) has managed to acquire 1043 acres for open space in the last seven years and is aiming for a goal of 4000 acres (out of a total of 20,000). "We are trying to get all the open space land we can, as fast as we can, and by any means (legal) that we can," says the Conservation Commission chairman. "It is a real big job and a very important one. Protecting our natural resources is, of course, not only for the survival of the human race, but it is for the benefit of every community in many ways and especially financially. We realize that if we are going to get land, we must get it very soon. We have in mind bonding the town for perhaps $150,000 and really putting on a land-buying drive."

Lunenburg is lucky enough to have land left to buy, land that has not yet been developed. What about areas where the concentration of population and industrialization has used up available land? They may have to create open space areas by tearing out the buildings to create "an amenable environment." That, at any rate, is one proposal offered by the firm of Eckbo, Dean, Austin and Williams, consultants to the State of California. Their plan envisions the freezing of broad tracts of open land, purchase of key land areas or development rights. "It is a fact," says their study, "that if the nicest and most useful open spaces that are still left in our urban metropolitan areas are to be preserved, fast action is necessary."

Of the 126,000 acres of open space recommended by the study for outright purchase in Southern California, "almost 80,000 acres are in high danger of being urbanized by 1975." Of the statewide total of 9.4 million acres recommended for preservation, "about 1.6 million acres are considered almost certain to be urbanized by 1975."

The study proposes "a balanced program of acquisition and control" to keep buffers of open space around the fast-growing suburbs and established cities, preserve beaches and waterfronts for public use, make freeways into green corridors, build a system of bicycling, riding, and hiking trails within and between major open areas close to our cities, preserve floodplains and marshes and fish spawning places, and save the best soils for their best function, that of growing crops for present and future generations."

One would suppose that the land pinch would be felt most severely on the East and West coasts. Yet, even the ample farmlands of the Midwest are being swallowed up by industry, population growth, and transportation ravages.

Illinois, for example, ranks near the bottom of the list of all states in outdoor recreation land per capita. This is why the Open Lands Project was formed in 1963, as a foundation-supported program of the Welfare Council of Metropolitan Chicago. A report of its first five years shows the following gains:

The public has acquired one of the finest remaining virgin forests in Illinois, a 623-acre tract at Beall Woods in Wabash County, and the Illinois Department of Conservation is moving toward a similar acquisition at Goose Lake Prairie, one of the last living examples of the great American prairie. It will involve some twelve hundred acres.

The Open Lands Project has also had an impact on urban-land problems. Quoting from the Project Report, it becomes apparent that groups such as this can act as a land lobby and keep areas open by alerting the public to their possible destruction. "Not all conservation issues involve any great amount of land. Particularly in a densely populated urban community such as Chicago, major public issues can arise over a relatively small physical tract. So it has been in the controversy over McCormick Place and various proposals for landfill in Lake Michigan and concerning the construction of office and apartment buildings on the lakefront. Individually, these actions have involved only a small amount of acreage, but they reflect an unresolved philosophy of land use in Chicago which has its counterpart in virtually every major city in the nation."

Quite deliberately, any number of communities have decided to bank open space, to buy it now with town funds so that it will not be available for development. They may use this hoarded land at some later date for a school site, recreation complex, or town office building; or, keep it open to serve as a balance to town growth. They have profited in more than one way if they have had the imagination to buy now. Everyone seems to agree that land prices are bound to go up, and so it makes good sense to buy when they are relatively low. Secondly, they have bought time when they bought land. When land pours onto the building market, a community is faced with a spurting growth that can only mean one thing—higher taxes.

Financial Facts of Life

There are those who insist that since people pay taxes, the more people you have in a given town, the more taxes you will collect. However, these same people are using town services, and this costs everyone money. One small New England town calculated the cost of buying eighty-five acres of open space vs. letting it go for development to bring this fact of life home to the voters. They figured that each new house would cost the town $900 a year, over and above what it would pay in taxes. The thirty-seven houses which could have been put on this property in question would have meant an additional cost to the taxpayers of $33,000 each year. This figure would certainly rise as town services became more expensive over the years. The portion of a new school, necessary if the subdivision were built, would cost the town $80,000. Over a five-year period those thirty-seven houses would cost $245,000, and this only if all operating and building costs remained stable. On the other hand, the eighty-five acres could be had for $67,500 (using state funds; less, if federal funds came through). Needless to say, the town voted to buy. Stuart Chase, economist and long-time member of Redding's Planning Commission, says quite bluntly, "The more open space we can hold, the lower our future taxes will be, and the pleasanter the town."

Many towns have begun weighing the advantages of a land bank against unbridled development. A conservation plan for Wayland, Massachusetts, presented citizens with these considerations:

Dwindling ground water supplies—brought about by increased building—could lead to an expensive municipal water system;

Flooding problems—produced when floodplain acres are opened to development—could require expensive dredging or protective devices;

The pollution problems which force a central sewage system at enormous costs.

Wayland conservationists pointed out that if two thousand acres of the least suitable, buildable, accessible land were bought by the town and kept in its natural state, there would be a net saving on the tax rate of $175,000 each year on the average. "This is the estimated financial gain secured by protecting water resources and the general quality of the environment."

Conservative voters may turn down land purchase because they feel they are already paying high taxes. But, this is a shortsighted economy. Or, they may resist keeping space open by allowing recreation complexes to go in, maintaining instead that the town should be purely residential. One Connecticut town turned down a golf course on three hundred acres in 1964. "They'll live to regret it," said the developer who proceeded to plan 249 houses on the property. During October of 1967, sixty-six school-age children moved in and they're still coming. Instead of taking the golf course, the town now has to build a new school or two.

Guiding Growth

The use of open space to guide growth is gradually being accepted by planners. State planners are trying to get this message across, and it is filtering down to the local level.

The horrors of undirected growth can be seen quite clearly in California as this example from *Cry California* shows:

"If all the land put into urban use in Santa Clara County between 1947 and 1956 had been placed in one parcel, that parcel would have consisted of about 26 square miles. But development in Santa Clara County was so disorderly that there existed in 1956 not a single square mile in a 200-square-mile area which had not been invaded by one subdivision or more. The result was that the entire 200-square-mile area was in effect held hostage, for eventual development."

Zoning has a bad name with both good guys and bad. It symbolizes suburban exclusiveness to the advocates of open housing. It means a cut in profit to the land profiteers.

When zoning is applied with an eye to saving natural features, preserving a total environment, directing growth where it will do the most good and least harm, it should be welcomed. Zoning can and should be used to protect health, welfare, and safety standards. In the process, it can also make large building lots mandatory and thereby help a town estimate the number of people who can be comfortably accommodated on a given piece of land. This is not "zoning out people" as some have charged. It is, instead, "zoning in the amenities."

Some towns have called it "conservation zoning" in an effort to improve zoning's image. True conservation zoning starts with the goal of designing growth so that essential natural areas are preserved. Zoning should be "for" something, not "against" it.

Perhaps the best example of conservation zoning is wetlands preservation. Connecticut, for example, has tried to put its salt marshes, stream banks, and inland swamps off limits for building. Some towns are now trying to write ordinances to protect inland wetlands. (See page 289.)

As Roland C. Clement, vice-president of the National Audubon Society, has pointed out, salt marsh acres were not particularly valuable until after World War II. Farmers cut salt hay on them or leased them for duck shooting privileges, but such land was considered impossible for building. When the heavy dragline and hydraulic dredge were perfected in the postwar years, it became possible to scoop up the bottom of the bay and fill the marsh, making it dry land.

Clement reports that "in the last generation or so, Connecticut has sacrificed 50 per cent of its coastal marsh in this way. The point is that the advent of earth-moving technology has changed the rules of the game by greatly increasing land values and has created a greedy scramble for cash."

By filling in his marshland, the owner could sell it for 3000 per cent above the old price, Clement estimates. "Such financial windfalls are called capital gains. But unlike unearned income, we tax only 50 per cent of a man's unearned capital gains! So, many people got rich selling former 'wasteland.'" (New Connecticut tax laws have reduced these profits.)

How enterprising of them, some people are sure to say. Can you blame them for seeing the possibilities in "unusable" land and exploiting them? After all, that puts poor land on the tax rolls and provides building sites for people and commerce. Those opposed to such crass development techniques have made an excellent case for preserving marshland as essential to the food chain. Without the wetlands we are, quite simply, endangering our survival.

The speculator is interested in making building sites where there were none. His value is pure marketplace ethic—or lack of it. The community is rightly concerned about the disappearing landscape, the lost opportunity for recreation, the degradation of the environment that will come in the wake of such unplanned development.

Clement suggests that concerned citizens do more than simply push for laws protecting the wetlands; he wants to do away with capital gains tax, "stop subsidizing landscape changes."

"A proper tax on these capital gains will slow down land destruction, lower land prices, and provide enough tax income to enable communities and other governmental units to buy sensitive areas and give them the protection they must have if they are to continue making life livable on this planet."

With land as scarce as it is, developers are bound to build on highly unsuitable sites. They are driven to areas which are inherently fragile. All you have to do is leaf through the building trade magazines to find stories about turning "the impossible site" into a house lot.

If a town wants to stave off the inevitable plundering of the countryside, it should institute conservation zoning. No filling in the wetlands, no tearing down the cliffs, no building on a slope with more than a certain percentage of grade, no gravel removal. By the time you have fenced in the developer with dozens of restrictions, he loses his taste for the impossible—and, of course, cheaper—site.

Back in 1967 the citizens of Wayland, Massachusetts, voluntarily agreed to restrict development on wetlands. They adopted a law which prohibited man-made changes along the banks of six brooks. At the town meeting which passed the law, there was the expected opposition from landowners who maintained that they had a right to do what they wished with their land.

Speaking in favor of the new restriction were other old-timers who thought it was a good idea to protect the whole town against pollution which might be caused by a few. Lewis Russell, whose family has lived in Wayland for generations, summed up this point of view by saying, "Sure, it's a matter of rights. But that doesn't mean you can stand on your own land and shoot somebody standing on his." The law was adopted by a vote of 362 to 42.

Develop It Properly

When land is developed properly—with a maximum attention to open space—everybody wins. The developer can make a decent profit without gouging the land and the community, without building as close to the limit as zoning allows. It helps to have a model to follow, and the nonprofit development companies can provide a good example. (See page 307 for a sample incorporation form.)

In Lincoln, Massachusetts, the Rural Land Foundation, Inc., was organized "to see that land which is going to be subdivided anyway is subdivided properly." When a large tract goes on the market, this group stands ready to make an offer which compares favorably with commercial bids. If the owner elects to sell to the Rural Land Foundation, Inc., its members borrow the money from a bank—on their personal notes—for the initial investment. Paul Brooks, indefatigable conservation worker in Lincoln, describes the next steps. "With a bank loan guaranteed by the members, the Foundation buys the land, and employs its own landscape architect to make a subdivision plan, reserving a sizable tract of open space to be held by the Land Trust. It then markets the lots, which needless to say are larger and—particularly because of the open land—more attractive than they would be if a real estate speculator were trying to squeeze out the last penny of profit. In its first trial, this enterprise has worked without a hitch. The guarantors have never had to worry about their commitment. And, since this is a non-profit organization, any favorable balance constitutes a revolving fund to be applied again as need arises."

It may be significant that the Foundation was born in a town like Lincoln, which has considerable local pride in its environs. The town has a rich historical heritage. It is Emerson and Thoreau country. Although Lincoln's populace is affluent and educated, aware that the land must be protected and a substantial amount set aside for open space, support for its conservation program reaches into every social strata. Lincoln has had zoning since 1929 and it has been supported by old-timers and newcomers alike.

Bob Lemire, chairman of Lincoln's Conservation Commission, has made sure that everyone in town understands the importance of land preservation. He is particularly concerned that the children of the town grasp the idea that they have a heritage worth preserving.

When Lemire speaks to schoolchildren he introduces himself as "the biggest landowner in Lincoln. I own over eight hundred acres. I'm sure you'll all agree that that's a lot of land. Does anybody here know how big an acre is?"

After the children guess two thousand feet, forty-two

hundred feet, Lemire says, "An acre is just under forty-four thousand square feet. See that ball field outside? I'd guess that's about four acres. You've all been to Mount Misery . . . that's about two hundred acres. Anyhow, that gives you some idea of how much land I've got. Now then, how much land do you have?"

One after another gave his family acreage as two. Then, as Lemire tells it, "one youngster in the back of the room smiled and said that he also had eight hundred acres. 'That's my secret,' I said. 'Each one of us here owns over eight hundred acres in Lincoln. At today's prices, that makes us all millionaires." Everybody in Lincoln knows what a prize they've got and they want to keep it. They have a common interest in fending off the speculators. A common heritage to protect.

Are there any good developers?

Yes, of course. But good developers are not born, they are made. Every land speculator has a natural, and understandable, urge to get his dollar's worth out of the land. He isn't about to give it away. But, when confronted with public opinion and public land-use plans, he may decide his is better off making some concessions to a balanced environment.

Cluster is the magic word among developers for the kind of land-use plan which seems to satisfy everybody. If a town permits this kind of exception to zoning, the builder is allowed to cluster his houses together, thereby saving on road costs, and the remaining open space is given to the town or land trust or to a homeowners association.

In Madison, Connecticut, the cluster concept has worked

extremely well. The town has a more open look thanks to these blocks of green scattered through the subdivisions.

However, if the developer succeeds in building more houses on his acreage than normal zoning would allow, the idea of cluster is self-defeating.

A town may have all the apparatus it needs to secure land—a conservation commission, an open space plan, and the announced intent to preserve scenic and natural resources. Still, nothing happens. Study after study is commissioned. Experts are brought in to analyze the town's land use and recommend procedures and priorities for the future. Still, nothing happens.

The innocent citizen thinks that he is being protected when, in fact, the powers that be are stalling, buying time until open land goes off the market into the hands of developers.

In one New England town the Conservation Commission has repeatedly recommended purchase of some ten parcels for a reasonable sum. The commission knows it is getting a run-around. Said one member, "Every time we go to the Board of Finance for approval, they think of some question they haven't yet asked and then table it while we go off to get the answer." State and federal funds which would be forthcoming if applications were made are locked up in the selectman's office because he hasn't filled out the proper forms.

What is needed here is what every town needs—an active and vocal public opinion working for land preservation. How do you build popular support for open space, to the point where a town will vote its tax dollars to buy land? How do you get a land trust going to serve as the private arm of an acquisition program? How do you implement town regulations on dredging, filling, mining so that community resources are protected?

You have to light a fire under people, make them appreciate the terrible price they will pay if they don't move now to save the land. You show them how it's done, how other towns have done it to their everlasting credit and benefit.

6

Positive Protest

Mobilizing public opinion against an environmental threat takes a tremendous amount of time and effort. You have to make everybody see that property values all over a community will be affected when one portion of the land is downgraded. It's not hard to arouse the people who are directly and visibly endangered, but their protest may be brushed aside as pure self-interest. Community self-interest is the key to productive protest. When you can get everybody involved and actively insisting that the landscape must be preserved, you have a good chance of success.

Occasionally an environmental issue will sell itself because the threat is so outrageous. So many properties and people are touched that public opinion simply erupts of its own accord. (With, of course, some help from those practiced in the arts of activism.)

The case of the Connecticut Power Line is an awesome example of what can happen when a big industry makes plans for expansion without calculating either the impact on the environment or the response of the people.

In the fall of 1970 the Connecticut Light and Power Company sent a letter to eleven towns advising them of a plan to build a 6.25-million-dollar 345-volt line through the heart of some of the most beautiful land in the state. The line would run for thirty-nine miles, consuming some two thousand acres. The company announced that it had not pinpointed the route, but it would fall somewhere within a mile-wide corridor.

No one at CL&P had any reason to anticipate trouble. Not only was the company adept at maintaining good relations with town officials, giving them a free lobster dinner every year and providing town recreation facilities on its man-made lakes, but it had recently instituted something called "open planning," or "early public decision." Instead of simply buying up land for its power projects and then announcing where the line would go, CL&P, under the direction of its parent company Northeast Utilities, invited public officials to hear what goes into planning process. Northeast announced, with some pride, that it wanted to "provide an opportunity for open discussion of major utility facilities before they were formalized."

To that end, CL&P invited area officials to meet with "members of our engineering and environmental staffs" on December 10. Like many other companies which use sizable tracts of land for their projects, and which are pollution-prone, CL&P had employed an "in-house ecologist" to, presumably, minimize enivronmental destruction. Cynics suggested that this was mere window dressing, that company decisions continued to be predicated on profits and that the house ecologist was there to rationalize them.

Peter Stern, Northeast's house ecologist, opened the December 10 meeting by saying that "explicit consideration of the environment" had influenced the proposed plan. Using overlays to illustrate his points—in the approved Ian McHarg fashion—he showed lands which would not be traversed by the corridor. These were highly developed areas, ridges which would silhouette the 65 to 115 foot poles against the sky, state- and community-owned recreation lands which, he said, should be off limits for any commercial development.

Curiously, for an environmentalist, he did not identify conservation acreage as worth preserving.

The only map that town officials could study at close range was a standard highway map, marked with a felt pen. Some officials had trouble locating their towns because they were blotted over with the ink. When asked if CL&P did not have more detailed maps for each town, showing precisely where the line would go, company officials said they did not.

Town officials pointed out that the corridor would cut through conservation lands. Some had been bought with town funds, others were financed with state and federal monies. This acreage was as inviolate as any community or state-owned recreation lands. Private land trusts and the Nature Conservancy held title to some of the lands, and these were protected by deeds against development. The proposed high-lines would also run across the Saugatuck Reservoir, one of the most scenic areas in the county, and stretch out over Lake Lillinonah. If the company were to live up to its expressed concern for environmental protection, how could they justify this kind of planning? Why not put the lines underground?

The vice-president in charge of engineering dismissed this as far too expensive claiming that the cost would be $143 million as compared with $6.25 million. "At the present rate such an undertaking would double the electricity rate."

CL&P did appear shaken in its certainty that it had covered all bases when the question of traversing publicly owned open space land came up, and said it would meet again with representatives of the town conservation commissions, land trusts, and the Nature Conservancy. However, those who attended the meeting came away with the feeling that the corridor was set. Company officials said they would take the criticisms into account and that arguments for the line would be heard at the Public Utilities Commission hearing on December 28, at 10:30 A.M.

Area newspapers carried full accounts of the meeting and the public soon learned what was in store for them.

CL&P had clearly not counted on the public indignation which swelled in the wake of newspaper stories describing the meeting. A map showing the proposed line was printed and area residents then realized what was happening.

"We Didn't Want to Alarm People"

For some months people had been puzzled over the white markers which appeared on front lawns, stone walls, in the middle of roadways. These were for the benefit of CL&P engineers who were marking the route from the air.

CL&P men explained to those who asked, that the white

arrows were "for the helicopters flying out of Sikorsky."
Asked later why CL&P had not played straight with the
populace, one v.-p. explained, "We didn't want to alarm
people."

When the word went out that the line would run perilously
close to landmark houses, along untouched valleys, through
the backyards of newly developed acreage, the alarms were
sounded in earnest.

On December 22, just before the Christmas weekend, more
than a hundred people met in Bethel to plan a counterattack. Obviously, the PUC hearing, scheduled for the Monday after Christmas, had to be postponed. *Life* photographer
Arthur Rickerby and his wife, Wanda, spearheaded the movement to postpone. They urged everyone present to write,
wire, or phone their elected representatives in Hartford
and express opposition to the line. "Ask them to give us
thirty days before the PUC hearing.

"CL&P has been working on this plan for five years,"
said Rickerby, "and they file it November 30, show it to the
towns ten days later, and expect to get their okay by the
end of the month."

Charles McCollum, first selectman of Bethel, expressed
the feeling of his constituents when he charged that CL&P's
tactics were "an insult to the intelligence of the people. It's
just another case of the big corporate structure going to the
Public Utilities Commission, which won't come down out of
its ivory tower to investigate the situation on the scene. So
now it's up to the poor guy making a hundred per week
to go sixty-five miles to Hartford to plead his case. But the
trouble with that is that we have to go to the PUC without
knowing anything about what we're opposing."

The local press was unsuccessful in getting CL&P to specify precisely where the line would go, although the company insisted that they wanted only 250 to 300 feet within the mile-wide corridor.

Opponents of the power line dramatized their case with photographs of existing 345 lines which dwarfed the landscape they traversed. Rickerby's son put together a scale model of his neighborhood, showing how the proposed line would look in relationship to the houses and trees. It was a chilling presentation.

Someone pasted together a large map, much more detailed than the one CL&P had given local officials, so that residents of the area could locate their properties and see how close the line would come.

As the date for the post-Christmas hearing grew closer, public outrage intensified. The Rickerby house became a headquarters for the movement-to-change-the-hearing. Wanda Rickerby told the local press that they "had phone calls from people all the way from Massachusetts to Long Island Sound. And they're not just people whose land is threatened by being on the right-of-way. They're people who are simply concerned with environmental issues."

The public pressure blew CL&P's cozy, virtually private, hearing on the day after Christmas wide open when the PUC conceded that the short notice "was kind of rough" and granted a six-week extension.

Bethel, Weston, Easton, and Redding residents formed an action group called FLEC (Fairfield Litchfield Environmental Council) to raise funds for legal counsel, technical advice, and publicity. Roxbury, Bridgewater, and New Milford organized their own group called ACUTE (Active Citizens Urging Transmission Ecology).

Arthur Rickerby urged ACUTE to work with groups forming in other towns. "People should be brought together. I'm trying to impress on you the influences of public opinion. You have to use the media. These things are railroaded through as fast as possible before public opinion is formed. One of our rights is to influence government."

Power line opponents showed over the ensuing months just how powerful the people can be. FLEC was modeled on BLEC (Berkshire Litchfield Environmental Council), a group which was fighting Northeast on a pumped storage facility in the Berkshires.

BLEC had already made people aware of the utility's callousness to property values. Now FLEC poured it on. PUC spokesmen said they had never seen such an outcry, and in such a short time, on any issue they had handled. Opponents of the line rallied support by cheering their cohorts on with reminders of successful protests held all over the country. "If they'd done this five years ago, they could have forced this down our throats." Those days are gone forever. The days of submission to the do-no-wrong giants are over."

Sophisticated Infighting

When CL&P decided to run its line through sparsely settled countryside, it probably thought that the absence of people would make it easier for them to ram through the project. In actuality, the inhabitants of these open lands were precisely the ones they should not have tangled with in the first place. Writers, artists, advertising and public relation executives, engineers with Connecticut companies, they had taken to the hills to find peace and quiet. When disturbed, they reacted like angry hornets. They had fought hard for their remote territory, and were not about to have it taken away from them. More importantly, they were wise in the ways of communication techniques, and they knew enough about the technical aspect of the project to be able to argue intelligently against it.

Elmer Garrett, an engineer who had retired to Roxbury, could, and did, come up with alternate proposals to save the environment. The Rickerbys and others in the publishing business knew how to get the most coverage out of the media.

Many of them had fought earlier battles in other places and they knew precisely what the game plan should be. Bill McGeorge of Roxbury, who had tested himself with the New York City Rent Control Commission, told ACUTE: "You need a lawyer. Let the Public Utilities Commission look after itself. They're well taken care of. Don't go up to the PUC with your hat in your hands. It'll end up over your ears. The more time you have to make a political stink, the more power they'll lose. These people are going to play dirty with you; you have to be prepared to play dirty with them. It's that simple. I'm sorry if I undercut anyone's idealism in what the establishment is like, but that's the way it is."

Someone suggested buying stock in Northeast. "If everyone bought just one share and went to one meeting, we could raise a lot of hell as stockholders."

"I'd even be willing to buy a hundred shares," another said.

Frank Glick suggested a strike against CL&P: "A little strike might upset their computers. We say if you don't tell us what you plan to do, we won't tell you what we have in the bank."

Another predicted that the company would yield in the face of publicity about its rates and lack of research. "One thing the utilities are most afraid of is a Congressional investigation."

In the weeks that followed FLEC, ACUTE, and hundreds of unaffiliated citizens worked to get their officials on record as opposing the power line. In town after town, the selectmen, conservation commission, planning commission, made statements critical of CL&P's proposal. The local press covered the activities of FLEC and ACUTE almost obsessively. Everything they did made news. They formed committees, elected officers, raised money, hired consultants, issued statements, and circulated petitions. They seemed in complete mastery of the uses of the media.

The PUC finally announced that they would hold their hearings on March 1, at Danbury, not Hartford. This change in date and place was a victory for the citizens who had never ceased pressuring their legislators to pressure the PUC.

FLEC would be represented by Dr. Alexander Kusko, president of his own firm of consulting engineers and on the teaching staff of MIT, plus David Sive, a specialist in environmental law who had fought off Con Ed's generating plant at Storm King. His credits also include the winning battle against the BASF chemical plant at Hilton Head and halting the Hudson River Expressway. Two Connecticut lawyers—Russell Brenneman and Haynes Johnson—with reputations as environmentalists would assist them.

Working for That Better Way

In a statement released to the press, one member of FLEC attempted to set the record straight on what the power line opponents hoped to gain through protest. There had been letters in the paper from people who feared brownouts if the power projects were halted. Other criticism came from those who doubted that the FLEC group was motivated in the public interest. They implied that a hard-core band of environmental fanatics was bent on depriving the public of its God-given right to enjoy the comforts conferred by abundant electricity. Some of the writers were employed by the utility.

The FLEC statement tried to allay fears and put the group on the side of responsible progress.

"FLEC is not, per se, in opposition to all improvements in the Northeast Utilities Grid System.

"Flec is not attempting to assume the responsibility for the design of, or to recommend engineering approaches or criteria for, those improvements.

"FLEC is directly concerned with seeing that these improvements are conducted with due consideration for the environment as well as for the small, but significant, portion of the public that will be directly affected.

"FLEC is wholly in favor of the application of new technology and the use of available facilities in a more efficient manner to reduce the detrimental impact of uncontrolled growth on the environment and the community.

"FLEC demands that any group proposing impacting construction spend more effort in implementing less devastating approaches to preserve the best of what we have as we grow in the future.

"FLEC asks that all groups, corporations, industries, etc., plan their growth as though they themselves would have to live within the environment they so seriously affect.

"FLEC is trying to take a position of reason and understanding in the middle of diverse opinions . . . We seek a practical solution of reasonable cost, in terms of dollars and resources, so that our state will not be brought one step closer to becoming a 'transmission line' waste land.

"FLEC takes the position that the 'lowest out of pocket' cost to the utilities and therefore to the consumer, cannot be the sole determining factor in any project which will affect so much.

"In short, we think that there is a better way than the way that it has been done in the past, and the way that is being proposed now—and we are working to find that better way."

The Public Cross-Examines

As February wore on, CL&P spokesmen made the rounds of civic groups in the region, pressing their case for the line on the simple argument that "we need the power." They brushed aside any suggestions for alternate routes along the new Route 7, along existing power lines. They insisted that the cost of undergrounding was prohibitive.

Meantime, local citizens became more informed and inclined to demand information which CL&P either did not have or did not care to divulge.

At one meeting, Daniel R. Forger, division manager for

CL&P, was pressed for an accurate definition of the line through Easton. He finally invited a representative of FLEC to display its map so that the citizenry could see at last that the line in Easton would cross Black Rock Turnpike, follow Rock House Road, North Park Avenue, North Street, Knapp and Maple roads.

In Weston, Mr. Forger turned aside all questions about the effect of the line on radio and TV reception, insisting, too, that a power line in your backyard did nothing to lower real estate values. His remarks were greeted with laughter from a knowledgeable crowd. Perhaps his most astounding remark, given CL&P's avowed environmental conscience, was this one. He stated that open space was not "property," or "anyway anyone's home." To members of the audience who had given their land, or sold it at a sacrifice so that the community would be protected against unbridled development, this was a shocker.

Asked by the engineers in the audience about new technology which would put the lines underground, Mr. Forger professed ignorance. Or, as the frustrated reporter put it, "CL&P seems to have no knowledge of this cable, at least none that it is about to put to practical use in Fairfield County."

Businessmen in the FLEC group totted up the amount of money CL&P was spending on advertising and sales versus research into that better way of conveying power. The statistics were dramatic enough to draw gasps and boos from the audience. Several million were spent on promoting sales, but only $250,000 on research.

As each town in the path developed its own expertise on power lines, it was perhaps inevitable that alternate methods would attract proponents. The solidarity of the opposition began to crack as first one group and then another came out for a different solution. Towns which were far away from the new Route 7 thought it would be nice to build the line along the new highway. "Let's put all the eyesores in one place." Naturally, those in the path of the road were not enthusiastic about the prospect of high lines adding to the desecration of the area.

Said one resident of the Route 7 area, "running the lines along the road would make 'multiple use' a euphemism for 'multiple horror.'"

FLEC leaders urged the towns to band together in a common cause and not allow the natural desire to find a solution in somebody else's backyard divide them. Rickerby said, "We should make CL&P defend their application. They must answer our questions first." An opposition which could not agree on alternative solutions would make an easy target for the power company.

Joanne Brooks, who had supervised the mammoth job of gathering petitions against CL&P in the snow and ice of early winter and who had personally talked to hundreds of affected residents, felt there was common agreement that the ultimate solution would have to satisfy everyone. "There has been no desire on anyone's part to protect their own property at the expense of another's. The prevalent feeling seems to be a mature and wholesome desire to work out a permanent and equitable solution for the entire transmission problem." She added, "It is a constantly rewarding experience to live in a town where people love and appreciate their environment and are ever ready to defend it."

On March 1, CL&P presented its case for the power line

to the PUC at a public hearing. The arguments were the same ones the company had been repeating for months. There would be a power shortage without the new line. The line had been planned with environmental considerations in mind. There were no alternatives—such as a different route or undergrounding—which were acceptable.

As the lawyer for CL&P put the company technicians through a carefully rehearsed question-and-answer discussion of these positions, an overflow' audience of homeowners in the area listened intently. Their turn would come. To encourage speakers to lose their mike fright and say their piece, FLEC hoisted a sign which read: EVERYONE. THIS IS YOUR HEARING. YOU MAY SPEAK. PLEASE BE ENCOURAGED TO USE THE MICROPHONE. GIVE YOUR NAME. GIVE YOUR RESIDENCE. GIVE YOUR OPINION.

A Passionate Protest

Dozens of individuals rose to speak against the proposal. A sampling of their statements gives some idea of the passionate protest which the power line inspired. They looked like prosperous, middle-class homeowners, but they sounded like "radicals" as they questioned the assumptions of unlimited growth.

From Weston's Alfred G. Frisk: "I . . . and many other residents commute to New York and other distant points, spending three to four hours a day in travel, only because we feel it is worth it. For, when we are home, it is not in a beehive metropolis, but in our own bit of natural surroundings. Through the years we have fought consistently against the encroachment of industry upon environment—against commercialization in all forms that would create chaos and ugliness.

"Therefore, when a utility company attempts to gut forest lands with a slashed swath of desolation and cross our lakes and reservoirs with power lines and the obliteration of many acres of Weston's Natural Conservancy, this is reprehensible in its very concept. We know we must resist with all of our will.

"To curse society with the philosophy 'the public be damned' can no longer be tolerated. It is our duty to save for the generations to come as much of our natural environment as we humanly can and to undo the ravages and blights that have been created over the past decades."

New natives like Frisk were joined by old-timers. Thomas Wallace IV of Woodbridge explained that the line would "cross many choice areas of wooded open space which are part of a three-generation trust.

"It comprises almost four hundred acres of land which has been owned by our family since the early seventeenth century, having been part of a Crown Grant to my forebear William Clarke. The land was invaded by the British during the American Revolution and the house was burned after it had stood for well over a hundred years. We live in its replacement built in 1795. Obviously our roots in this land go very deep and our attachment to it is very strong.

"The threat of invasion by CL&P is far more horrifying than that of the British because it would be far more permanent. There could be no rebuilding of the natural beauty which it is their intention to destroy."

Real estate agents and appraisers testified that the line would surely bring property values tumbling down in its wake.

Conservation organizations were on record as opposing the project. Area legislators jumped on the bandwagon and made ringing denouncements of the utility's plan. Representative Stewart McKinney called it "a travesty and rape of the Connecticut countryside." "I am not a doomsday conservationist. I don't pine for the good old days. But, this is premeditated environmental pollution advanced under the guise of environmental protection."

Representative Ella P. Grasso predicted that public response to this crisis heralded "a new ethic of public rights."

Selectmen, conservation commissions, planners read their opposition into the record. And, a petition carrying over six thousand signatures protesting the project was delivered to the PUC. Speaker after speaker emphasized the cost to the community in lowered property values and reduced tax revenues. The line was planned without considering town plans —"thirty-five years of planning and I might say expensive planning" could be wiped out, said one official.

Reader's Digest editor James Daniel, once selectman of Weston, wondered how CL&P had the power to undo all the careful work he and others had put in trying to preserve the landscape.

"This is appalling. When local citizens and local governments labor to do something to save the shrinking countryside, are we only preserving low-cost rights of way for the public utilities? Is every bit of open space destined to be defiled for commercial purposes?

"Some years ago, when I was a reporter in Washington, the highway planners almost got away with taking over Rock Creek Park for a superhighway. At that time one of the Washington commentators made the comment that, to highway planners and utility men, any bit of set-aside open country is as alluring as a clean sheet hung out on the wash-line. At the very sight of that lovely white space some 'bird' feels the irresistible impulse to let fly at it."

The Basic Questions

A sizable number of speakers attacked the utility for not exploring alternatives. Fred Clemens of Redding quoted Senator Lee Metcalf of Montana, who reported that Northeast Utilities spent only 2 per cent (or $169,757) of its advertising budget on research and development. He went on to say: "The company mounted a huge campaign to sell us electricity that they now tell us they cannot deliver. Now they want to carve up our countryside to ship in power from hundreds of miles away . . . I suggest, that, before being permitted to move one shovel full of dirt, Northeast Utilities be required to mount an R & D campaign equal to the ad campaign that got them into the present power mess . . . Let us stop, put down our shovels and chainsaws, and pick up our pencils, and slide rules. There is a better way to meet our power needs."

Although many speakers acknowledged that the need for more power did exist, a sizable number refused to concede this point. Others stoutly maintained that there would be no basic shortage if we would eliminate frill usage. "I am deeply concerned about the need for more power," said one woman. "Is it to be used to electroplate more aluminum beer cans, to service more badly sited factories in the cities along the Sound, to air-condition more office buildings in Manhattan?

"We are here today because a private, profit-making firm,

buttressed by the regulatory power of the state, may exercise this freewheeling dominion over a large swath of landscape . . . The presumption of this whole procedure is that it serves a social purpose. We not only have the right but are impelled by social necessity to challenge the utility company and the Utilities Commission to explain their long-range projections for this area, their plans to deal with real, that is, social needs, and their proposals for future discouragement of haphazard growth in population and power consumption in this region . . . Otherwise we will be the first to go under."

Another speaker added, "Decoratively spotlighted bridges, the neon carnival of Times Square, all the electric blankets and clocks of New York are not worth, to me, the rare wooded hills and valleys of Connecticut. I am aware, however, that neon signs and electric appliances are more profitable to the utilities."

Speakers continued to line up for the mike as the hearing wore into its third day. Toward the end, playwright Arthur Miller, speaking for his neighbors in Roxbury, gave the proceedings an electric charge as he eloquently protested the project. He, too, wondered, "how much effort has been put into seeking ways to avoid the defilement of my landscape.

"When I open my electric bill I am treated to recipes for cakes and puddings and a seemingly endless series of lectures on the virtues of privately owned rather than publicly owned electric light companies.

"I would like to say to the public utility industry that it is your responsibility now to come forward with alternatives to this project. The burden of proof is on you to investigate alternatives and to demonstrate that no other means is conceivable to carry electricity.

"And if you say that such research will take years, the only intelligent answer must be that it will be worth years, when what is at stake is the preservation or the destruction of one of the chief resources of Connecticut.

"It is time to plan, but to plan broadly and with a practicality that vaults beyond this corridor of wires, slicing down the belly of the state. Let planning take on the vision of Emerson's most practical observation. 'The sky,' he wrote, 'is the daily bread of the eyes.'"

At several points in the three-day hearing, David Sive, representing FLEC, asked the company for source material to justify its figures on future power needs. He and other lawyers, representing towns and individuals, would have the right of cross-examination at a later date. But, for now, Sive was clearly interested in pointing up CL&P's reliance on a traditional growth formula, one which could be questioned in the light of a dawning environmental conscience.

Even before the hearing was concluded, PUC chairman Eugene S. Loughlin volunteered that CL&P would have to pinpoint the route for the line and not simply ask for a mile-wide corridor. CL&P asked if the PUC would grant "interim approval" so the company could then work on a specific location. The chairman refused, saying that they could not do so without "prejudicing our final decision."

The impressive line-up of citizen power at the hearing had clearly put the PUC in a very visible and vulnerable position. Commented one PUC spokesman, "The popular image of the PUC is not good. We represent the public. They don't believe that, but we do." Several area legislators went out of their way to comment on the PUC's insensitivity to the public interest. "Frankly, I don't think the PUC has been properly responsive to the public," said Senator Edward S. Rimer. "But I think they've been awakened to reality, that they're not sitting to merely represent the needs of the utilities."

House Minority Leader Francis J. Collins added, "They should be pretty well aware it's not the same ball game. They can't just put a line on the map anymore and say, 'That's where we're going.' The utility companies have to become more aware of the fact it's a two-way street."

FLEC Chairman Rickerby observed, "The ordinary citizen shouldn't have to do this. The lawmakers and the PUC should be the questioners, not just umpires that call balls and strikes."

Legislative Help

The rebellion of the people against CL&P's idea of progress was reverberating in the halls of the Connecticut Legislature. In early February, State Representative Frank Ciampi and State Senator George Gunther introduced a bill entitled "The Public Utilities Environmental Standards Act."

The proposed law called for a power facility evaluation council, funded by application fees from the utilities. The council would review all proposed electric facilities and either okay them or turn them down, making their judgment on environmental compatibility and public need. Without approval by the council, no company could exercise the right of eminent domain and condemn land for the construction of new facilities.

Most important, the council would be made up of government agencies, including the PUC, but it would include representatives of major state conservation organizations. Other voting members would be state legislators representing districts affected by specific power facilities under consideration.

FLEC saluted this new piece of legislation and threw its considerable publicity resources into fighting for it. Said Rickerby, "This is a monumentally important bill for the State of Connecticut because it will balance our need for electric power against the destruction of our environment. It offers safeguards and protective devices which are badly needed, and yet in no way interferes with the construction of new facilities which can be certified as necessary and environmentally sound."

The utilities girded themselves for a new battle with the environmentalists. Anthony E. Wallace, president of Connecticut Light and Power, used many of the same arguments used for the power line. He warned of brownouts if the bills were passed or power rationed. He claimed that "the level of economic vitality and industrial productivity are directly related to the production of electricity."

Representative Francis W. Ciampi questioned Wallace carefully at a hearing before the State Legislature's Environment Committee. "Why is it that putting lines underground is always the consumers' cost? Why isn't it a CL&P cost for a change? CL&P says it is doing all it can for the environment. If that is so, why are we all here? Why are all these bills before us if there is nothing lacking on your part?"

Wallace admitted that the company had not done all it could for the environment in the past, but said that CL&P had "come up against the realization that improper planning can destroy our most priceless resource—land."

It might be noted that without the infuriated outburst of the citizenry, CL&P would have continued its traditional planning procedure, that is, go where the land is open and cheap. Understandably, Wallace gave his antagonists no credit for setting higher public priorities. Instead, he implied they were fanatics and warned legislators not to "overreact to well-intentioned individuals who somehow feel that those who produce power are doing something evil."

Getting Results

The PUC announced at the close of the three-day hearing that it would reconvene on May 3. But a week later, CL&P asked for a six-month postponement "in response to sentiments expressed last week during the hearings." The company said it wanted to explore alternate routes and methods of transmission. It woud study "the impact upon public interest of transmission facilities located on a specific route within the 'corridors' it proposed at the hearing." Acknowledging the criticism it had felt ever since the proposal was first aired, CL&P said it "planned to confer with the officers, boards, and commissions in towns that may be affected by any possible routes in order to obtain and consider their views and recommendations before resubmitting its plan to the commission."

FLEC had filed a motion with the PUC to dismiss the application completely. When CL&P asked for a postponement, Arthur Rickerby commented, "It is certainly a victory, but it is a long way from final withdrawal of the threat to our environment which this giant transmission line poses. We are settling in for a long and expensive legal battle and we are going to need every bit of help we can get."

The jubilant power line foes had no time to celebrate. They were busy trying to pass the bill to create an environmental council to pass on all power siting projects. And, they were afraid CL&P might co-opt the environmental issue by working out a compromise plan which would still be unsatisfactory. "FLEC, of course, reserves the right to question the basic need for the line and the date on which your claims of need are based . . . because the CL&P application was withdrawn our experts were never able to exercise the right of discovery, that is, examination of this material in your files."

On May 13 the State Senate unanimously passed a bill which would establish an environmental council to review applications by utilities. The utility companies continued to lobby vigorously against the bill, warning of a "breakdown in electric service," "a significant electric cost increase," and said the bill would cause "poorer service." Stratford Senator George Gunther, who co-sponsored the bill, called these warnings "just so much propaganda tripe. If we have brownouts, it's because the utilities lacked the foresight of planning properly and their overselling . . . The bill would merely put the skids on utility attitudes which contribute to the 'rape of Connecticut.' "

The other sponsor, Representative Francis Ciampi, paid tribute to the environmental activists who had indirectly produced the bill. "The exciting thing about this is that this is the people's legislation. It is the result of the citizens speaking out, demanding that the special qualities of Connecticut be preserved."

Just before the House was due to vote on the bill, Connecticut Governor Thomas J. Meskill announced that he would veto it. Environmentalists were stunned and went to work on their legislators to work on Meskill. A few minor changes were adopted which House leaders promised would not dilute the bill. "I'm not interested in a watered-down bill," said House Speaker William Ratchford.

The bill passed the House and Meskill allowed it to become law. However, he had the last word when he appointed his members of the council, none of whom pleased the environmentalists. Ratchford was allowed one appointment and, to the delight of the power line foes, appointed Rickerby.

Some Lessons

The power line fight is instructive because those who took part in it used every known activist device, except a sit-in, to demonstrate their feelings. In fighting hard and constructively, they won the respect of the press: "FLEC did not just stand up, say 'no,' and stop there. It engaged legal and engineering consultants versed in power transmission. It presented challenges to facts and figures presented by the utility. It got hundreds of people to attend the hearings in the towns. It got many hundreds more to express their view individually.

"It challenged not only the utility, but it challenged the PUC, as the state regulatory agency, to provide what one speaker termed 'active and affirmative protection' of the public right and interest.

"In short, it demonstrated what concerned citizens can do when they are willing to work together."

It also demonstrated the willingness of so many citizens to spend time and energy mastering the details of a complicated technology, studying maps, making phone calls, and carrying petitions. They learned a lot, and we can learn from their fight—and others—what works and what doesn't.

Before boards and commissions can make a decision, they have to look at the record of a public hearing. How many people spoke for or against the proposal? How many petitions were received? Letters, telegrams? Sheer weight of numbers counts, so every effort must be made to get the public to commit itself.

You have to assume that the other side will be developing its case, persuading people to come over to its side and sign petitions, make calls, and write letters. The sooner you can get the petitions circulating, the better chance you have to capture the largest number. You can make your case as you make the rounds. It helps to carry maps showing exactly what is proposed. You must be prepared to answer questions on the details of the proposal. The best strategy is often enough a delaying tactic. You are protesting because the public hasn't had enough time to study the situation. Perhaps you can point out that the governing board hasn't anticipated the cost and consequences. Wouldn't it be wise to put off a decision until everybody can look at the facts and discuss them? Most people, even those who are reluctant to be for or against something in public, will sign a call for more study.

It is important to reach citizens from every area and have them represented on the petitions. It is equally important to get as close to 100 per cent in the affected area. The petitions should reflect the strong opposition of those immediately touched, plus a general disapproval rising from the community.

Get everyone to turn out for the hearing. Interestingly, the advocates of a change are usually weak at getting a crowd, although they may be very effective at rounding up petition-signers. The "aginers" are more likely to turn out in person. Encourage a big attendance by making phone calls, getting publicity in the paper, and sending out a mailing to alert the public. People are appreciative when a citizen group goes to the time, expense, and trouble of advising them of what's up.

Line up your speakers before the hearing and assign each one the job of making just a single strong point. One argument at a time, forcefully presented, is the best strategy. You can't afford to scatter your shots.

Don't divert the public with side issues. For example: some opponents of the power line began to argue for the ultimate solution, that is, restricted use of electricity. This only served to arouse people against them, those who thought this argument was unrealistic. Instead of focusing public resentment on the power company, they succeeded in deflecting it on themselves.

Pick one or two people who have a talent for interrogation. Instead of making flat statements—"You want that rezoning so your property will be worth three times as much when the highway condemns it"—you could ask, "What will the state have to pay for your property if it is rezoned now before the highway goes through?"

When you testify for a bill, be prepared for the indifference of the committee. Be brief and to the point. Don't snow them. They hate to be pressured. Don't assume they know what you're talking about or even have the background to understand. Just get your arguments on the record and in the press. Don't resent what seem to be hostile questions. You must understand it's their way of showing they are neutral when they play the devil's advocate.

Dramatize the Effects

At the risk of being criticized for being a doomsayer, hysterical, histrionic, you must spell out as vividly as possible what could happen if the first step toward change were taken.

When the Remsenberg (L.I.) Civic Association set out to defeat a proposed jetport at Westhampton Beach, they summoned up visions of an army of jets screaming over beach cottages and exclusive ocean-front property.

"This airport will turn into a decibel desert," the association's president predicted, "and those who enjoy and pay for the enjoyment of the natural resources will suffer."

Mrs. Charles Quay presented a petition with 3622 signatures protesting the jetport to Suffolk County legislators. The petition left nothing to the imagination: "It would result in air pollution and noise beyond the tolerable levels, as well as further depletion of our critical water supply." It would, the petition promised, produce "a Kennedy Airport here in Westhampton."

Never, never let your audience forget that one crack in the armor, one special dispensation, one intrusion is going to bring more of the same. The Scenic Hudson Preservation Conference stated this argument most persuasively when it pointed out that "this proposed hydroelectric plant is a potential forerunner of other industrialization of the Hudson River

Gorge. If one hydro plant gets in, a precedent is set for more already planned. If one form of industry is let in, others will claim similar right. The principle applies not only to the Hudson Highlands and the surrounding area, but also to such magnificent sites as the Grand Canyon, the Redwoods, the Great Swamp, etc. If our case is lost, it could mean debasement of much of the national beauty and resources of our countryside to the rule of the marketplace. This concerns the whole nation!"

There is no substitute for a field trip when you are trying to stop a project. Letting the people see for themselves is the strongest case you can make. Often, an open house or walk can convert the most resolutely opposed.

The Stevens-Coolidge Place in North Andover was probably saved as much by the enthusiasm of the eight hundred people who came to an open house there, as by any other single strategy in the campaign.

The citizen group that has worked for six long, strenuous years to save Staten Island's natural areas from superhighway destruction relies on Annual Greenbelt Hikes to keep the citizenry steamed up and the issue before the public.

Westport (Connecticut) Save Cockenoe Island Committee produced a homemade color movie showing happy commuters basking in the sun on an unpolluted, uncrowded, sandy island beach. "Now can you picture an atomic power plant sitting right here?" the narrator asked. The committee's slogan was "Fishin' not Fission" and that, in itself, conjured up quite a picture of alternate uses.

One of the great slogans is posted on Route 209 near Dingmans Ferry, Pennsylvania, by opponents of a plan to dam the Delaware River at Tocks Island. It reads: "No

more shad, oysters, farms, forests . . . Eat an Engineer for
Lunch, tomorrow. Nix on Tocks, Future Pollution Level
430." Put the message where it counts, is the moral here.

When Congress created the Chesapeake & Ohio Canal
National Historical Park in 1970, this act capped sixteen
years of indefatigable citizen effort and action. In 1954 the
185-mile stretch of land along the Potomac was slated to be
turned into a freeway. Citizens would not be able to enjoy
one of the most remarkable parks in the United States had
it not been for a well-publicized hike along the Canal.

The idea came to Justice William O. Douglas after he
read an editorial in the Washington *Post* saluting the Bureau
of Public Roads for dreaming up the freeway.

Douglas proposed that "the man who wrote your editorial
. . . take time off and come with me . . . One who walked
the canal its full length could plead that cause with the
eloquence of a John Muir. He would get to know muskrats,
badgers, and fox; he would hear the roar of the wind in
thickets; he would see strange islands and promontories
through the fantasy of fog; he would discover the glory
there is in the first flower of spring, the glory there is
in a blade of grass; the whistling wings of ducks would make
silence have new values for him. Certain it is that he could
never acquire that understanding going 60, or even 25, miles
an hour."

The editorial writer agreed to the hike and when news of
the project leaked out hundreds of others clamored to go
along. Only thirty-seven were invited, representatives of environmental organizations. But, as the group hiked along,
they were joined at various points by the public and press.
Douglas recalls, "The hike excited all the communities along

the river. Dozens of people joined us, walking a few miles; at times we had several hundred trailing us, making us look like Coxey's Army. All the local newspapers sent reporters to be with us the day we entered their respective territories. The local radio and TV stations got interviews as we stopped for lunch. CBS, NBC, and ABC television had a man with us every day.

"Schools closed and classes came down to greet us as we passed. Some wrote and sang songs in our honor.

"Adult groups picketed us, proclaiming their desire for a freeway.

"The good people along the Potomac greeted us to honor us not as individuals, but for what we stood. We hiked—and in 1954 the automobile had not so possessed us that hiking was news. Behind the hiking were the conservation principles for which we stood—elbow room for people who wanted to camp, pure river swimming pools, hiking and cycling trails, and an inland canoe way 185 miles long.

"This was what we talked about. We never said a word against the freeway; we only emphasized the *plus*."

Sell the Plus

When New Jersey residents were faced with the prospect of a jetport in Morris County, some of them went to work to get 3750 vulnerable acres set aside as the Great Swamp National Wildlife Refuge Wilderness. The jetport scheme then had to be dropped because the National Wilderness was off limits.

The Town of Oyster Bay (N.Y.) gave the U. S. Government 3100 acres of wetlands to use as a wildlife refuge in the hope that this would forestall a proposed bridge over Long Island Sound. The land lay in the path of access roads to the bridge. Once the Government accepted the gift, the state of New York would be stymied in plans for the bridge since it could not condemn federal land.

A landmark house, historic site, publicly owned recreation and conservation land are generally off limits. So it is important to get more of them. However, just about the only thing the highwaymen, bridge builders, utility people are afraid to tinker with is a cemetery. Projected roads skirt them carefully.

When developers began to creep over the Tiburon Peninsula off San Francisco Bay, there seemed to be nothing anyone could do to stop the leveling of the land and filling in of wetlands. One threatened landmark, St. Hilary's Church, attracted the attention of Mrs. Robert Bastian. In 1959 she formed The Protestant Protective Society for the Preservation of Old St. Hilary's Church and proposed buying the landmark from the Roman Catholic Archdiocese for ten thousand dollars. A leading botanist certified the site as "one of the most interesting and remarkable and beautiful wildflower gardens in California (and therefore in all the world)." Certainly it was worth saving and if it could be spared the developer would be halted, because as Thomas Howell, curator of the Department of Botany at the California Academy of Sciences, put it: "Procedure to save this floral diadem is simple. All that is required is to let the area alone, absolutely and always. It must not be disturbed, landscaped, planted, weeded, irrigated, or walked on."

After an endless struggle to raise the funds, Mrs. Bastian and her group succeeded in putting title to the property in the hands of the Landmarks Society. The apartment houses which would have engulfed the spot were sidetracked. All year round the rare cache of wildflowers, which continue to occupy their natural habitat, bloom and give pleasure to Marin County residents.

Touching the Power Base

You must win the support of elected and appointed officials if you hope to make your case. Go to them well in advance of the hearing and sound them out. If you feel they will hurt your cause, then leave well enough alone. Don't pressure them for a decision or you may get the one you don't want. Instead, concentrate on officials who are with you.

Hire your own experts if you can't count on public servants. In the past sixteen years the C & O Canal Association fought for its Potomac Park. They were obliged to defend their position against a formidable array of opponents. The Army Corps of Engineers wanted to dam the Potomac so they could flush the river of its sewage. The association's experts recommended sewage disposal plants. Then the Corps maintained that the dams were needed to store water in case of drought. The association's hired engineer demonstrated that there were over a billion gallons of good water in the Potomac estuary, enough to protect Washington against any drought. In 1970 conservation groups finally pushed through authorization for a pumping station to make the most of this reserve.

Editorializing on the efforts of conservationists to reroute a proposed Federal highway through the Joyce Kilmer-Slick Rock forest, a wilderness area in Tennessee, *The New York*

Times commented: "If necessary, they are prepared to go to court to save the dream of an integral Joyce Kilmer wilderness. It is ironic that private citizens have to use their own money and energy to accomplish what they pay their public servants to do."

What's more, even well-financed and veteran conservationists are up against formidable odds in their everlasting fight to save the land. As Brooks Atkinson, retired drama critic of *The New York Times* put it as he described the impact of a proposed power line on the Catskills: "We are expected to defend ourselves against a huge political and technological organization that can pay the salaries of executives, engineers, attorneys, and public relations specialists, pay their expenses to meetings, pay experts and witnesses, pay for surveys, promotion, and publications. It is a fully staffed state within a state . . . I hope the genuineness of our concern for an unimpaired environment will compensate for the meagerness of our resources."

Anyone who has fought in the conservation cause knows that there are no final victories. Whether it is the nature of the problem—new crises arising wherever natural resources are threatened—or the stubbornness of the opposition, this battle to save the land will go on and on and on.

7

Building Local Safeguards

It is easier to prevent a disaster than stop one. Much frenzied citizen activity on behalf of the environment would have been unnecessary had these same concerned citizens been able to anticipate trouble and build safeguards against it. This is hindsight, of course, and will be resented by many who are fighting hard to save the environment. It is said in the spirit of helping those who have no protection. It is never too late to plan against even more outrageous invasions to come. If a community does not have the most rudimentary mechanisms to guide sensible growth and protect the environment, it will surely find itself continually at the barricades. If it uses every technique in the book—planning, zoning, conservation commissions, land trusts, and watershed associations—its citizens can feel reasonably secure that property values will be maintained.

If decisions on land use are not going to be made by the marketplace, the law of supply and demand, communities must insist upon a land policy made in the public interest. Decisions on the way a town develops should be made by all the citizens. They are stockholders in the town corporation and have the right to review all proposed changes in corporate environment. Few would dispute the fact that growth cannot be left to chance.

State laws differ, of course. What is permitted, even encouraged, in one state may not be possible in another. Still, there are certain basic protections that communities can enjoy if enough citizens know about them and work to set up the enabling machinery.

Every town needs to assess its natural resources and identify what is worth saving. You start with an inventory of what you have. What are the soil characteristics? Which soils are suitable for building and which, because of slope and poor quality, are not? The town's water system should be mapped. Which wetlands are vital to long-term production and storage of drinking water?

Some communities choose planning; others have it thrust upon them by state, regional, or federal agencies. In order to qualify for grants to construct housing, sewers, water treatment facilities, a community must demonstrate that it can plan for its own needs. To take just one example, money to buy open space is not forthcoming from a government agency unless a community has adopted an open space plan showing the most desirable conservation and recreation acreage.

You must project land use well into the next century. How much land will be needed for housing, schools, agriculture, business and industry, roads, recreation, and conservation. These projections can come as a shock. So much the better. Town officials may have to be jolted into planning for present and future needs.

Obviously no town can afford to buy all the land it will need. Does your town have a land trust or similar organization set up to accept gifts of land for public use?

You need enforcement machinery. Who will make the zoning laws stick? Who will see to it that a long-range plan is adhered to so that land suitable for open space is not swallowed up by development? Who is going to be the watchdog for the total environment? "With a conservation commission on the scene," says environmentalist Gay Ewing, "people feel that they can at least do something about it."

One of the marks of a civilized society is the extent to which it works to protect the public interest. Many communities have instituted planning and zoning boards which discipline development and protect the environment from total destruction. In the last decade, particularly in New England, the conservation commission has joined them, giving communities even more hope that property values may be preserved. Conservation commissions operate on a broad front. They are protective, guarding natural resources against erosion and pollution. They are preventive, with their soils maps showing the least desirable areas for development. They are prescriptive, with their recommended ordinances to save the wetlands and control dig and fill. They are predictive when they recite the horrors to come if steps are not taken— right now. The first big step is to set land aside for town use, conservation, and recreation.

However, if a commission never bought an acre of land, it

could still justify its existence by acting as a watchdog to prevent environmental abuse. Commissions have fought gravel mining. They have successfully campaigned against billboards and junk-car lots. They have campaigned against DDT, Sevin, and the careless use of pesticides. They have halted the wanton cutting of trees, and prevented the silting and erosion of streams.

Yale professor David M. Smith has defined the potential of a conservation commission in spine-tingling terms:

"The planning and zoning commission has the rather negative regulatory power of defining what is barely tolerable, and, therefore, permitted. The conservation commission, on the other hand, is free to work for what is desirable even if it must persuade regulatory agencies or legislative bodies to act."

Persuasion requires education and many commissions try to build an informed citizenry by exposing them to environmental problems. They show films, distribute leaflets, and hold open meetings, run field trips, and conduct programs in the schools. They have a strong constituency because the tide is running with the conservationists and the growing importance of commissions reflects a strong public interest in environmental protection.

"Who's in Charge Here, Anyway?"

Writing about "Conservation Commissions in New England," Andrew J. W. Scheffey, professor at Williams College, notes a new militancy among conservationists:

"People are becoming increasingly vocal over heretofore accepted by-products of progress and prosperity—unkept parks and polluted waters, cluttered roadsides and befouled air—and are demanding to be heard. Opportunities are arising for whole new areas of involvement by private citizens, civic organizations, business interests, and local communities."

The new conservation deals with nature's impact rather than nature's grandeur. The old conservation, symbolized by Teddy Roosevelt, Gifford Pinchot, Yellowstone and the Grand Tetons still captures the American imagination. But, more and more, we want to know how to protect our own backyard, feeling—rightly or not—that the mountains and open ranges have the protection of governmental specialists and the constant scrutiny of national conservation organizations.

As Scheffey points out, "our contemporary industrial complex makes it possible to transform large areas of landscape in a matter of hours or days, and present-day science has introduced a broad range of new intrusions into the environment . . .

"Whether in a new suburb or an older neighborhood, the changes and the reactions follow a similar pattern. They may involve a park about to be dissected by a new highway, a marsh drained, a stream put underground, or a sledding hill leveled for a shopping plaza. Too bad it had to go: wasn't there some other place; might anything have been done about it; where will the kids go now; what will come next; is it worth it; who's in charge here, anyway?

"The last question provides the key. Community participation in public issues has long been accepted as an elemental test of democracy, yet this concept has never really been incorporated into conservation planning and practice . . . Much of the potential power to structure a community's growth lies in the will of the people living there. Yet until recently there has been no formal procedure for determining public attitudes toward the environment; no vehicle to influence the public and private landscape-shapers. With the rise of town Conservation Commissions in New England, a community response has become possible."

The conservation commissions of New England are increasingly "in charge" to the delight of preservationists and to the dismay of the destroyers. In some towns, they are invited to have a hand in the planning of land use, the protection of the environment through zoning. In other towns, they must force their way onto the official scene, reminding their fellow officials of what they take to be the public interest.

Imagine "bird watchers" having power over land use. Some say this is the province of hardheaded businessmen. Indeed, planning and zoning commissions are often overloaded with engineers, realtors, and businessmen who are accustomed to thinking of growth as good. Conservation commissions, on the other hand, are staffed with residents who try to preserve what exists, who actually resist "progress." Naturally they are apt to rock the boat and upset the plans of those who could assume—before environmentalists gained power—that business attitudes would prevail. In town after town the conservation commissions have sought to establish new official attitudes about what is best for the community. They have made many friends and not a few enemies as they challenge old assumptions and, in some cases, the town fathers who have set another course for the community.

Feeling that they are on the side of the angels, conservation commissions have often acted in a pre-emptory, officious style, which is bound to handicap their efforts.

Conservation commissions can turn people off with their insistent questions about pollution and erosion, their one-track high-mindedness on clean and green. Perhaps because they are newly formed and relatively untouched by the compromising factors of public office, they can be wholly idealistic. They can opt for the ideal solution and not worry too much about what it will do to somebody's pocketbook if he isn't allowed to take out the gravel or fill the wetlands.

Broad Powers

Conservation commissions have broad powers, but they must seize them. They have been charged with, to quote New Hampshire's Enabling Act, "the power to maintain, improve, protect, limit the future use of or otherwise conserve and properly utilize open spaces and other land and water areas within their city or town, and shall manage and control the same . . ."

In a number of communities, the commission is powerless because it is working within the system to the point where it accomplishes nothing.

In others, they have made powerful enemies because they took their job seriously. The chairman of the Springfield (Mass.) Conservation Commission believes that commissions cannot be above politics. "You've got to fight. You've got to educate the public. We advise loudly. That's our only weapon. It's nice to try to win friends, but in some matters we don't care if some people don't like us."

When the conservation commission bill was introduced in

the Massachusetts Legislature in 1957, it caused "little controversy or commotion," says Scheffey. He believes this was because no outlay of funds was anticipated.

Three years passed and there was no conspicuous mushrooming of commissions in the wake of the legislation. Only 19 had been created, leaving 332 communities commissionless. The Commissioner of Natural Resources, Charles H. W. Foster, who was to become a power in New England's conservation politics, decided to survey the unpromising situation town by town. He decided that poor communication was responsible for lack of interest. Most communities simply did not know enough about the potential of a commission to want one. Foster set about remedying this with a public relations barrage. But, his most important finding concerned funding. Without the promise of a grant-in-aid, communities were not motivated to form commissions.

The law was amended in 1959 to, as Scheffey puts it, "permit the establishment of Conservation Funds, supplementing goodwill and persuasion with the prospect of financial incentive."

Money provided the spur. In 1960, commissions were created in 25 towns, doubling the number in existence. They doubled again the next year and by 1969, commissions were established in more than 275 communities.

A Land Inventory

The commission's first job is to inventory town land so that it can assess present and future problems. How much wetland? What natural areas must be preserved? Can the map be worked out so that natural areas are linked by trails?

What would be the hazards of development on poor soil? With a soils map in hand, done by professionals, the conservation commission is then able to make recommendations to the planners and zoners. The commission also should draw up an open space map, showing lands which it feels should be kept open. These are properties worthy of acquisition for any number of reasons—to provide an oasis of green, to save a scenic or historic site, to guard against pollution, particularly where a town's beaches or marshes are concerned.

"Save the wetlands" is a conservationists' battle cry. It can mean preserving a beach from dig and fill, keeping oil slicks at bay, putting shorelines into protective custody so the public can enjoy a beach forever as a national park. These are the dramatic accomplishments.

But, the interior wetlands also deserve protection. Anyone who has a summer cottage on a lake knows that detergents, septic runoff, and unbridled development can kill the water system and turn a vacationer's paradise into a weed-filled bog. Protecting the lakes and streams and marshes is the conservation commission's responsibility. How can it prevent destruction and deterioration? A wetlands ordinance is one solution. It might, as one does, "regulate the dredging, filling, deposition or removal of materials, the diversion or obstruction of water flow, the placement of structures and other uses in the wetlands and water courses of the town." The object is to protect these areas from gravel mining and fill. It also cuts down on construction in areas which are unsuitable for development. If a septic field must be placed so many feet away from a stream or marsh or pond, an ordinance can effectively limit the number of housing units on a given property. (See page 289 for model.)

One major objective in making an open space map is to dramatize the need to secure certain prime parcels as open space in perpetuity. Without the map, showing town priorities in acquisition, there is little chance of government funding. With a comprehensive map, a town can realize the most ambitious open space policy.

In 1967 the Cape Cod town of Dennis, Massachusetts, appropriated $652,000 to buy fourteen hundred acres of land, representing almost 11 per cent of the total area of the town. The price was not exorbitantly high for seashore property, but it did amount to quite an investment by the town's thirty-two hundred registered voters. They were solidly behind the purchase, as shown by their nearly unanimous vote to buy. Clearly, the Dennis Conservation Commission had done a splendid job informing the public on the urgency of land preservation. Its chairman, William McLeod, had, in fact, made a clear-cut case for land acquisition two years before the money was voted. He said then: "If I were asked to explain in simple terms what the Dennis Conservation Commission is trying to accomplish, I would state unhesitatingly that it hopes to cultivate a greater reverence for the land in its community. The land will be here long after its present owners have died and have been forgotten. But what the present generation does to the land can either enrich or cheapen the lives of generations to come."

Other town officials do not always share conservation's enthusiasm for land acquisition. They fear the out-of-pocket costs. They resist removing the property from the tax list. And, some of them may have other plans for working the land.

When the Weymouth (Mass.) Conservation Commission

set out to acquire 237 acres of wild lands bordering the Black River, they met strong opposition from the town's selectmen. The cost was reasonable—$113,000—contingent upon preserving the area as untouched open space. The selectmen wanted to buy the property, but they wanted to mine it for gravel.

After an intensive public education campaign, the Conservation Commission was gratified by a vote in favor of the open space, preservation buy. "How fortunate we are to be able to have it and leave it as it is . . . Once you're inside it, it's like another world."

The disappointed chairman of the Board of Selectmen expressed another view: "We've purchased a piece of property which not only the whole town, but everyone can use. To me this is asinine."

More Than "Beautification"

Thoreau must have had conservation commissions in mind when he wrote: "it would be worth the while if in each town there were a committee appointed to see that the beauty of the town receive no detriment."

Many commissions concentrate their entire effort on what Lady Bird Johnson called "beautification." They sponsor "clean-up, fix-up, paint-up" campaigns. They plant trees, preserve wildflower patches, tidy up public beaches, and thin the woodland so that specimen trees can flourish.

Some commissions exert influence on commercial areas, persuading businesses to tone down their architecture, choose quieter colors, or place advertising more unobtrusively, all in an effort to control visual pollution. They have also tried to initiate recycling programs.

Here and there in the records of conservation commissions you find a whiff of real action, a suggestion that they have met "the interests" head on.

A commission investigates the city dump, let's say, and publicizes pollution permitted by other public agencies. Or, it makes known its views on sewage disposal and alerts the voters to possible contamination of water supply and recreation areas. (A number of commissions have voted phosphate bans.) When a highway is widened or constructed, the commission is often vocal in its objections to an encroachment on natural areas.

Commission chairmen are all too aware that some officials would like to keep them powerless, restricted to bird watching, harmless nature study. William Morrissey, who headed the Newtown (Conn.) Commission, once got his frustrations off his chest with a plea for a strong, coordinated effort to correct environmental abuse:

"We have been putting out brush fires. What we need is an ordinance that can put 'teeth' in our attempts to protect the wetlands, rivers, streams, ponds, and swamps that are now being polluted. We must have an over-all plan, a definite list of needs, and the tools with which to accomplish our purpose as a commission."

Without these tools and without the support of other town officials, conservation commissions are left with no power except the power to expose anti-environmental schemes. One such project surfaced in Newtown in June 1971, when the Conservation Commission branded a park plan as nothing but "a massive gravel operation." Town fathers proposed making a thirty-acre park out of a steep and rugged property which, they admitted, would have to be leveled before it could be used. The commission was all in favor of acquiring the land for open space, but noted that it was too rough for any use except hiking and picnicking. To put it in shape for other types of recreation would require a gravel-mining operation that would take at least twenty years and result in not a park area, but "a vast oasis of rubble."

One member of the commission said, "The time has come for the Conservation Commission to stand up and speak its piece." He said that although conservation was a hot subject, "everyone treats us like poor relatives."

When a commission tries to superimpose environmental values on a community, it usually wins cheers from the populace, with the exception of those property owners who hope to make a buck off the land. Most people welcome regulation of pollution and erosion. However, in the spring of 1971, some Connecticut commissions found themselves on the wrong side of an issue. The forests of the state were being stripped by cankerworms and gypsy moths, but conservationists were opposed to aerial spraying.

The Conservation Commission of Ridgefield, Connecticut, took the unprecendented step of becoming a party to a suit to stop the mass spraying. The commission contended that it would be derelict in its duties if it did not protect the wetlands under its custody from receiving a dose of Sevin.

"One of the cautions on the package label of Sevin is: 'Avoid contamination of Food, Feed, Water Supplies, Streams and Ponds.' Since all but one small parcel of land under the commission's custody has water or wetlands or both, it was a legitimate request that these not be sprayed from the air with this product."

The suit aroused strong feelings both pro and con the commission. First Selectman Mortimer J. Woodcock was boiling mad: "I feel that the Conservation Commission has acted in very poor taste . . . They are accountable to the voters of Ridgefield and surely should show a reasonable reaction to a vote of the town. I feel that the members of the commission could have acted as individuals without criticism, but as a commission, subpoenaing their own government to court, is both unbelievable and intolerable . . . We should do all we can to protect our trees, but let's also forgive our zealous if misguided friends. Please forgive them, Lord, for they know not what they do."

Later in the year the Conservation Commission again clashed with the selectmen, but this time they had Planning and Zoning on their side. Acting upon the recommendation of the Conservation Commission the Planning and Zoning Commission had refused other town officials permission to fill in a 2.6-acre wetlands area for a playing field. This so infuriated the first selectman that he proposed a referendum to decide the fate of the wetlands and also to allow townspeople to vote on whether or not town property should be exempt from zoning regulations.

Ridgefield voters decisively defeated those who would have filled in the wetlands—by 1197 to 471. They were even more firmly opposed to the idea of putting town property off limits to the zoners and defeated this item by 1450 to 199.

Ridgefield's experience suggests that conservation commissions can be a thorn in the side of officialdom, but if they are to be effective and do their job these confrontations must be expected.

Conservation and Development

The most imaginative spokesmen for the conservation cause repeatedly remind us that we cannot simply be against, we must be for something. We must offer a better solution to land use, better regulations against land abuse.

William H. Whyte goes so far as to link conservation and development. "The powerful commission is a conservation *and* development commission," he says. "It gets in on the planning stages in the town's development. Conservation commissions should plan the open space in land to be developed in the future so that there are tie-ups between open space parcels. Developers can then build around the open space plans. It is very important that commissions work toward being able to influence plans in their towns at the planning stage in order to enforce proper land use."

Whyte knows as well as anyone that commissions will meet opposition from special interests. He suggests that commissions work with developers to help them make the most of their land, saving natural features and building on the best soil. Whyte is an advocate of cluster zoning, a device which permits a developer to cluster his houses on desirable building land, leaving the wetlands, natural features, and open space untouched.

He had said, however, that the phrase "cluster zoning" creates the wrong image—"the doughnut rather than the hole." Charles Little, formerly of the Open Space Institute, agrees: "Whoever invented the term 'cluster development' should get an F in public relations." Little expresses the views of many who ask, "Clustering? You mean houses all pushed together? That's what I've been trying to get away from. Doesn't sound like a very good idea to me."

Cluster might find more supporters if stress were laid on what was being saved. Some have suggested "ecological zoning" or "conservation zoning" and that is more descriptive of the goal. However, it's a hard concept to sell because residents who are accustomed to a uniform pattern of large lots fear that any departure from conventional zoning might open a town to downzoning. Developers are wary, too, of any cluster plan which obliges them to build the same number of houses they would be permitted under the conventional scheme. True, they can economize on roads and utility lines because the houses could be put closer together. But they eye the open space that's spared and see, quite naturally, the potential for more houses.

Several years ago, Robert E. Simon, whose reputation as a conscientious builder rests on the imaginative job he did as developer of Reston, Virginia (America's first new town), bought some three hundred acres in Pound Ridge, New York. He planned a comprehensive development, dredging a sizable lake to use as the focus for the development. However, a money shortage led him to start on a piecemeal plan. He applied for permission to build on twenty-one three-acre plots. Some townspeople saw the danger in this kind of orthodox development, and, because they were concerned about the natural and historic features embedded in the tract, asked the Planning Commission to withhold approval until a thoroughgoing ecological study was made.

One such study had already been made by an interested citizen. Harmon F. Newell, Jr., a local carpentry contractor, had devoted two years to examining the potential of the Simon tract. He had even built a four-by-six-foot three-dimensional model of the property and adjacent land which included the town park. Newell has lived in Pound Ridge for over twenty-five years, walked the property, camped out on it as a scoutmaster. He identified twenty-odd acres of Indian Hill as unique because it had never been touched by man. Newell hoped to arouse bipartisan support for conservation zoning, a device which would allow Indian Hill and the wetland around it to be saved as permanent open space. If the builder were allowed to put his houses closer together so that he got the same number on the three-hundred-acre tract, the wetlands and unspoiled areas could be preserved.

Newell prepared five charts relating the ecology of the area to various aspects of planning plus eight hundred feet of color film he had taken of the property. He had tried earlier to persuade the Pound Ridge Conservation Advisory Council —of which he was a member—to sponsor an official study of the property. When other members refused, he resigned and did the job himself.

Newell's work aroused the community, both pro and con cluster zoning. Many felt that giving one developer a special concession would open the door to downzoning. But others could see the merits of ecological zoning aimed at protecting vital historic, scenic, and wetland areas.

In late July 1971 the Pound Ridge Planning Board approved the subdivision. The chairman said it had no alternative because it met all town zoning requirements. Harmon F. Newell was present and still fighting. He proposed that the twenty-five acres representing the Indian Hill Section of the development be purchased by town subscription and added to the thirty-seven-acre Halle Ravine Nature Conservancy which it abuts.

In November, Simon addressed an audience of townspeople at a meeting on open space zoning and called conservationists "insidious, subtle, and dangerous." He insisted that "the only way you can save anything is by clustering" and he felt that he had been defeated in his proposal to cluster by conservationists opposed to downzoning.

Harmon Newell lost no time in countering Simon:

"I would suggest that Mr. Simon is a fox in the suburban chicken coop, eyeing the hens, roosters, and chicks . . . Mr. Simon says that three-acre lots will become one-acre lots or condominium sites. He says the only logical open space planning is 'tight clustering'—multi-unit housing. These statements are contrary to the environmental need of a low-population density in Pound Ridge . . .

"Last summer Mr. Simon submitted, and the Planning Board under existing zoning ordinances, had to approve, a plan of large lot development with no open space protection. Last February I wrote to the *Patent Trader* that 'Mr. Simon has done little but talk to alleviate my alarm . . .' My opinion is hardening."

Some weeks later Simon laid three plans for development before Pound Ridge. The first two were conventional but Plan Three would save Indian Hill, while preserving 83 acres of open space. However, Simon asked permission to build 100 units instead of the 64 permitted by zoning. Sixty of the units would be townhouses concentrated on 9.3 acres. Newell said he did not favor any of the prosposals but he thought a plan might be worked out which would be economically and environmentally sound.

Looking Ahead

A good plan must offer new ideas, new approaches to preservation, and not simply celebrate the status quo.

Take, for example, the "Comprehensive Development Plan for 1985" produced by the Nassau-Suffolk (L.I.) Regional Planning Board. The plan was organized around the theme of "corridors, clusters, and centers." The object was to save Long Island from "being paved over from shore to shore," by saving large chunks of open space. The potato farmers who own huge tracts of desirable land far out on the Island would be given the privilege of selling off 20 per cent of the fields for dense development. But the remaining 80 per cent would be deeded to the community. The farmers would have the privilege of remaining on the land and working it.

Other Long Island communities faced with the prospect of an invasion of new residents demanding schools and other services have prepared planning documents which suggest the use of preferential tax treatment to encourage the farmers to hold their land and easements. If the farmer will grant a negative easement to the town, promising not to develop his land, he will pay lower taxes.

In another move to stave off ticky-tacky development which would destroy Long Island's over-all land values, Lee Koppleman, director of the Suffolk County Planning Board, recommended that the county acquire nine hundred acres of undeveloped land to complete a cross-Long Island green belt.

"Suffolk still has a chance to build buffers—we can prevent communities from running into each other."

Most communities need the services of professional planners. They need the technical assistance, the mapmaking, chart-drafting skills. They should hear about solutions to problems which have worked in other towns. This is what they hope they are buying when they engage outside planners. But, they may have to fight for it. Instead of approaching each new project on its own merits, designing a plan to fit a particular community, the professional planners may try to superimpose stock plans for a stock suburbia on an unsuspecting town.

Bringing their slide rules, their grim prophesies of inundating growth, they convince their new client that all is lost anyway. They are the outriders, bringing news of communities gone down the drain because they didn't plan. Yet, to many the salvation they offer seems less a plan than a self-fulfilling prophecy. Plan for the industry because it wants to settle on your borders. Plan for the shopping centers because the new highway will attract customers. Plan for the apartments because people are moving out of the cities.

When a community resists the prepackaged future ordained for it, the planners shake their heads and murmur about looking backward, about not facing reality, about wishful thinking.

It is up to the public to make planning and zoning commissions and their consultants realize that there is a powerful and vocal segment of the public very much concerned with the town. These taxpayers and voters don't have to settle for the lesser of two evils. They can insist upon planning that preserves the best of what they have.

The spur must come from citizens. Commissions are wary of moving too fast and too far off center. They wait until they are pushed and prodded to make decisions. Too often the pusher is someone who wants to exploit a land-use decision. The developer of a large tract of potentially valuable commercial land comes in and requests a change of zone. Subdividers hack up the land in a conventional design. Builders pull out gravel in the guise of lot improvement.

A plan is only as good as its enforcement. Shorthanded volunteer boards simply can't keep an eye on every builder every minute. When the damage has been done, the culprit will claim hardship.

"I forgot," the developer said guilelessly when asked to explain why he built a house closer to the lot line than zoning permits. "It was a human error," his attorney added, saying that it is only the third time in eighteen years that his client had made such a mistake. He did agree that the placement of the building "kind of ran amiss" and apologized, insisting that the surveying stakes had been moved. One neighboring resident asked, "Is this a way to pay a fifty-dollar fine to avoid zoning regulations?"

Zoners increasingly find themselves up against developers who ram their projects through, risking court cases and intense public disapproval.

Controlling Big Development

Towns still lucky enough to have sizable tracts of unspoiled land within their boundaries can expect to be vulnerable to large-scale developers. When they come calling they will court the town fathers with promises of environmental protection, dazzle them with visions of tax revenues and increased activity in local building trades. Their architectural plans may be most impressive.

Once the foot is in the door, however, and zoning laws have been abandoned or adjusted to fit the reality of the "new concept in housing," the town may find it has a tiger by the tail.

Heritage Village, in Southbury, Connecticut, is but one example.

In 1964 the Paparazzo Brothers took an option on a seven-hundred-acre tract owned by Victor Borge and Alfred P. Kreuger, who invented the Scotch tape dispenser. It was zoned large-lot residential at the time, but the citizens of Southbury decided that the promise of tax benefits implicit in a housing complex limited to people without school-age children was too good to pass up. In one night, after months of heated debate, they threw out zoning so Heritage Village could come in; later they restored zoning so the rest of the town would be protected.

Heritage architecture, designed by a California firm, with its shed roofs and rough siding looking appropriate for New England, won a fistful of awards from architectural and building groups. A tidal wave of publicity followed each new construction. *Look* called it "A 20th Century Brigadoon with golf course attached." The *Christian Science Monitor* explained: "What the architect and builders are trying to develop—and critics so far say successfully—is a gentle village where the residents can trade the hustle of the city for the quiet of the Connecticut hills."

That quiet was due to be shattered as soon as the Paparazzos developed the commercial side of this project. A handsome, imaginatively planned barnlike shopping bazaar rose on the site, attracting visitors from all over Connecticut, New York, and Massachusetts. First to feel the impact was the town road feeding into Heritage Village. With the increase in traffic this old, single-lane connector which snaked its way tortuously into the valley and across a precarious single-lane bridge into "Brigadoon" was made obsolete.

Clearly, a modern east-west road and new bridge would have to be built to the tune of a half million dollars or more. Who would build it? Town or developer? The antiroad groups, calling themselves the "Concerned Southbury Taxpayers Committee" charged that town financing of the road would be a "dangerous precedent . . . every developer in Southbury, and Connecticut as well, will take note of this and will expect and indeed demand that the town pay for his access roads based on this precedent."

In referendum after referendum the town voted down the road. But, predictably, Heritage Villagers themselves pushed the road through when they packed the hall to vote in a town budget with the $500,000 road money included.

Southbury's disenchantment with Heritage focused on the road money, but town residents have other complaints.

The developer has been charged with polluting the Pomeraug River in his construction activities and sued accordingly.

Heritage has been given any number of variances to allow it to disregard the codes which govern planning and building in the town at large. The developer was, until recently, according to the local press, "batting 1,000 with the Zoning Board of Appeals."

Most significant of all, Heritage Villagers attempted to

break the political structure of the town and raid the Republican caucus. More than a hundred Villagers turned out to elect their own slate of candidates at a March 1970 caucus. This triumph was short-lived when "the regulars" called for a primary and won.

However, Southbury residents can see the handwriting on the wall. Heritage Villagers will, by 1973, number five thousand and that's equal to the population in Southbury itself. "It's one thing when you hear about five thousand people and another when you see them," one resident complained. "They're going to control the whole town. We can't stick together the way they do. It's a fight—the town against the Village."

What about the highly touted tax advantage which Heritage was supposed to bring Southbury? It had been estimated at close to one million dollars annually.

Despite some money coming in from the Village, Southbury's budget jumped 77 per cent in 1971. Why? Because Heritage developers have withheld taxes pending a resolution of their lawsuit claiming unfair assessments. The Board of Finance has had to raise the mill rate to compensate for the loss of income. If the town must bear the cost of the new bridge and east-west road, taxes will go even higher.

The cost to the town, the return—or lack of it—on its investment in Heritage Village cannot be measured solely in dollars and cents. First Selectman Robert E. Harroff conceded that the tax revenue was welcome, that an influx of business and professional men settling in the Village provided a pool of mature talent for town boards and volunteer organizations.

On the debit side, he criticized the Village-Town feud, the

abrupt demand for town services—like roads, medical facilities, and fire protection. "Demands on this town are often distorted," Harroff said. "There is a vast difference between the town's obligations and responsibilities to residential property owners and its obligations to commercial interests."

Predictably, Henry J. Paparazzo disputed the disadvantages to the town and reminded the selectman that: "When the basic plan for Heritage Village was first approved in 1965, it was agreed by Southbury town officials, the planning commission, and engineering consultants that an access road would be built to accommodate the traffic to and from the Village and it was the town's responsibility to build it."

He also insisted that medical services were being developed in the Village and a volunteer ambulance organization was under way.

Old-timers remember it just the other way. They say that in 1965, Louis Paparazzo agreed to build the access road if the town would build the bridge at a cost of $100,000. They feared that if the Villagers push through the budget request for $500,000 this will be only the beginning. The town will have to relocate and rebuild other roads to service new Heritage condominiums. They know, too, that when the Paparazzos pull out upon completion of their complex, the town will be asked to accept the roads within the Village and maintain them even though they were not built to town specifications.

It is only a matter of time before the Paparazzos will move out of Southbury, leaving their Village in the hands of the condominium owners.

In 1971 it became known that they had been quietly picking up land in Amherst, Massachusetts, and were now ready to apply for a zoning change so they could build a two-thousand-unit complex.

The secrecy of the maneuvering bothered the Amherst people. No one knew anything about it until some 630 acres were safely in the hands of the Paparazzos. Then cocktail parties and conferences brought the deal out into the open. It was to be called "The Commons." How appropriate a name for such a New England setting.

The promises the Paparazzos made to Amherst sounded familiar to the Southbury Planning Commission:

"A new concept of community planning . . . utilizing the natural beauty of the site . . . emphasize the preservation of trees, rustic areas and untouched woodlands . . . this type of planned community will be harmonious with the area. We intend to create the kind of environment and facilities . . . that will be an asset to Amherst."

In addition to housing units, there would be the shopping bazaar, golf course, and of course the "new road."

At a public hearing on the project Amherst residents proved themselves to be more sophisticated and searching in their questions about the project than Southburians had been in 1964. For one thing, they could analyze the impact of Heritage Village, Southbury had had to guess what it would do. For another, the professors in the area could contribute detailed and factual information on the probable impact of two thousand units on the environment, the development of Amherst, and the future of its schools and the tax base. The Commons would not be restricted to retirees, and families who moved in from outlying areas would surely put a strain on the school system.

"Would you promise to build a school and give it to the

town?" the developer was asked. "We are not prepared to do that," was the not unexpected reply.

Many people were clearly disturbed by the prospect of turning Amherst into a haven for displaced suburbanites. As one put it, "Are we not, with The Commons, taking the big and irrevocable step toward becoming another Bronxville, Scarsdale, Wellesley, Bryn Mawr, Darien, or some other well-groomed, well-heeled, upper-middle-class suburb?"

One resident insisted that opponents of the project were not against growth *per se:* "Amherst has never—to my knowledge—and never should try to exclude any individual who wants to live here and share these blessings with us. What *should* be opposed are real estate developers who would build beyond the projected local need for housing, who would attract to their predominantly high-priced, upper-middle-class developments people from far and wide, some of whom will probably never hear of Amherst until they read the glowing advertisements."

A Snowballing Effect

Peter Farb, a professional ecologist who lives in Amherst, drew a comparison with Aspen, Colorado, to dramatize what might happen:

"Like Amherst, Aspen grew and a need developed for housing, particularly low-income. But instead of providing only for the natural, internal growth, Aspen closed its eyes to the consequences of allowing developers to build much of the real needs of the community. Amherst apparently is about to take the same step; instead of the several hundred units, mostly low-income, needed for internal growth, Amherst is about to allow the Paparazzo organization to construct two thousand middle and upper income units.

"As soon as Aspen opted for development, a snowballing effect resulted that could no more be halted than an avalanche. Despite the developers' assurances that there was no hazard, the new building overtaxed the sewage system and a stench lay upon the town; water quality suffered and unexplained stomach ailments increased . . .

"And, what happened to the low-income housing, the original justification for Aspen to take the path to development? It got lost in the scramble for profits. And the quality of life that had attracted developers to exploit Aspen in the first place? That also evaporated as cultural events became prohibitively expensive, roads and streets jammed with traffic, streams, open sewers."

In the summer of 1971 visitors from Amherst descended upon Southbury to discover at firsthand whether Heritage had been a blessing or a burden.

Paul Richardson, chairman of the Southbury Planning Commission, left no doubt in the visitors' minds about the enormity of the impact a Heritage Village might make on Amherst.

"This is one of the toughest situations I have encountered in fourteen years on the commission," he said. He recalled the many disputes the town had had with the builders. "We have had problems in drainage. There are no gutters. The architects are from California and oppose them on esthetic grounds. Storm drain design is poor."

Said Richardson with the weariness that comes after years of doing battle with a rampant bulldozer, "They go ahead and tear up town roads without even asking for a permit. You are up against a very aggressive and energetic developer."

The crux of the problem here as elsewhere lies in enforcement. "If you have good zoning and good planning and good inspectors, then you can do things the right way. You could avoid the mistakes we have made.

"Like a lot of other builders, they will not do anything they don't have to do. Our principal problem has been getting them to comply with our building code and other regulations.

"In one condominium cluster of fifty buildings, only three were built where they were originally shown on the site plan; the others were one hundred to five hundred feet away. Part of this is the fault of a weak zoning enforcement officer. Enforcement is out of the commission's hands.

"They make changes in plans without coming back to us. Local builders protest that we are letting them get away with murder."

One of the more outspoken opponents of the project, Richard Beamish, wrote long, thoughtful letters to the Amherst *Record* raising fundamental questions about the advantages of packaged communities.

"The assumption here is that you, Mr. Paparazzo, are the lesser of two evils. Why must we live with either evil? If development so far has been ugly and unmanaged, can't we establish some quality control over it in the future—through new zoning and other means—as some enlightened communities have done?

"And so it seemed to me, Mr. Paparazzo, that the choices put to us are both unacceptable: the piecemeal blight of the past, or your gigantic, tastefully planned suburb of the future . . .

"I can picture Amherst and its surrounding towns ten or fifteen years hence . . . The hills and valleys of this once pastoral land would be clustered with endless (though tasteful) suburbs. The flagship development-pace-setter and tastesetter for the rest is 'The Commons.' The others, showing the same profitable respect for New England tradition, bear names like 'Sugar Maple Groves,' 'The Orchards,' 'Pelham Woods,' 'Thoreau Pastures,' etc. The real town commons, sugar maples, and apple orchards have long since gone . . . except those that have been spared for ornamental purposes. In this vast sea of Suburbia a few small islands nevertheless remain—Lawrence Swamp, the Holyoke Range Park, the Amherst College Bird Sanctuary—to give some slight substance to the advertisements that still doggedly tout the charms of country living."

Or, as Holly Whyte once observed:

"The woods and meadows that so attracted new residents disappeared as soon as developers got around to building on them, and if the residents wanted to find what other natural features would be next to go, they had only to check the names of the subdivisions being planned. When a developer puts a woods into the name, or a vale, heights, forest, creek or stream, he is not conserving; he is memorializing. Subdivisions are named for that which they are about to destroy."

The hardest questions fired at the Paparazzos concerned benefits to Amherst.

"What is this development going to do for me?"

Paparazzo answered with commendable honesty, "It will not solve the problems of Amherst."

"Will it compound them?"

"I have no way of knowing," Paparazzo admitted, "how many will come out of Springfield to live here or whether that's good or bad."

Residents could judge for themselves just how bad it could be when they heard the developer estimate that sales would be about 250 units a year for seven or eight years until the two thousand units had been built. The developer did agree with one suggestion that advertising be limited to media within thirty miles of Amherst.

The big question of the evening came when someone asked Paparazzo: "If you found out that we residents of Amherst do not want the town to grow that much, would you stop?"

Paparazzo answered: "We are business people interested in making a profit. We are professionals interested in doing the best job we can. We need your assistance. You have the option of continuing the kind of development you have had in the past. I would not come into town and buck a community."

Even before a formal town meeting to take a vote on the project the Zoning Board of Appeals turned the proposition down.

The town meeting voted tentative approval of Amherst Fields if the developer would come back to the town with a proposal "on a scale of about one-half that of the original plan." A committee to study the potential growth of Amherst was appointed, clearly prompted by the Amherst Fields debate. "How big do residents want their town to grow?" A question for Amherst and, indeed, for all communites to face and discuss.

People Make Plans Work

When a specific threat engages the imagination of endangered homeowners, they can rise to unexpected heights of protest. But, the best way to avoid the disaster is to plan for a community's development.

Fortunately the citizen activist can turn to local government and insist that his planning and zoning boards, his conservation commission, act in the public interest. The rise of land trusts and watershed associations provides other private means to save the landscape.

In most communities, town boards and commissions are staffed with volunteers, elected by the townspeople, or appointed by the mayor or selectmen. They get their jobs by way of politics and usually receive no remuneration for their tireless work.

It is important to recognize that the best plan in the world, the most detailed zoning regulations, the most ambitious open space plan will not protect a community if the people charged with administering these documents are fundamentally opposed to protection of natural resources.

This brings us back to politics. Too many environmentalists still believe that because they are on the side of the angels the opposition will yield gracefully to their demands. They may win the battles over a highway siting, a threatened industrial complex, or an enlarged shopping center, but lose the war when they fail to challenge appointments or nominations at a party caucus or at the polls. They then have to fight again and again as their efforts are subverted by those in office.

Time and again citizens have discovered, to their horror,

that the best case in the world against an environmental disaster is brushed aside by the people who have political power.

In earlier times, before environmental sensitivity developed, we believed that it made sense to put builders on zoning boards, real estate men on the Planning Commission. After all, they had certain expertise, although some suspected it was like putting the fox in the chicken coop. There is still a hankering for the good old days. As one consulting engineer to a planning commission put it, "I would be perfectly happy to have three reputable people from the building trades on the planning commission. It would make more planning sense. But, we have a cross section of the town on the commission, and in our society, this is the only way we can do this." To that comment, one might add, "Thank God."

Now that there is more pressure to keep the public interest, rather than the private purse, represented on commissions, there is more opportunity for citizen involvement. The environmentalists must seize it, must run for public office, must force their way into the decision-making inner circle. The best local safeguard of all is the continued service of public-spirited men and women in office.

8

Getting Outside Help

It's only natural to feel powerless, at bay, unable to spring into action, when you hear that someone with money and influence has designs on your personal landscape.

Quite by chance you learn that "the State is going to widen 58," that the area airport is to be "studied for possible expansion," that three hundred acres have been acquired by a syndicate for housing, light industry, and shopping.

Even when you keep a weather eye out for signals that the winds of development are blowing your way, you can be taken by surprise. One homeowner who weekends in the Berkshires makes a point of reading the local paper from cover to cover so she'll know what's going on. She got a rude shock not long ago: "I learned that a huge new shopping center was planned for Great Barrington. It was the first I'd heard of it. I wanted immediately to join a group, or start one, but it's difficult to take the first step if there's no ongoing organization."

Neighborhoods which have been spared the onslaught of civilization may have never felt pressured to form a home-owners group. When danger strikes they must hastily put one together. The task is made immeasurably easier if they are aware of help which may be available to them from public and private institutions and well-established environmental activists.

Within a radius of fifty or a hundred miles you can find at least one "environment nut" who will lead you to the sources of power and influence. How do you find him, or her? You start calling—the soil conservation man in the district, the county agent, the garden club, the high school science teacher. If your town has a conservation commission or a land trust, call their officers. Often the League of Women Voters has studied land and water use and heard experts testify on wise management of both. They may know leaders on the conservation front, people who like nothing better than to lend their names, contacts, or energies to a cause, help novices organize quickly in an emergency.

The conservation movement is incestuous. People are tied by strands of funding, interlocking directorates, common projects, one to another. There are dozens of groups but a core of influentials. Once you get a lead to a leader, you will find the conservation establishment opening up.

When your neighborhood is under siege you must not only muster local troops, but summon infighters, trained in other environmental battles. It could be a lawyer, like David Sive, known for his effective legal defense of the environment. Or, a chapter of the Sierra Club which would be willing to help. Or, an Audubon group able to put up the money to study the impact of a proposed project. Or, the Nature Conservancy which might advance the money to option a threatened tract of land, helping you buy time so you could raise the funds yourself. Or, a respected scientist who will give you facts and figures, the ammunition you need to nail down a clear and present danger to human life and the environment. Or, an environmental circuit-rider like Dick Pough who, because of a lifetime spent in the cause of conservation, knows all the short cuts, all the power levers to push or pull.

The Missionaries

Richard Hooper Pough has been an officer, director, or member of virtually every important conservation organization in America—not to mention his connections abroad.

When asked to run over the ones he is on active duty with at the moment, Pough (pronounced "Po") produces a mimeographed sheet which lists twenty-seven "current affiliations." They range in influence and visibility from "The Boone and Crockett Club" to "National Audubon," from "The Fauna Preservation Society" to "The Nature Conservancy." Pough considers them all equally important to the cause and takes a proud parent's satisfaction in those he has brought to life and sustained through his own unique fundraising efforts.

Pough is the key to the conservation establishment. His own career dramatizes the evolution of the movement—from passive nature study to active intervention on behalf of the national environment, from the Museum of Natural History, where he set up the "Hall of Forests" in the fifties, to the courtroom where he testified for "the integrity of Storm King Mountain" against a utility powerhouse in the sixties.

Pough's father was a chemical manufacturer and teacher, his mother a biologist and teacher. After taking a degree in engineering administration and chemical engineering at MIT in 1926, he followed his father's profession, but a fascination with birdlife and a very real talent for coaxing money out of the well-heeled produced his own hybrid career by the thirties. The depression was his ally in helping him move over from hard production to hard preservation. Since times were lean he decided to follow his own interests.

A stint at Audubon—1936 to 1948—gave him the impetus to do his *Audubon Bird Guide,* first published in 1948 by Doubleday. It has sold nearly seven hundred thousand copies to date and is selling just as steadily now as when it first came out. The income is important because Pough serves a good many of his conservation projects without pay. "My wife claims I am allergic to money—'You just fight it off,'" Pough says with considerable satisfaction.

Since he is obviously not self-serving, he can drive a hard bargain for his causes, come away from a luncheon date with a check for $100,000, money to rescue a wildlife sanctuary, pay for a publishing program, put his protégés on the payroll of any of a dozen projects he has cooking at the moment. (He loves the good life when somebody else picks up the check. "My Texas millionaires take me," he says, recalling a particularly lavish lunch in Manhattan.)

He knows who to see and which strings to pull. He is

an absolute gold mine of information about sources of help and how to reach the patrons of the conservation movement. His phone rings constantly with pleas to intervene in one battle or another. One of his most useful services is to hold the money for *ad hoc* groups seeking an honest broker who is beyond reproach. He works best behind the scenes, where he has influenced more than one decision which saved the landscape for posterity.

In any battle where land preservation is the key, Pough is the man to see.

He gets more pleasure out of raising a million or two to save an endangered island than he would ever have gotten from making that million for himself. But the pleasure must surely arise from the size of the portfolio of open lands he has accumulated for his conservation clients since the 1930s. As a tremendously effective fund-raiser, the man who knows where all the coin is buried and how to magnetize it for open space purchase, he has put into public ownership thousands of acres worth millions of dollars.

His success derives from a kind of double empathy. He knows what it's like to be poor and he can fairly feel what it must be like to be rich. Sympathetic to those who want to save the land but can't afford to buy it themselves, he is happy to put them in touch with those who can write the checks. He tries to persuade the rich to loosen their purse strings in their own self-interest, and is a walking encyclopedia of information on tax benefits which will accrue to land philanthropists. Nor is he unmindful of the enormous pleasure large tracts of open space confer on country squires anxious to preserve the illusion of a frontier land on their doorstep. Quite possibly, Pough's greatest achievement has been the

Nature Conservancy, an organization which to date has helped set aside thousands of acres across the country.

The Nature Conservancy goes back to 1916. A University of Illinois zoology professor, Victor E. Shelford, organized the Ecological Society of America. Shelford cataloged all the known remaining pieces of wilderness then extant in the United States. He wanted his society to go after these pieces and preserve them in an unspoiled state. "A few samples of the fabric of nature," says Pough. Members rejected his proposal, claiming that it was "undignified" and "inappropriate for scientists." Shelford then created something called "The Ecologists Union" and that didn't get off the ground either until Pough came along. "They simply needed some businessmen in there," he says, citing Avery Rockefeller's comment, "Let's get some land."

In 1950 Pough went to a conference in England and was exposed to the National Trust System. He remembers thinking, "Let's change the name (of the Ecologists Union) to the Nature Conservancy."

It was an inspired idea and Pough teamed up with George Fell, who came from Illinois, to man a small office. "He had no particular source of income," says Pough, "but his wife got a job and I was with the museum."

Pough and Fell decided that they would concentrate on just one objective. "We were just going to save land, one thing and one thing only." Fell is credited with thinking up the device of a revolving fund for land purchase. Patrons provided seed money to buy endangered areas, thereby giving area residents time to raise the cash. When the money was repaid, the Conservancy could move on to save another tract.

The Conservancy

By 1960 the Nature Conservancy had preserved some four thousand acres but was sorely handicapped by lack of money and one major, ill-considered project, which was draining its revolving fund. Alexander B. Adams helped put the Conservancy on the road to solvency with its present hardheaded attitude toward saving land, an approach which has been wildly successful.

By 1970 the Conservancy had preserved 150,000 acres in forty-one states and the Virgin Islands—up 146,000 acres in a decade. Adams is a former FBI agent who is also a devoted nature man. He has respect for business techniques and businessmen, many of whom have become valued friends and patrons of the Conservancy. After reorganizing the Conservancy headquarters, bringing in management experts like President Thomas Richards who once worked for IBM, persuading the Ford Foundation to make grants to the Conservancy as well as provide a $6 million line of credit for land acquisition, Adams retired in 1969.

Today the Conservancy headquarters resembles, in the words of the *Wall Street Journal,* "a high-powered real estate agency." Nobody there is ashamed of the description. Adams says bluntly that the Conservancy needed people who "could make a revolving fund revolve." Says Tom Richards: "To win a land conservation battle today, you've got to use the same skills private industry uses."

Suppose you were to turn to the Conservancy for help. A choice wooded ledge is up for sale to a developer. It commands a striking view, is sited in the heart of other conservation country and should be preserved. You'd like to know if the Conservancy would buy it, take it off the market and keep it as a nature study area. You call your state Conservancy chapter and they show immediate and reassuring interest in the project. You make a date for an inspection by one of the Conservancy's field men.

If the project is a major one, the field man might come from a regional office of the Conservancy. He will look like an Ivy League forest ranger, ask searching questions about the ecology of the area in question, and agree with you that it must, most certainly, be preserved. Then you get down to the business of what the Conservancy can, and will, do.

Suddenly this nice young man has become a hard-nosed bargainer. What could the community put up in the way of cash? How many contributors can be counted on? Have you considered asking the town to buy it with a bond issue? The mirage of that six-million-dollar credit line from Ford vanishes over the horizon. Slowly you begin to understand—the Conservancy tries its damnedest to get somebody else to pull the fat out of the fire. If all else fails, if you can't raise the money any other way, they may come to your aid, but you need all the leverage you can get—friends at court, people like Pough who have their ear, support from every conservation organization you can enlist—if you are to get anywhere. Without its realistic appraisals of what a community can and should do to save itself, the Conservancy would have bogged down in handouts long ago. Its record of saving land is outstanding and its reputation as an honest broker in the field of conservation real estate has inspired many property owners to donate acreage to it. Indeed, the majority of its 450 land-save projects have been acquired through gifts.

What the Conservancy can do is to give you the courage to move ahead and get the land—by private subscription, by public purchase, or by persuading the owner to sell some and keep some open. Discussing the project with them can lead, after the initial depression, to a renewed resolve to put that land in trust.

Land philanthropists have come to look upon the Conservancy as a watchdog. If they give their acreage to a civic or charitable group they want to make sure the terms of the gift are respected. And so, they may give the land with a reverter clause to the Conservancy. If the beneficiary does not hold the land in trust, the Conservancy can step in and take it back.

Pough is experienced enough, and sophisticated enough, to know just how important this watchdog role can be.

"I have found that organizations like the Boy Scouts and Girl Scouts are long on patriotism and citizenship, but short on civic responsibility when land is involved. These organizations hold numerous tracts that I have every reason to assume were given to them in the belief that doing so insured the lands remaining always green and open. In case after case that has come to my attention, instead of turning land no longer useful to them over to the community for park purposes, they have sold it to the highest bidder—invariably a developer.

"The records of colleges and universities are no better. If the trustees see some way of gracefully turning such land into cash, they frequently do so. I know of one case where a friendly condemnation was apparently arranged in order to break the terms of the gift and turn the land into cash—land the condemning water company later sold at a nice profit to someone willing to buy it so that a second attempt could be made to see that it remained a natural area.

"The Nature Conservancy never looks on land as a marketable asset. It always considers itself a trustee of land in its care and transfers it only to those it feels sure will use it carefully and properly. And it is hardheaded enough to do it only with airtight, adequate legal safeguards that it wishes in this respect will be observed."

Local land trusts look upon the Conservancy as a partner in conservation. They may add a reverter to the Conservancy in deeds conveying land to them. If the local trust should ever go out of business their holdings would go to the Conservancy.

The Conservancy does its job superbly well. And that's all it wants to do. It is not into conservation education like Audubon. It may respect the militancy of Sierra, FOE, and activist conservation groups, but this is not its style. Some critics have assumed that it does not get embroiled in the action because it does not want to offend industrial and business interests which support it with cash and gifts of land. Conservancy spokesmen deny this, of course, claiming that they must concentrate on what they do best—saving land. Happily, their work is buttressed by other, more militant organizations carrying the lance into battle.

Sierra and FOE

Someone once described the typical Sierra Clubber as "white, affluent, far better educated than the average man and a little holier than thou."

Before Dave Brower came onto the scene in 1952, the club was strictly for Californians and only a certain class of Californians was welcome. You had to be sponsored for membership, but if the club didn't like your style, you could be blackballed. But as more and more Americans looked around for an organization which would fight to keep the country inviolate, Sierra's membership became a true mixture of conservationists. It grew in numbers from seven thousand to seventy-seven thousand.

Under Brower's direction Sierra took an aggressive stand against the giant marauders of the earth. Sierra was credited with stopping the building of two dams which would have flooded parts of the Grand Canyon. Brower's unforgettable advertising campaign—"Should we also flood the Sistine Chapel so tourists can get nearer the ceiling?"—brought the message home to many Americans who might not otherwise have fought the issue or joined Sierra. Sierra helped mightily in the war to save the Redwoods. It also protested the Disney plan to build an "Alpine Village" at Mineral King inside the Sequoia National Forest.

When the Internal Revenue Service ruled that Sierra was no longer tax-exempt because of its vigorous lobbying, that its efforts to stop the damming of the Grand Canyon were "too political," an internal war developed.

Brower split off with FOE (Friends of Earth), which is openly political, and seeks no tax exemption. Sierra continues its good work with less flamboyance and more executive assurance.

If you were to seek help from Sierra, how would you go about it? Let's say you'd like to have Sierra take up the fight against a proposed bridge which might land in your backyard, against the threatened desecration of the local wildlife preserve.

Depending on your location you could call one of these Sierra "Representatives for Conservation":

Peter Borrelli at Sierra, New York City

Lloyd Tupling at Sierra, Washington, D.C.

Brock Evans at Sierra, Seattle, Washington

John Ela at Sierra, Madison, Wisconsin

Jack Hession at Sierra, Anchorage, Alaska

John McComb at Sierra, Tucson, Arizona

Michael McCloskey at Sierra, San Francisco, California

These experienced conservation infighters could tell you how to get local legal counsel, how to mobilize public opinion, or how to make the media aware of your crisis. There are thirty-seven Sierra chapters across the country and each one of these has subgroups. For example, the Atlantic Chapter includes three groups in Pennsylvania, one in Ithaca, New York, a Mid-Hudson group, a Northern New Jersey and a Southern New Jersey group. You would want to contact the groups in your area and explain the problem. They would discuss it at a meeting and if they believed in your cause would stand behind you.

FOE *is* Dave Brower and if you can reach him and persuade him of the merits of your case, you gain his personal opposition to a project and his name will carry weight. FOE is shorthanded, limited by its lack of funds, unable to move against any and every crisis brought to its doorstep by outsiders. Naturally, Dave Brower and his organization have their own projects, big enough and time-consuming enough to absorb their own energies. They have the best will in the world but are simply not equipped to participate in every environmental battle. Nor do they have the extensive chapter setup that Sierra enjoys with its large membership.

Audubon Takes Action

The Audubon Society has a long and honorable past. It is the whitest of the white-shoe conservation groups. Its bird watchers have long been the aristocrats of affluent, influential upper-middle-class America. But, until the environmental crisis of the sixties roused them to action, they were only a potential, not very potent, force for preservation. Once aroused, Audubon chapters around the country showed what they could do.

Officially, Audubon did not change its image until 1969 when the Board of Directors announced a new policy. It sounds safe enough, but its application has given Audubon a new activist image:

"To promote the conservation of wildlife and the natural environment.

"To educate man regarding his relationship with, and his place within, the natural environment as an ecological system."

Audubon Magazine, which had undergone its own editorial transformation, commented: "Action and education, not appreciation and enjoyment alone. The whole environment, not birds alone. Does the general public yet have this image of us? How did we come to it ourselves?

"Knowing that choices affecting our environment significantly are made almost daily somewhere in this country, we are resolved to fight those whose effects will be adverse to that environment."

Whenever a great national environmental issue is raised Audubon is sure to be on hand. It was largely responsible for stopping the jetport in the Everglades. It counts the saving of the Red River Gorge and San Francisco Bay as accomplishments it helped achieve through a coalition of similar organizations.

These are big-time, big-league campaigns and you would expect the great conservation institutions to put their money and expertise on the line. But, says the average homeowner, will Audubon help me save my own backyard?

The answer is a qualified yes—if you have a local or state chapter convinced that what you want to save is important to the ecology.

For example: Audubon chapters in Minnesota and St. Paul have been fighting for years to keep a jetport from landing on the 23,000-acre Carlos Avery Wildlife Management Area.

Three Texas chapters of National Audubon brought a lawsuit to prevent the construction of a golf course in Meridian State Park, naming as defendants the Lakeview Recreation Association and the executive director of the Texas Parks and Wildlife Department.

When the Tacoma (Washington) Audubon Society campaigned against a proposal to convert the delta of the Nisqually River into a deepwater port for industrial development, it published a prospectus outlining the scientific rationale for keeping the delta "as a natural biological laboratory and wildlife refuge." The language the society used in pressing its case was eloquent: "There is not, but there should be, a Department of Solitude. It is one natural resource still undowered by alphabet and is recognized as valuable only by bird watchers and view watchers. Along the crest of the west bank of the Nisqually Delta lies a developer's dream. And perhaps an ecologist's nightmare. For people like to build on crests and look across the natural terrain to distant vistas of reach and sound, rivers and islands, woods and wildlife."

The society contended that a "view loss" worth at least $2,120,000 should be counted in any calculations of natural resources to be destroyed if the delta were developed.

Audubon is particularly strong in defending natural areas from encroachment. In some communities local chapters are making strenuous efforts to reserve prime conservation lands before it is too late.

Not long ago a group of concerned conservationists in Greenwich, Connecticut, banded together to organize a survey of the natural phenomena in their neighborhood. The Greenwich Audubon Society put up fifteen hundred dollars to hire Diana Starr Cooper, a graduate of Yale School of Forestry, to research the water resources, geology, and vegetation in the area. The point of the study, according to Patsy and Gray Taylor who handled the fund-raising for Audubon, was to "determine ways in which we can conserve and enhance our environment."

Elvis Stahr, the aggressive president of National Audubon, leaves no doubt about the society's commitment to "a decent world."

In his relentless round of speechmaking, he likes to use this telling paragraph: "The really big problems of the environment have resulted from man's own actions. Infinitely more damaging than nature's dramatic storms and earthquakes are what man does day in and day out. Curiously, many of the problems can be expressed or suggested in terms that also begin with the letter 'P': population growth, pollution, persistent pesticides, power plants—from automobile motors to jet engines to atomic reactors—plowing, paving, plundering, power tools—from bulldozers to deep drills —politics, quick profits, public passivity, and lack of intelligent planning."

The Academics

Even the smallest town has a science teacher who can provide supporting evidence in the battle against environment abuse. Nearby private and public colleges, the state university, are full of academics, justifiably indignant over the rape of the landscape and attendant pollution. They are playing an important role in bringing problems to public attention.

W. T. Edmondson, a limnologist (specialist in the study of lakes), who taught at the University of Washington, helped reclaim Seattle's Lake Washington back in the fifties. One of Edmondson's students, a young ecologist named George Anderson, had noticed that the lake water looked "different" and had taken samples to show his mentor. Edmondson was alarmed by the presence of an algae called *Oscillatoria rubescens*. This meant that the lake was dying because sewage was being dumped into it.

Writer Daniel Jack Chasan has pointed out that, "If he (Edmondson) had been the only person already concerned about Lake Washington, all he would have had to show for his concern would probably have been a well-documented case history of eutrophication. But there was a core of politically knowledgeable and energetic people who were also concerned, were already working on the problem, and were prepared and eager to put Edmondson's findings to use."

Getting Lake Washington on the road to recovery took years of citizen effort. Activists put a bill through the legislature which made it possible to set up a metropolitan organization with jurisdiction over sewage disposal. By 1968 sewage was being pumped around the lake instead of into it and the lake had made a dramatic recovery.

James Ellis, a lake homeowner who led the citizens' drive to reclaim Lake Washington, calls Edmondson "a powerful weapon. We couldn't have done it without him. He was our data bank. We needed emotional appeal, but we already had that . . . Edmondson gave us the facts we needed to answer our critics. He provided the authority to back up what we were saying."

In an article describing the fight to save the lake in the *Smithsonian Magazine,* Chasan quotes Ellis as explaining: "We wanted him to say what he did. We were looking for someone to say it. But when he *did* say it, he made us feel that Lord God was standing right behind us on this one."

Recognizing a responsibility to inform the public of ecological consequences, many scientists have spoken out on the environment. Barry Commoner and Paul Ehrlich are perhaps the best known, but there are hundreds of others who work to help beleaguered citizens build the best case they can against destruction.

The Funders

The conservation cause has been richly funded over the past decade by foundations which thought it was safe. They approved the notion of being for something nobody could criticize. Their executives and trustees were members of a class which valued nature and the outdoors. What better way to spend your tax-deductible dollars than to preserve the landscape?

The Ford Foundation has been the prime source of money for conservation research, land acquisition, and, until the new tax laws muffled any hint of political action for tax-exempt groups, environmental intervention. Consider these milestone grants made by Ford during the crucial sixties:

September 1965, Save-the-Redwoods League. $1.5 million matching grant, to be used toward the purchase of the Gold Bluffs area and to encourage the league's own fund-raising.

December 1965, Nature Conservancy. $550,000 grant for administrative support over three and a half years.

June 1966, Open Space Action Committee. $150,000 grant to support efforts to acquaint landowners, officials, and civic leaders with the need for preservation of open space in the New York metropolitan area.

June 1966, Chester County Water Resources Authority. $240,000 grant for planning an experiment in open space preservation of the upper branch of Brandywine Creek, some thirty miles from Philadelphia.

March 1966, Massachusetts Audubon Society. $375,000 grant for the operation of a Shared Services Center, supplemented by $10,350 in December 1967, to produce photographic slide shows on conservation.

October 1966, University of Wisconsin. $120,000 grant for fellowships for lawyers in land-use law.

July 1967, Conservation Foundation. $450,000 grant for regional planning and leadership development.

Gordon Harrison, program officer for Ford's Environment Effort, defines the thinking behind the grants this way:

"To educate people and resource managers to ask themselves the right questions about their jobs. What, specifically, does this mean? The developer doesn't have to cut every tree on the lot; he doesn't have to pave every street to every half acre. There are better, less disturbing ways of doing many things in nature. The Foundation has supported some educational programs and we will continue to try to develop the habit of asking ecological questions.

"The second thing we are trying to do is to strengthen what I call the 'think twice' mechanism: those instruments that compel or persuade people to pause before engaging in vast environmental engineering projects. One of these mechanisms is the conservation organization, whose essential role is to say, 'Stop and think.' We are particularly interested in supporting such organizations in their efforts to become more professional . . .

"A second think-twice mechanism is land preservation itself . . . it is easier to reverse a decision that holds land open than it is to reverse a decision that develops it. So one can justify a good deal of land acquisition and preservation simply on the grounds of holding open some options for future generations . . .

"And, finally, a third mechanism we have begun to look into is the use of the law as an instrument both of action in preserving the environment and for public education."

Thanks to Ford money some stars developed in the conservation constellation. Perhaps the brightest is Ian McHarg whose landmark book *Design With Nature* (Doubleday) emerged from his work at the University of Pennsylvania.

Ford helped finance McHarg's Pennsylvania effort and also contributed mightily to McHarg's ambitious natural design for the Brandywine Valley. Ford hoped that McHarg's "ecological imperative" would influence land-use planning and "bring up a new breed of planner." Their hopes have been partially realized. The in-thing is a "McHarg-type plan" in which transparent overlay maps—one for soil characteristics, say, another for scenic and historic factors, another for the wetlands—are combined to indicate the "givens" which should shape development. The concept has begun to shape the thinking of planners, but in its pure McHarg form has not yet accomplished all it might.

Another star who came up through Ford financing is Joseph L. Sax, whose book *Defending the Environment* was written under a grant from them.

Ford has been a steady, constant friend to Audubon, the Conservation Foundation, and other established organizations which needed an infusion of money. The conferences, publications, and consultancies which have resulted have been used by thousands of amateur land-savers.

Many Ford grants are designed to produce a breed of professionals and consultants who can help citizens move to save the environment on a broad front. Perhaps the best known environmental consultant group is the Open Space Institute. Once called "The Open Space Action Committee," it was funded by Ford in 1966 for $150,000. Its management, two ex-advertising men, Ned Smith and Chuck Little, were gifted promoters and sold the idea of land preservation hard—some thought too hard—in their handsome, slick magazine, *Open Space Action*. The small field staff helped many communities crystallize their open space program and learn

how to go after desirable tracts of land. They claimed to have
saved over four thousand acres valued at five million dollars.
In 1969, Ford gave them another $300,000 "to further their
transition from being largely dependent on foundation grants
to being able to generate most of their income from the
services they perform and from their publications."

The magazine *Open Space Action* folded soon after and
the office is now manned by Ned Smith and field expert
Richard Galantowicz. Anyone seeking their help must be
prepared to pay for it. But the fee is modest considering the
expertise they can provide. Little's book *Stewardship* is available from the Institute, along with other publications, and is
probably the most persuasive appeal yet made to the potential
land philanthropist, worth sending to anyone who could give
land.

Legal Help

Environmental law has attracted young lawyers' interest
in public interest suits. And, a number of established firms
have made their reputation in a short time by handling well-
publicized environmental litigation.

David Sive is one. An active member of Sierra and FOE,
his credentials as an environmental lawyer include Storm
King, Hudson Highway, and Hilton Head. He also represented FLEC in the fight against the Connecticut power line.
A deceptively soft-spoken man, Sive is practiced in the art of
drawing contradictory facts and opinions out of the defense.
In the most gentlemanly fashion he leads his adversary down
the garden path until he has extracted damning testimony
from him.

Roderick A. Cameron, who heads the Environmental Defense Fund, is another well-known environmental lawyer. So is Victor J. Yannacone, Jr., who has been involved in many cases on Long Island as well as the Florida Everglades suit and several DDT battles.

The Environmental Law Handbook (Ballantine/Friends of Earth Book), written by two lawyers, Norman J. Landau and Paul D. Rheingold, lists other specialists in the emerging field of environmental law. It also outlines the concepts of law which can be helpful to any individual or group seeking redress under law.

One of the most significant observations in the book is made by Anthony A. D'Amato, a professor of law at Northwestern. Writing in "The Bulletin of the Atomic Scientists" (reprinted in the *Handbook*), Professor D'Amato warned: "Convincing a court to accept a public-interest lawsuit in the environment area is mostly a matter of strategy and education . . . One type of strategy is to emphasize the threat to property values in a case against an environmental pollutor. Courts are most inclined to find that a plaintiff has standing if his land values are threatened than if he complains that his health, physical or mental, is impaired. This tendency may be only slightly due to the fact that courts are more 'at home' with questions of wealth rather than questions of well-being. A more important reason for the tendency is that courts have been historically convinced that land is unique."

In other words, an impact on the environment which reduces the value of the land, even its scenic value, is recognized by the courts. Says D'Amato, "The threat to land and property values seems to add an element of specificity to a lawsuit."

Suppose you decide that the courtroom is the proper arena for protest. First, you must get legal counsel, someone trained to know whether you have a case. Lawyers who are not experienced in trying environmental suits may be negative about your prospects of winning so it is better to start with a specialist, a lawyer who likes to try these cases and can make an educated guess on your prospects for success.

Lawsuits cost money and if the point of the suit is to stop a threat instead of to recover damages, your lawyer is not going to be conspicuously rewarded by cash if he wins. However, any number of conservation groups have been active in the courts and their war chests have been put at the disposal of lawyers who agree to work for costs. If you can interest one of the major conservation agencies in your case because it would set a precedent, you may be able to get them to foot the bill.

Another approach is to form a group with an eye to splitting the cost of legal services. When the Connecticut power line first loomed on the horizon the group which formed FLEC knew they would need legal counsel. In a few weeks they had raised several thousand dollars from their membership and were able to approach David Sive.

Lawyers, as you might expect, are sold on the idea of going to court. They are generally cynical about the prospects of citizens' intervention in the planning process and believe that most of us get the runaround when we question the wisdom of private or governmental projects which are a threat to the environment. But, they point out that officials in both the public and private sector are afraid of court cases. As Joseph L. Sax puts it, "for public officials the initiation and pursuit of such litigation is often a signal to reconsider their positions or to adopt postions formerly avoided." Sax believes and other lawyers agree that the courtroom offers citizens an opportunity to participate directly in environmental decisions and on an equal basis with their adversaries.

The Politicians

Your elected representatives are there to protect you when your property is threatened. After local officials have been contacted, you should get in touch with state and federal politicos serving your district. They have an obligation to become involved and if they drag their heels you can always make their apathy known through the press. As one outraged homeowner put it, "What good is government if not to protect the land from its enemies who would exploit its people and devastate its land for profit."

Some have found to their sorrow that politicians are unwilling to fight the Highway Department, let's say, or the State Development Commission. But, the older attitude that those at the governmental level must make common cause against the people is fast disappearing. When challenged to make a choice—between supporting the bureaucracy or the people—any realistic politician picks the people.

There's too much at stake. When you confront an elected official with thousands of names petitioning him to do something—and that means thousands of votes—vs. the executives of one company, you can pretty well guess what side he is going to take.

One housewife who successfully waged a campaign to keep a small section of a state highway from being widened learned that she could, indeed, make her elected officials rally behind

her. "Our politicians are there to do this for us. It's no
good to moan and groan about a problem. You should take it
to the top. At first, you can't find out what's going on. You
have to be loud and persistent, which is a shame, but the
politicians do swing around when they see there's a sizable
group behind you."

You always need bipartisan support, and it's not hard to
get when the issue is hot enough to burn everyone. Mrs.
Sylvia Dowling, a leading opponent of a proposed 800-mega-
watt plant which Hartford Electric Company wanted to
construct on Stamford Harbor, represented a number of
neighborhood associations and Stamford Democratic Clubs
in the fight, although she, herself, is a Republican.

You have to lobby for what you want. Remember that
industry is lobbying all the time.

When tiny Cockenoe Island, just off Westport, Connecticut, was acquired by the United Illuminating Company, the
residents of nearby Westport, Connecticut, realized that they
had lost their traditional swimming, boating, picnicking area.
In place of a vital community resource, they were faced with
the prospect of an atomic generating plant to be built on the
island.

Community protest culminated in legislative action. Two
bills were introduced in the legislature to give the town of
Westport power to condemn the island. One read: "The
power of eminent domain granted to any public utility
company in this state shall be subject to the superior right of
a town to take property in its jurisdiction by condemnation."

Westport residents came to Hartford in droves to plead
for the bill. State Representative Stewart B. McKinney left
no doubt that the legislation was aimed at United Illuminat-

ing's take-over of Cockenoe. Let's save these islands so that some year—fifty or a hundred years from now—people will know what it was to have one piece of property that doesn't have something built on it."

Threatened with the bills, the utility decided to sell the island to the town of Westport for some $200,000. Ironically, the town was offered the island before United Illuminating bought it and at half the price. There was one cliff-hanger still to come. The town's planning and zoning board voted against the purchase, but the Westport Representative Town Meeting overruled this decision. State and federal aid covered 75 per cent of the purchase. The town kept its recreational facility, the delicate ecological balance in the waters around the island was saved from disruption, and all because the people got up on their hind legs and demanded that their elected officials vote for the environment.

Public Protectors

More and more states have instituted environmental councils, review agencies, commissions charged with site location for industry, development, power plants.

You can find out if your state has any machinery which could control or prevent local problems by calling your state senator or representative.

A Vermont law gives its "Environmental Board" the power to issue or deny permits to large-scale developers. The developer must prove that the project will not cause "undue" pollution or soil erosion. It must dovetail with existing land use plans and it must not have an "undue adverse effect on the scenic or natural beauty of the area, esthetics, historic sites, or rare or irreplaceable natural areas." The developer must also demonstrate that the project will not cause "unreasonable highway congestion" or an "unreasonable burden" on governmental services. This may mean a new school, built expressly to take care of a sudden influx of schoolchildren.

Maine's "Environmental Improvement Commission" is charged with approving all major developments across the state. Its most important power is the right to license and regulate oil terminal facilities. Not long ago it turned down, after five months of hearings, a proposal for a $150 million oil refinery in Searsport, Maine.

Illinois, Michigan, New York, Washington, Connecticut, New Jersey, Michigan, Rhode Island, all have some kind of machinery to control environmental abuse on the state level. Governor Tom McCall of Oregon has pushed more than a hundred conservation and environmental protection bills through the legislature. The state's Department of Environmental Quality was recently given authority over automobile pollution. And, reflecting public displeasure over the power of the highway lobby, Oregon voters earmarked $1.3 million in state highway funds to be used, not for concrete ribbons, but for hiking and bicycling trails. Earlier, the electorate had voted to protect five hundred miles of unspoiled river country from commercial development.

The states have roused themselves to create protective agencies, task forces for clean air and water. Citizens have every right to turn for help to specialists at the state level. However, you should be forewarned. Help is not always forthcoming. The regulatory agencies drag their feet. They do not leap into action—to test the water, to stop the dig and fill, to order a cleanup. It can be a disillusioning and frustrating experience for the trusting, those who believe that once the machinery to protect the public interest has been established it will move.

Conflicts between agencies often serve to immobilize the action. If the Department of Transportation wants to run a road through open space and if the Department of Natural Resources wants to preserve it, the battle will take place deep in the heart of bureaucracy. The agency with the most clout —that is, the most funding—will win out. Only rarely is the public privy to these internal rivalries.

At the heart of the problem lies a governmental tendency to pack regulatory boards with representatives of the very industry they are expected to regulate. Ralph Nader has accused California of allowing its Water Quality Control Act to be written by polluters for polluters and claims it is a fraud on the public. "If California were consistent in this pattern of writing law, burglars would be writing the burglary laws."

Joseph Sax believes that those agencies responsible for looking after the public interest fail to do so because they are blinded by their "insider perspective." Says Sax, "a central problem of government lies in the vast area of administrative 'discretion' that often masks submission to the demands of powerful interest groups . . . Regulation in the name of the public interest can no longer remain a two-party enterprise carried on between the regulated and the professional regulator. Effectuation of the public interest must begin to embrace the active participation of the public." Happily, a mass movement by the public, an urge to become informed and effective, is taking place. But not without a struggle. The insiders want to keep the action for themselves.

The Competent Amateur

Wherever you turn for help you are likely to run into monopolistic professionalism. Experts, government officials, special boards and commissions, the conservation establishment are all guilty of resisting an appeal from the grass roots. They want to handle the big issues. "We can't fool around with every little local group," one highly placed foundation man said. "We don't think that little guys in little towns can solve these problems."

In point of fact, it is the little guys who are solving them all the time. Housewives, accountants, college kids, doctors, writers, artists are becoming quasi-experts on the environment. They have had to learn for themselves because the insiders have done their best to withhold information to make the business of environmental protection seem far more arcane than it actually is.

Pough does not hesitate to criticize the foundations for ignoring the grass roots conservationists:

"Somehow I could never convince foundations that the nation's struggling conservation organizations and the 'civically alive' citizens that compose them were the only hope for securing action before environmental problems grew to disastrous proportions.

"They (the foundations) should have used the members of these groups—most of them intelligent but not rich—as infinitely precious resources to be backed to whatever extent was necessary to insure that their message reached the whole American public.

"Instead, the stock answer I got to my appeals was, 'We

don't support organizations. The members should do it.' The result, of course, was that these groups never had the resources they needed to gain access to the mass media and the public at large.

"The only hope of making our democracy work in these days of big business, vested interests, etc., with their powerful well-financed, self-serving lobbies, is to make sure that groups of civically alive citizens, with no ax to grind beyond a concern for the common good, have sufficient support so that their voice is heard. This they have not had and the blame lies largely with those who denied them the funds that could have given them that voice."

Fortunately, many have found their voices, mastered the most difficult disciplines with sheer hard work and persistence. Having won through, they are more than willing to help other amateurs, to share their knowledge and strategies with nonprofessionals.

Find one of them, a self-taught, true amateur, who has acquired his expertise the hard way, and you will be treated to an impressive display of know-how.

Writing in *West* Magazine about environmental activists ("Right On, Lillian!"—7/11/71) Elinor Lenz identified the "distinguishing characteristics of this emerging species . . .

"Citizen activists seem to have more time than other people, although perhaps this is an illusion. Certainly they have a superabundance of energy; this is necessary in order for them to hold on to their jobs, families, and sanity while simultaneously preparing presentations for the planning commission, writing letters to the editor, attending meetings of the Sierra Club, and running for the school board. They're an articulate bunch, or they eventually become so, and knowledgeable,

especially about local government. They know about esoteric
matters like zone applications, zoning regulations, deed restrictions, and the laws governing initiatives, referenda, and
recalls. They can tell you how the councilman in their district
votes and why . . . why the Departments of Harbor, Airport,
and Water and Power should be subject to a city council
rather than an independent audit (because, as Ralph Nader
says, in order for power to be responsible it has to be insecure
—and because citizens can exercise some control over the
independent departments).

"Citizen activists know why it is that matters of city-wide
concern such as rapid transit, urban renewal, and planning
for growth receive far less attention than street resurfacing
and rubbish removal . . . They can cite chapter and verse
on the difficulties of getting things done in Los Angeles—
because of the excessive fragmentation: too many power centers operating like independent fiefdoms with no coordinating
machinery, so that if you want to pressure for better water,
air, or recreational facilities, you have to deal with separate
jurisdictions at different levels of government and bone up
on the bureaucratic jargon of each one.

"Let a citizen activist buttonhole you at a dinner party
and he'll brief you on the faults in the present city charter (no
clear-cut allocation of power between executive and legislative branches, and lack of communication channels between
citizen and government), on what's wrong with the county
government (five bodies in search of a head), and what's
happening in Sacramento (the special interests pretty much
run the show up there, so he claims, which is why so little
environmental legislation gets through)."

There's a lot that's right with big-time conservation, but

much that is wrong. The faults become glaringly obvious when people in trouble seek help. Anyone who has followed conservation news over the last few years has a romantic view of the professionals—an image of a Big Brother able to set things right. This is, of course, asking the impossible, but when citizens do knock on the door of private or public institutions in search of help, they may come away deeply disillusioned. They learn that the people inside are absorbed with their own projects, that they are scratching hard to make a meager living off their professional skills, that they really have little time to fool around with a project that isn't truly grand in scope. There is only so much money, so much time, and they refuse to be sidetracked.

So, what can you do? Try every avenue, every lead. Don't stop at any one stage in your journey for help. You may find someone who will take the time to listen, to offer a good suggestion, to provide a model to follow, make a few phone calls, or show you how to apply pressure. In the long run, however, you will be relying on your fellows, those who have a personal stake in the outcome of the battle. You could do a lot worse.

9

Some Tough Questions

Obviously, we cannot go on with business as usual if our survival is at stake. Yet, many concerned and conscientious business and industrial leaders worry that no-growth philosophy will create as many problems as it might solve.

Nagging questions hamper our efforts to resolve the environmental dilemma. Can we have jobs and the good life? Where are we going to get the power for goods and services? Property owners who have fought strenuously for their place in the sun are often conflicted about the ethical questions raised by suburban enclaves. Are the conservationists simply keeping people out in the name of environmental purity? Should the suburbanite enjoy fresh air and green pastures while millions of other Americans are stifling in the cities? The environmental activists receive as many brickbats as bouquets. Some resent their hard-line resistance to traditional American growth values.

Why should a bunch of fanatics be allowed to throw sand in the wheels of progress? Often enough, they are in the minority, yet they can stall a project with protests and lawsuits. They always seem to be "agin" something.

Elvis Stahr, president of National Audubon, has taken this particular criticism to heart and addressed himself to it: "Actually, our approach in the conservation movement is *not* limited to in court or Congress or wherever sounding alarms, awakening concerns, and fighting defensive battles—though frankly all of this continues to be necessary, and much too often. We *do* have constructive ideas and we seldom oppose anything blindly. Rather we do, day in and day out, insist on the use of *foresight*. There are better and worse ways of doing nearly anything; we therefore try to insist that *alternatives* be studied before irrevocable choices are made. In my home state of Kentucky, we'd call this horse sense, yet in some industrial and government quarters it's considered very radical. The fact is, we conservationists are basically very conservative; we abhor waste and boondoggling, and we oppose charging ahead on expensive projects whose consequences haven't been thoroughly studied and considered . . . our position is that when you don't know, be careful, be cautious; try to find out *before* you make the leap—let's quit learning so many lessons the hard way."

Economic Growth Zero?

Yes, say the critics, but what do we do while the research is going on? Are you saying that we should never cut down another tree, never build another road or dam or development?

The best answer to this has been given by Joseph L. Sax, who advocates legal muscle to protect public resources:

"Just as a landowner or first homebuilder in a neighborhood may not enjoin all subsequent homebuilding just because it would impair his unrestricted view of the scenery out of his living-room window, the public, as a holder of rights has no absolute claim against developments which will affect that right. The public right to public resources, like private rights, must be subject to the reasonable demands of other users, whether they be factories, power companies, or residential developers."

The key to solutions lies in the word "reasonable."

Alexander Adams has expressed Sax's view in much the same language. "We cannot save everything, but we can save a reasonable part of it. And the objective of conservation is to draw the line. I do not believe we should leave every forest untimbered, but I do not think we should timber every forest. I do not believe that every single marshland in the United States should necessarily go unfilled, but I do not think we should continue our present course of filling them all indiscriminately. I do not believe that we should go without highways, but I also do not think we should cut down an irreplaceable grove of redwoods in order to build one.

"Unfortunately, we have failed to draw many lines. Instead we are using all our resources for all purposes with the result that they are all becoming downgraded to the lowest use. We employ our rivers as sewers for factories and towns, and at the same time we try to enjoy them for fishing and boating. But they are now sewers. We have only the mildest of local restrictions on the location of factories and other commercial buildings. As a consequence, if the present trend continues, we will have a land dotted with factories. We need dams for flood control, irrigation, and municipal water supplies, but we do not have to turn every river into a lake . . . Someone should be coordinating our activities and be responsible for the outcome. But in terms of our environment, we are a leaderless nation."

Who Is to Decide?

When you have competing uses for land, and a struggle between profits and preservation, who will determine how the land is to be used? We have no coordinated land policy and so each battle is fought locally and the most vocal, the most influential element wins.

Fortunately there is a movement toward integrated departments to protect the environment. Instead of competing bureaucracies, each with its own empire to protect, the trend is toward merging them. If you put engineering with agriculture, transportation with natural resources, you may force some consideration of the impact of man-made projects upon natural resources. Will a particular dam or road or building enhance the quality of life or destroy it?

The point is to ask questions. And, ask them of everyone concerned. As Audubon's Elvis Stahr puts it, "If you ask an engineer whether a dam could be built in a certain stretch of river, you will get an answer, a very reliable one. If you ask him whether it should be built, you may—though of course you may not—get a different answer. To get the best answer, however, you should ask the right questions—whether that dam could and should be built—and you should ask that question not just of the engineer, but also of the economist and the ecologist. Up to recently, that last fellow was never asked at all!"

The public not only has a right to ask questions, but an obligation to do so. Instead of being resisted as a nuisance factor the environmentally aware citizen should be thanked for demanding answers and for insisting that his public servants prove to him that their projects are not going to diminish his investment in the environment.

Incessant questioning of experts who were once considered to be a law unto themselves not only gets citizens into the decision-making process, but it educates the general public on environmental issues.

When the Atomic Energy Commission proposed building Long Island's first nuclear power plant the plan was greeted by a storm of public protest. The Lloyd Harbor Study Group hired environmental lawyer Irving Like to represent opponents of the project. His strategy was to examine witnesses in a hearing conducted by the AEC. Like admitted that his case was primarily a "no-win" contest and that he expected the permit to be granted. However, he contended that getting testimony on the record would be a powerful means of educating the public to the hazards of such a power plant.

Where's the Power Coming From?

The siting of power installations is probably the hottest environmental issue going. Nobody wants high wires in their backyard or ruining the open country. Nobody wants to live near a polluting power plant. And, few are convinced that nuclear power plants are safe enough. The Atomic Energy Commission holds that radiation effects are "negligible," but respected scientists—Gofman and Pauling—insist that they are "disastrous."

We are concerned here with what the citizen can do. He cannot answer the hard questions about the safety of nuclear power. He can only weigh the answers of the experts. But, surely, he would rather have the AEC err on the side of caution.

President Nixon's "Message on Energy" stressed the importance of designing and building nuclear power plants to reduce environmental impact. It also called for the development of controlled thermonuclear fusion sources of power. This would present fewer environmental costs than our present nuclear fission techniques. Even more hopeful is the possibility of developing solar power. The President commented: "The sun offers an almost unlimited supply of energy if we can learn to use it economically."

If we do not know precisely what effect our present nuclear power plants will have on the human race, then we must certainly not build anything that is remotely hazardous. Many of the environmental suits currently being aimed at nuclear power plants could be settled if the AEC would build safeguards into the design. Rod Cameron, director of the Environmental Defense Fund, says, "We don't want to be obstructionist in these cases. We simply want to make sure they are designed with enough environmental safeguards." When satisfied, the protectionists are quite willing to cooperate. Environmental groups in Michigan and Minnesota dropped their objections to nuclear power plants after officials agreed to make design changes.

Many citizens are worried not so much about brownouts and blackouts as they are about the terrible human and environmental price they might have to pay for power. Some would rather cut down voluntarily on power consumption. Others have suggested upping the price for frill usage to the point where the electric toothbrush and back scratcher would be so expensive to run that people would abandon them. Of course, it will be said, immediately, that appliances count for very little in the total consumption picture. But it's a start. We could be more efficient, as consumers, in our use of power. And, there's little doubt that the power companies could reform their system to make the best use of the power we now have at our disposal.

More Efficient Power Distribution

Richard L. Ottinger, former U. S. Congressman, who has spoken out consistently on environmental issues, suggests a regional reorganization of the nation's generating and transmission capacity. "Power should be produced at the location where it can be produced most economically and with least ecological damage, regardless of company jurisdiction.

"The Federal Power Commission should be authorized to require regional power planning, to approve all construction and to resolve location disputes with adequate provision for protection of the environment. The F.P.C. would also be empowered to require interconnection of all systems . . .

"The major present obstacles to regional production of power and its transportation to the areas of need are (1) inadequate private utility cooperation, (2) inadequate F.P.C. authority, and (3) the existing rate structure which establishes power rates for the private utilities based primarily as a return on invested capital . . . The incentive is for companies to increase invested capital (their rate base) by building their own production rather than by buying power from other systems."

Congressman Herman Badillo has also suggested a "nationwide power grid" which he says is the only way we can "achieve electric reliability while protecting our environment." Instead of building plant after plant in the densely populated Northeast, for example, power could be imported from the West. Not only would this "create a spinning reserve to take care of emergencies," but it could provide a source of energy which would eliminate the need to overburden existing fossil-fuel plants. And, the need to build more of the same.

The government's system of fuel and power regulation is so contradictory that our power problems have been compounded. A nationwide Associated Press survey discovered:

"Over the past decade, practically unnoticed, the energy industry has become a near-monopoly with major oil companies moving to take control of gas, coal, and uranium production. The Federal Trade Commission and the Justice Department's Antitrust Division only recently expressed mild interest in the situation.

"For years the FTC regulation of natural gas rates has been aimed at keeping prices down. At the same time, state regulation of domestic oil production has been directed at keeping prices up. The two products frequently come from the same fields. The F.P.C. admits 'an element of inconsistency' in the policies.

"While many electric utility companies struggle to find enough coal to get through the winter months, the nation's coal producers are selling $900 million worth of coal every year to foreign customers. Federal authorities have ruled out the possibility of imposing export controls for the time being on the grounds that foreign money is vital to the nation's balance of payments situation."

A coordinated energy program is obviously a first step toward managing the energy crisis efficiently. The public can, and should, insist upon government intervention if private utility companies are not doing the job. And, those same private utilities should bend every effort to educate the public to use less, not more, energy. Charles Luce, chairman of New York's Consolidated Edison, raised "the serious question of whether we ought to be promoting any use of electricity."

Until we have exhausted all avenues of research which could lead us to safe, clean, cheap power, the consumers of power—householders, industry, business, and government—should join together in a common resolve to hold the line on consumption. We have been wasteful, extravagant, and more inclined to expand power sources rather than conserve the energy we have at our disposal. We have paid a terrible price for the luxury of limitless electricity—a price that until recently was considered to be simply the dollar sign on the electric bill. Actually, it represents the depletion of our natural resources and the rape of the countryside.

As Ed Chaney, a National Wildlife Federation lawyer, pointed out: "We waste electric power as if it were cheap and easy to get. But if you look at what strip mining has done to West Virginia or Southern Illinois and Indiana you see that it wasn't cheap after all. If we ever see, as a people, what strip mining is doing to our country, I'm sure we would insist on some other answer, and less use of electricity may be a temporary solution while we find other means of generating power."

We can no longer afford to be the big power spenders. Not while we still haven't come up with a satisfactory answer to the question: Where's the power coming from?

Ecology or Jobs?

John Cole, editor of *Maine Times,* has not dodged the question thrown at him, as he puts it, "at every public dialogue on the state's future. No matter what the nature of the occasion, if it is a talk about Maine, the question is asked with amazing consistency. It goes like this: If the environmentalists want to 'save' Maine, how do they propose to see that Maine people are able to earn a living wage?"

The conservationists are against oil depots in Maine's deep blue harbors. They fear the onslaught of industry. They resist jetports. But, say the critics, they make their money somewhere else, use Maine as a vacation or retirement land. They can afford to be simon-pure.

Cole's answer to the question "How are the working people of the state going to earn a decent living if the conservationists want industry kept out?" is a simple one. Maine's superb natural environment can yield the jobs. Fishing, tourist services, lumbering, these can be developed to a higher level without seriously injuring Maine's magnificent environment. His objective is to "allow all Maine people to make a good living without destroying their good life."

Maine's conflict over jobs vs. environment can be matched in state after state. Instead of analyzing an area's natural resources, its native potential for jobs, the easy way is to

seek "new industry." This, Cole believes, is a disastrous road
to follow. "It takes a great deal more thought to make better
use of what's here than it does to import another shoe
factory, refinery, or manufacturing plant. All that takes is
a sales job, the offer of low taxes, low wages, and a tolerant
attitude toward industrial polluters. It's much more difficult
to do some real skull-knocking about how to creatively
manage Maine's present resources so they not only produce
more, but sustain and reproduce themselves at greater rates
than they do now."

It is fashionable to talk about "trade-offs" these days.
You have to give a little to get a little, put up with some
pollution to get an income. In Maine there was a lot of talk
about trading off jobs for a possible oil spill. This Cole felt
was unconscionable. "We don't see any way to justify more
oil spills in Penobscot Bay or anywhere else on the Maine
coast. This sort of reasoning can no longer be followed by the
people of this planet. We have been 'trading off' too long.
Hundreds of species of animals have been traded off into
extinction; the air has been traded off until it is no longer
safe to breathe for almost 80 per cent of the nation's population; the Great Lakes are dying because they have been
traded off to the steel and iron industry; Long Island is
running out of drinking water because its land has been un-
wisely traded off to millions of suburban New Yorkers; the
depths of the ocean are poisoned by trade-offs with pesticide
salesmen and mercury producers. Enough of trade-offs. They
are not discussible, in our opinion, in terms of what little
environmental integrity there is left."

Is Cole totally anti-industry? Not at all. But, he believes
in putting it in its proper place. One bright idea he has

advanced could save the prime coastal recreation land while accommodating industry and keeping local taxes down. He suggests putting heavy industry in a new inland site which is sparsely settled and able to take environmental impact. He proposes that the state foster the plan by choosing and preparing a mammoth industrial park, providing transportation and waste-treatment facilities. Cole recognizes the problems inherent in such a plan.

"As Maine's tax laws now stand, the new industrial communities will never be built. Because of the town-by-town property taxes which dominate Maine, no town which now has heavy industry would be willing to see it move to a remote industrial community; and the intertown fight over the prospective taxes to be gained from such a community would prevent its construction."

Cole's plan involves a revision of Maine property tax laws. He would spread the tax revenue from the state's heavy industry across the state. Each town would get a share whether it housed the industry or not. "Once the intertown competition to lure industry has been ended," Cole believes, "the planning of environmentally sound industrial communities can begin."

And, one might add, property owners who must fight a ceaseless battle against the incursion of industry can breath more easily.

Property Tax Revision

A recent decision by the California Supreme Court held that the state's system of funding schools through local property taxes is unconstitutional. The California decision was based on the contention that children in areas where property values were low were deprived of the quality education available to children living in areas where high property values generated lavish economic support for schools.

Whatever effect this decision will have on national education patterns it will surely have a far-reaching impact on local land use plans. Property taxes are high because schools take the lion's share of community services. As much as 80 per cent of a town's budget can go for school costs. If these were financed through the income tax or some other national or state alternative to the property tax communities would lose their taste for a broadened tax base.

Regional planners are forever advising us to create mini-cities, separated by low-density development, instead of urban spread and sprawl. But, the suburban competition for commerce and industry which may produce revenue but no school children has led us to ignore their advice.

We are also reluctant to welcome moderate-income housing for fear it will not pay its way, will bring an influx of school children but only a modest return in taxes. If the costs of education were no longer tied to the property tax, if quality schooling were provided across the board to all communities equally, this argument would lose its impact.

A community should be able to plan for its future without the eternal calculation of what sound decisions on land use will do to the property tax. Taking school costs out of the equation should free planners to apply themselves to far-reaching decisions on how best to preserve a green and pleasant land.

Given our free enterprise system, how can anyone tell a developer where to put his buildings or how to build them?

There are two ways to guide development—by using the carrot or the stick. Financial incentives, planning concessions which cut the cost of the total project, and subsidies represent the carrot approach. Sometimes the threat of a lawsuit or fine is the stick that get results.

Landscape architect Robert W. Ramsey of Tacoma, Washington, suggests forcing developers to pay a destruction penalty for environmental abuse. He believes the destruction value of the landscape can be figured as closely as its real estate value.

"Every square foot of original natural topography, every cubic foot of soil, every spring, creek, pond, swamp or drainway, every bird and animal, every tree and shrub has value that can be measured.

"If the developer eliminates these things by 'improving' through clearing, excavating, filling, dredging, refilling, regrading, covering with buildings and pavement, then he should pay to a public body of jurisdiction a destruction penalty equal to the appraised ecological loss incurred."

He believes that the threat of such charges "would divert the forces of necessary development into sites where it does the least harm to our future environment."

What would happen to the money collected on the penalties? Ramsey would spend it on acquiring public open space.

Where Will the People Live?

If our town's growth had stopped ten years ago, how many of you would be here now?

This question was asked at a town meeting called to hear

the proposal of a big-time developer. Some of those within
earshot might have felt a twinge of guilt at having slipped in
while the door was open. But most of the audience was
probably thinking, "Thank God, I'm here. I had the good
sense to move in. And I'm going to make sure that what I
worked for and saved for and slaved over isn't going to disappear."

Selfish? So is any investor—in stocks, savings accounts, any
capital enterprise. He would be accused of being the biggest
fathead in the world if he let someone raid his capital, lower
its value. So why is the biggest investment a family is likely
to make in its whole lifetime—its house and property—not
worth defending? Why must he suddenly yield to outside
forces intent upon diluting his equity?

Unhappily, the very factors which can keep a town clean
and green are the ones which come under attack when
developers try to crash its defense. Zoning, an open space
program, good town planning are heavily criticized by the
very people who yearn to move in because the place has
retained some quality. Of course, the grass is always greener.
Of course, some communities are quite special. But, that
doesn't mean that everybody should live there.

Isn't the urge to own property and control your own little
world just a way of dodging social responsibility to the city,
to the underprivileged? Isn't the suburbanite running away
from the real world to create his own private enclave where
he can be with his own kind?

True, he is running away from crime, noise, people. He is
trying to build a clean, green world and keep it that way.
But he isn't necessarily a racist, just a protectionist.

As Chuck Little, formerly of the Open Space Institute,

explained in *The Village Voice* when he reported on a conference sponsored by the Suburban Action Institute and the NAACP, the "Suburbs Don't Mind Blacks, They Just Prefer Green." Said Little: "Zoning has been used in a vain attempt to keep taxes down while keeping environment up . . . To a large degree, what worries suburbanites is not so much the blacks coming in, but the green going out . . . out of their pockets and out of their environment.

"The inherent proposition behind the idea of racist zoning is that congeries of affluent whites, living in their two-acre and four-acre zoned enclaves, get together to figure out techniques to keep out knee-grows. The proposition is not valid. Those suburban whites snuggled away in the woods want to keep out *everybody,* without regard to race, creed, color, or national origin. They are the most egalitarian bunch of snobs ever produced in the history of civilization . . ."

Aren't you saying: The last guy in is a rotten egg? You've got yours so who cares about the people beating on the gate?

Some communities reach saturation sooner than others and some communities regard as saturation, or near saturation, a condition which other more populated areas might think of as virtual emptiness. If an open-door policy would destroy the amenities, the essential quality of a place which makes it desirable, then perhaps it's time to call a halt.

The celebrated Forest Hills case illustrates this point.

Last winter George Romney's HUD and John Lindsay's New York City Housing Authority decided to build three public housing towers in suburban Forest Hills, Long Island, New York. Residents of the area reacted with outrage. Their critics accused them of not being willing to absorb the poor, the old, and the blacks into a protected enclave.

True, they were protesting the cost of the project to the individual taxpayer. They did not relish the prospect of the increased crime which, they assumed, would come in the wake of the newly transplanted disadvantaged. Nor were they eager to pick up the tab for escalated school and social services.

However, just as important was the impact this "impersonal human warehouse" would have on the pleasant scale of the community. Efforts to get the project reduced in size were unsuccessful. The twenty-four-story towers would dominate surrounding six-story buildings and the total impact of the project would surely reduce property values in the neighborhood. There was even some doubt that engineers could make the buildings safe. A soft subsoil provided a shaky foundation for the weight the towers would put on the environment, literally, of Forest Hills.

Both liberals and conservatives opposed the project. Queens Congressman Benjamin Rosenthal asserted: "This is a national test case to determine whether the movers and shakers of the housing industry in this country can do whatever they want or whether neighborhoods will be able to influence their own future."

New York's *Village Voice* newspaper, which certainly could never be located on the side of the Establishment, took up arms for Forest Hills: "With the present plan everyone is in danger. The residents may lose their neighborhood, and the poor may find themselves in another slum." It's not as if there isn't any more land out there. All you have to do is fly over this country and look down at miles of empty land to know that we have barely scratched the surface for housing. It's just that everybody wants to be where everybody else is. This tendency to crowd in on those who have established a beachhead, to demand space when all the seats are filled, has led to the most appalling crowding in the most desirable areas. Take the Atlantic corridor known as Megalopolis. There really is plenty of living space for everybody, so why ruin the lovely old towns? Why pack a green and open countryside beyond its natural capacity? Why spoil it not only for the guy who has his, but the ones who manage to crowd in.

Suburbs vs. the City

One prevailing myth about suburbia holds that its zoning laws have had an adverse effect on city dwellers. City people cannot move out to the suburbs because of the high-priced and scarce real estate. Some observers think this is a good thing. They agree with New York Housing Authority's George Sternlief that "the only thing that's holding our central cities together is the suburban housing shortage." He thinks that the high cost of property in suburbia keeps the city's remaining middle-class residents from moving out.

Alfred B. Del Belle, mayor of Yonkers, is convinced that if suburban zoning were relaxed "it would be the middle class that would move first. They would continue to vacate the cities leaving an increasing proportion of poor black and Spanish population." And, by moving they would further reduce the tax base and impoverish the city.

Suburbanites resent being told that their movement outward set the city on its downward spiral. Why not build up the central city itself? Instead of urbanizing the suburbs, let's put money, imagination, and energy into reclaiming the housing which already stands in the central city, is already serviced by sewers, water, and transportation. Let's make the cities good to live in and reverse the process of blight instead of allowing it to spread outward.

Increasingly, jobs are moving to the suburbs as outlying communities woo industry with the promise of good sites, near new highways, relatively low taxes. The Regional Plan Association estimates that 2.4 million new jobs will be created in the New York metropolitan area by 1985. Two million will be in the suburbs.

Is it fair, or even defensible, to rob the city of its livelihood by enticing industry to the suburbs?

The answer is no. What's more, when suburbanites try to have the best of both worlds—tax income from industry and a peaceful residential environment—they end up with neither. You can't have it both ways, not for very long. Suburbs which value privacy and open space should be prepared to pay for the privilege and do their best to prevail upon industry to stay close to the central cities where transportation is better, mass housing is easier to come by, and a large labor force is available. If a suburb falls for the line that corporations bring money but no problems, it will soon be disillusioned.

Civil rights leaders have brought suits across the country—in Missouri, New Jersey, New York—claiming that corporations which move into "restrictively zoned suburbs" must provide for housing. When RCA bought a 254-acre tract in New Canaan, Connecticut, for an estimated $3 million and asked the town to rezone it from residential to business use, a group called Suburban Action Institute filed a charge against RCA (March 3, 1971) accusing it of *de facto* segregation. New Canaan is zoned as a large-lot residential community.

Its schools are good and taxes high and presumably the population can afford the tariff. Those who wanted RCA in town argued that this kind of "clean corporation" would help foot the tax bill and that there would be no attendant problems. Not everybody was so sure.

Ervin Bickley, Jr., who is president of the Citizens Continuing Committee for Conservation, protested it saying, "This is a pretty little town and we want to keep it that way."

The local paper supported RCA and promised residents that the country atmosphere would be preserved. "We don't visualize any smokestacks, or neon signs, or huge paved parking lots."

The usual arguments pro—it'll reduce taxes—and con— it'll bring people—filled the air. Some prophets predicted that a big, influential company would have considerable say in zoning decisions. Eventually they might ask for a relaxation of zoning so that housing could be built for a torrent of middle-income employees.

The question eventually resolved itself around the question: Do we have to right to keep what we have? Or, as one resident put it, "Are you allowed to have a preserve? Or, because of the housing crush, do you have a responsibility to eliminate two- or four-acre zoning and open up the town? Most of us think you ought to be able to have a preserve."

One Selectman, Henrietta Rogers, approved Suburban Action's effort to provoke "responsive action" from New Canaan, saying that the town had not taken responsibility for housing the poor. She carefully hedged her comments, however, emphasizing that the choice was not really the town's, that pressure would eventually be brought to bear on

it to provide such housing and saying, in effect, wouldn't it
be better to give in gracefully and have a say in how much
housing and where it should be located.

Said Mrs. Rogers: "Local rezoning restrictions must be
eased not only for social reasons, but because if this does not
happen, then sooner or later our local autonomy or choice
will be taken away by the State Legislature. It seems to me,
therefore, the Institute's complaint should be directed at the
zoning laws of New Canaan—not at RCA."

The High Price of Housing

Mrs. Rogers, like her fellow townspeople, protested the
idea that zoning laws were enacted simply to be exclusionary.
"Their purpose was to preserve the rural character of this
small town, to prevent the leveling of the countryside, to keep
intact our open fields, winding roads, brooks, and old walls."
But, she pointed out, as have the critics of large-lot zoning,
when you set land aside you inevitably raise the price of home
sites. Housing becomes out of reach for low and moderate
income groups. No doubt about it, this is one of the thorniest
problems conservationists who also care about people must
tackle.

Isn't the high price of land which dictates the high cost of
housing and produces high taxes driving out the older citizen,
the young marrieds, low-paid workers who serve the community? Where are these people going to live if a community
uses large-lot zoning laws to preserve the landscape?

First, no one should be under any illusion that downzoning would result in low-cost housing. Developers will
charge as much for a house on one acre as for one on two

acres. Speculators see a chance for more profit when land requirements are reduced. They may talk a big game about the need to provide housing for low to middle income groups, but they are not about to build it.

The only way to provide such housing is through subsidies, governmental or private. In some towns, citizens have been sufficiently concerned about the lack of this kind of housing to form nonprofit groups to finance it. The hope is that civic-minded citizens will donate the land and a builder could be found to build the project at a reasonable profit.

Sheafe Satterthwaite, a staff member for the Center for Environmental Studies at Williams College, proposes a series of "development experiment stations" to assist the construction industry. "Most builders," he says, "cannot afford the risk of innovating or altering development patterns. Non-profit groups, assisted by government at all levels, should help to meet this need. Being acutely aware of the increasing development pressures upon land, conservationists have a special duty in demonstrating more appropriate accommodations of new construction to the landscapes they know so well. Especially, they should try to increase housing densities so as to compact development and thereby leave land open for public recreation and public amenities."

The environmentalists have put some constructive ideas into the discussion about the kind of world we want, indeed must have if we are to survive. Unfortunately they are often met with hostility or ridicule. They don't have all the answers, but they are looking for them. They are willing to mark time, hold off on decisions until they do get the answers. And, they have a few questions of their own which are worth considering.

Does every place have to look like every other place? Or, can we plan development, save the countryside so that we will have a varied environment?

What will you do when it's gone forever, when there is no clean water, fresh air, green and open space? Isn't it better to pull in the reins while there is still time to consider what we could forfeit if we don't ask the right questions and insist upon the best answers we are capable of getting?

Staying Power

In the summer of 1971 the Sierra Club and Nature Conservancy held a joint conference at Connecticut's Kent School to discuss, among other topics of mutual interest, power needs vs. the environment.

The year had been a landmark one for conservationists who fought against pumped storage facilities, new high-power lines, and nuclear plants. They had won some battles, lost some, and held the utilities to a standoff in more than one case. An "Energy Panel" made up of lawyers, environmentalists, and a utility spokesman would discuss the issues involved.

Charles Bragg, an executive with Northeast Utilities, opened the discussion by saying, with more humor than anyone had expected, "The enemy always rears his head first."

He paid tribute to the fortitude and skills displayed by conservationists, and acknowledged that his company recognized their influence. However, he confided, some people at the utility were simply biding their time. "They are saying," he told his audience, "that the kooks will peak."

The audience bristled, then laughed in disbelief. Bragg hastily reassured them that he, of course, knew that the movement was not on the wane. His real concern was that "we reconcile our needs and our environmental problems."

As the meeting wore on it became all too apparent that the utility would cling to its predicted 8 per cent growth rate in energy needs, that the environmentalists would not accept this as a given, that new, more efficient means of producing and delivering power were still on the drawing board and not budgeted for the immediate future.

The audience was full of "kooks," dignified, soft-spoken, articulate, and informed veterans of the environmental wars. They showed no inclination to abandon their crusading zeal. Indeed, as Dr. Rita Kaunitz, a member of the Connecticut Clean Air Commission, urged them to be "full-time citizens, battling both public and private sectors," they stirred appreciatively.

Yet, the question is provocative. Is this outpouring of protest against environmental insult a transient phenomenon? Or, will it solidify into an enduring power bloc? Will the movement to save the land actually reform our attitudes toward growth and profits? Or, will the protesters find that revolutionary change is not possible and abandon the field to the profiteers? Is the movement itself too casually organized, too leaderless, too diffuse to be effective over the long haul?

The Movement's Future

Two behavioral scientists—Luther P. Gerlach and Virginia H. Hine—have studied Black Power, the New Left, Student Power, and Social Action in the Church—among others— and have developed a yardstick to measure the effectiveness and durability of social movements.

Gerlach and Hine have also analyzed citizen attempts to save the environment. Some of their observations indicate that the factors many people see as handicaps are, instead, advantages.

Gerlach and Hine favor a decentralized movement organization over a pyramidal type, with a strong leader at the head. Conservation groups have been criticized because they are so loosely organized, there are so many overlapping and, indeed, duplicating groups. Actually, this could be a strength.

In 1968 Gerlach, associate professor of anthropology at the University of Minnesota, prepared a study of "Movement Dynamics in Action" for the Minnesota Association for Conservation Education. Some of his observations made in this "position paper" offer hope for the environmentalists, particularly his views on the network structure of successful movements.

"Any member of a small group is a potential leader and many indeed strive to be actual leaders since they feel that they have a duty to help the group succeed. If an ongoing leader falters or fails, or appears to sell out to the establishment, he will quickly be replaced by another.

"It is not unusual for a man to be a leader in one small group and a follower in another . . . An individual cell is encouraged to do its own thing, perform according to its own special capabilities afforded it by the qualities of its members."

A network of groups, loosely organized with spontaneous leadership, "also provides a very effective grapevine communication system and logistical financial support system."

Gerlach explains that when you have many different groups in a network, potential converts can join the one "whose goals, tactics, personal life styles, and backgrounds appeal to him." Most frequently they are drawn to a group because someone they know and respect and like recruits them. Their attitudes are changed through the interaction of fellow members, "not through large-scale 'propaganda' or public information."

As people work together to defeat a new highway or jetport or shopping center, they find their consciousness is raised to a new level. They are united against "the enemy." Indeed, Gerlach believes, "the participants in a movement characteristically perceive that they are facing opposition—unjust opposition. Opposition either real or merely perceived is necessary to promote the movement, to offer it a basis for its commitment process and a force against which to unite. Opposition optimum for movement growth is sufficient to be perceived as a threat and a challenge, but strong enough to be overcome."

"Bridge-Burning Acts"

Movement members must feel a sense of commitment. Gerlach is convinced that the commitment process includes "one or more bridge-burning acts, through which the new member identifies and is identified with the movement as against the established order of things . . . In the commitment process individuals stand on the firing line for their faith, face up to and in fact welcome opposition and persecution. Their acts are designed to incur the wrath of the established order."

When an environmental activist challenges the decisions of, say, his mayor, city council, or planning commission by writing a letter to the paper, making a speech, or circulating a petition, he is going on record against the establishment. He is putting himself outside the traditional power center and attempting to form his own power bloc. He can succeed or fail, but the risk he takes, the old bridges he burns, are certainly part of the commitment process. He can never be the same, never view established leaders in the same light. And, they will never again look upon him as one of them. From that moment on he will be regarded with suspicion. He has passed from comfortable suburban acceptance of the status quo to a questioning posture which may get results and which, most certainly, will make him chronically uneasy about the sources and distribution of influence.

If a group can see its efforts as a contributing factor to a major change in public attitude, one which may transform the system, it has more chance of persisting than if the group is formed simply to fight a single battle. Gerlach cites the case of environmentalists who have opposed construction of a major Twin City airport in Minnesota. "Members argue that they are not any longer merely concerned with their own interests or only stopping the airport. They feel that they 'have gone beyond this.' They now see themselves as conservers of the wildlife in the entire area, as opponents of exploitation, as people dedicated to a more adaptive relationship with the environment. They will turn their attention to other matters of ecological adaptation when their airport mission is accomplished."

Sampling the "Kooks"

In the summer of 1970 Gerlach and Hine prepared an "ecology questionnaire" to be distributed to the readers of *Natural History*.

In what some readers took to be an unwarranted assumption, Gerlach and Hine seemed to be implying that church reform, Black Power, the Peace Movement, Student Power, and the ecology movement have something in common. They asked:

Do you think that there is any connection between all of these various movements in our society?
(1) They are all aspects of one single wave of revolutionary change.
(2) They may be related but are still separate movements.
(3) I am uncertain in what I think.
(4) There is no connection between them.

In a transparent effort to get at the "bridge-burning acts" which lead to commitment, Gerlach and Hine asked:

If your participation in the movement has involved any risks, write in the spaces provided the numbers of any you have experienced.
(1) Expenditure of great time or money.
(2) Loss of friends.
(3) Threatening mail or phone calls.

(4) Pressure from employer.

(5) Serious family rift.

(6) Loss of job.

(7) Destruction of personal property.

(8) Jail sentence.

(9) Bodily harm.

More than seven thousand readers answered the question-naire. They were typical of the Conservation Establishment—college-educated, professional, upper income. Although some "raised vociferous objections to (our) questions about political and economic issues, especially questions concerning attitudes toward other protest movements in our society, these re-spondents were in the minority. Most (86 per cent) report that they do see a connection between all of the movements."

The most committed—those who did interact with others—had had "bridge-burning" experiences and had felt them-selves changed in the way they viewed themselves.

Significantly, the generation gap was not apparent in answers to the questions. The under-thirty group, women over thirty, and men over thirty in the professions, education, or social service were like-minded. They were strong ad-vocates of change. They questioned the assumption that economic growth is an unqualified blessing. They tended to "view the profit motive as outdated." They approved of civil disobedience—sit-ins and protest—to effect change. Engi-neers and businessmen over thirty were more conservative.

Gerlach and Hine concluded: "It might be wise, for those who are interested in social change, to stop thinking simply in terms of older and younger and to explore instead the possi-bilities of position in the social structure as a key to changing attitudes."

Toward a Land Ethic

This is the hope property power offers the movement to save the land. More often than not, people who own land wield influence—political, social, and economic. If this influence can be used to effect a change in values, a new attitude toward land, a conviction that it is a resource and not a commodity, we may be on our way toward land ethic.

In calling for a "land ethic," the conservation philosopher Aldo Leopold pointed out, "We can be ethical only in relation to something we can see, feel, understand, love, or otherwise have faith in."

Although Leopold was concerned professionally with big-time conservation he worried that "American conservation is, I fear, still concerned for the most part with show pieces. We have not yet learned to think in terms of cogs and wheels. Look at our own backyard . . ."

The protest against the erosion of property values in their own backyards has necessarily awakened many Americans to other values. They appreciate in an immediate and personal way the importance of saving the green earth. They, too, may be called upon to make a choice between profits and preservation. Should they sell their land to the highest bidder or give it to the local land trust. Will they be willing to pay a higher tax themselves so that large landowners can get a tax break and thereby be motivated to keep their property off the development rolls?

A man who works within the system all week, motivated by the profit incentive, may find it difficult to shift gears and become a land philanthropist at home. But, business attitudes and the business ethic cannot be applied to environmental questions. If man wants to preserve his own turf, he will have to swear by consistent values all week long and not piously profess himself a Sunday conservationist.

This is happening. Tough, hardheaded businessmen are fighting the good fight on behalf of their particular piece of green and in so doing they are becoming aware of how destructive the businessman/engineering mentality can be. Hopefully, their personal battles will transform them sufficiently so that when they are on the other side of the fence, wearing their business cap, they will have more comprehension of what we are doing to the national natural resource.

Ralph Nader has called them "whistle blowers," maintaining that a professional in the hire of corporate giants must be free to denounce antisocial acts by his employers. He should be able to draw "a line in his own mind where responsibility to society transcends responsibility to the organization."

Nader is right when he says that professionals "are among the first to know about industrial dumping of mercury or fluoride sludge into waterways, defectively designed automobiles, undisclosed adverse effects of prescription drugs and pesticides."

He might have added, the engineers are the first to know when a utility company decides to expand its empire. The local bank president or realtor or insurance man gets early warning of a plan to downzone in order to bring a new and alien enterprise to town. Should they speak up? Yes, if they value their environment. But, if they are looking for personal gain, alone, they will probably bide their time, keep quiet, and hope the uproar won't rock the boat.

They are caught between a natural desire to live the

good life and a hankering for good, old-fashioned profits. They would like to have it both ways. Who wouldn't? But, it is no longer possible.

It is disheartening, to say the least, to recognize a venal streak in one's fellow environmentalists. They will fight as hard as anyone to stop a road going through the neighborhood, but when new regulations to control building are introduced they scream "nobody's going to tell me how to use my land."

It will take a while to drive home the point that environmentalists must set an example, even if it means some financial sacrifice. If we expect the world to change, we must change our small part of it. We will have to subscribe totally, and not simply when it is expedient or convenient, to the philosophy that land is a community resource. Nobody should be allowed to exploit it, certainly not its owner. If we want to impose controls on others, we are going to have to submit to the same ones ourselves. The big developer and the owner of one building lot are entitled to the same privileges—and responsibilities.

John Fischer, writing in *Harper's,* confessed proudly that he had been "radicalized" by the environmental crisis to the point where he had lost faith in private property. "I am now persuaded that there no longer is such a thing as truly private property, at least in land. That was a luxury we could afford only when the continent was sparsely settled. Today, the use a man makes of his land cannot be left to his private decision alone, since eventually it is bound to affect everybody else. This conclusion I reached in anguish, since I own a tiny patch of land and value its privacy above anything money can buy . . ."

As Fischer goes on to point out, "we are all responsible for the survival of the human race and we can no longer afford the luxury of playing God on our personal acres."

"The Survivable Society," as Fischer sees it, "will no longer permit a farmer to convert his meadow into a parking lot any time he likes. He will have to understand that his quick profit may, quite literally, take the bread out of his grandchildren's mouths, and the oxygen from their lungs. For the same reasons, housing developments will not be located where they suit the whim of a real estate speculator or even the convenience of the residents. They will have to go on those few carefully chosen sites where they will do the least damage to the landscape, and to the life-giving greenery which it supports."

Fischer knows these are radical ideas, but he maintains they are crucial to survival. "The current excitement about the environment will not come to much, I am afraid, unless it radicalizes millions of Americans."

Do We Care Enough?

So, what's radical about property power? Private ownership conferring special rights to the land? Rights that can be used as a defense against any incursion by public or private interests. Isn't the concept of property quite simply an old, conservative idea which may no longer be viable? Why not total land reform? Give it all away. Spread the wealth. Share the acreage. Let's nationalize suburbia. We're all too property-minded.

The problem is, we aren't property-minded enough.

We don't care enough to be responsible stewards of our

own backyard. We think of land as a medium of exchange, not as a natural resource, capable of giving pleasure to us now and all the generations to come. We don't seize the opportunity to save community property and put today's green space in the bank for tomorrow's people.

Visitors to England are continually astounded at that country's respect for property. Landowners are supremely conscious of the continuity, of ownership, of the obligation to treat property as a living organism. The great English countryside has been preserved through a National Trust. Development is held in check through an intricate system of permissions granted by planning officials. When land is taken by the government the price paid is its raw value, not what it would bring if developed to the limit.

Clearly, the English subscribe to a land ethic, indeed live by it daily. Why don't we? British author John Fowles attempted to answer this question in an article he wrote for *Sports Illustrated,* a magazine which regularly covers environmental news. Fowles thinks Americans are hostile to "the overwhelming power of the wild land" because, historically, it exacted so much sweat and tears from early settlers and pioneers. Even more important, Fowles thinks, "is the intensely profit-centered aspect of the American spirit, also to be traced back to the Plymouth Colony days: the drive to maximize the financial utility of any undertaking or resource . . . What did it matter if you ruined the few miles around you when so much still lay virgin? Even today it comes as a shock, so used have we foreigners become to thinking of the United States as one huge polluted conurbation, to see how much wild America still lies between New York and Los Angeles.

"I am not belittling the energy and resources being presently devoted to conservation in the States but . . . perhaps this (in many other ways, admirable) national habit of thinking big helps explain why so many urban and suburban environments seem to have been written off by the professional conservationists as hopeless. But these are the environments where most people now live, and where the reintegration is most urgently needed if there is to be any essential ground change in the public attitude."

Like many Englishmen, Fowles is all for allowing nature to flourish, for enjoying it as much in miniature as on the grand scale. He believes in husbandry, in stewardship, in personal responsibility for the national estate. "The plastic garden, the steel city, the chemical countryside will take over. The government-run parks and national reserves may still survive; but *nature in ordinary life is in the hands of people in ordinary life.*"

Of course, it's quite true that millions of Americans prefer city life and wouldn't care if they never saw another blade of grass. Artist/writer Alan Gussow, a conservation activist working diligently to preserve the beauties of his Hudson River scene, discovered this truth one day when a group of black students challenged his assumptions about the intrinsic value of nature. Gussow had been discussing "what it meant to me to grow up on Long Island when you could still roam the undeveloped fields and walk winters on the deserted sandbars of Jones Beach. I spoke of the sharp delineations of seasons in Vermont where I went to college . . . If there was a thread running through my remarks, it was that people are physical, that we all live somewhere and that the 'whereness' affects us, forms our outlook, gives shape to our values."

One of the black students immediately disagreed: "All this talk about place, about the importance of place. Man, that's not what I care about. Hell no, it's not place that counts. It's life style."

The blacks agreed that "place was important only because it was where life happened. Aesthetics and nature were secondary."

The discussion was, in Gussow's words, "an ecologist's nightmare," and he came to realize that "it is naïve to assume that urban blacks, burdened by enormous social and economic inequities, would place any priority on open space —on nature in the city."

Recognizing this fact of life should not make Gussow—or the rest of us—any less anxious to save the natural world we value. There has to be room for both—a better city and a wilder world. And, the natural life style and freedom that suits us best, wherever we live.

Appendices

A Typical Land Trust Certificate That Could Be Used as a Guide for Other Communities

CERTIFICATE OF INCORPORATION
REDDING LAND TRUST, INC.

We, the incorporators, certify that we hereby associate ourselves as a body politic and corporate under the Non Stock Corporation Act of the State of Connecticut.

FIRST: The name of the corporation is REDDING LAND TRUST, INC.

SECOND: The Town in Connecticut in which the corporation is to be located in REDDING.

THIRD: The nature of the activities to be conducted, or the purposes to be promoted or carried out by the corporation, are as follows:

a) To engage in and otherwise promote for the benefit of the general public the preservation of natural resources of the Town of Redding, including water resources, marsh land, swamps, woodland and open spaces and the plant and animal life therein and the preservation of open land areas of historical significance;

b) To engage in and otherwise promote the scientific study of and to educate the public regarding local natural resources including plants, animals, birds and other wildlife;

c) To acquire, by gift, purchase or otherwise, real and personal property, both tangible and intangible, of every sort and description and to use such property in such manner as the Trustees of the corporation shall deem appropriate to carry out one or more of the above purposes;

d) To use all property held or controlled by the corporation and the net earnings thereof exclusively for the benefit of all the inhabitants of the Town of Redding and other corporation members for the conservational, educational and scientific purposes for which the corporation is formed as set forth in this article.

FOURTH: No part of the corporation's income shall be distributed to, nor any pecuniary profit from the operation of the corporation accrue to, the benefit of any officer, director or employee of the corporation except reasonable compensation for services in effecting one or more of its corporate purposes.

FIFTH: The classes, rights, privileges, qualifications, obligations and manner of election and appointment of members are as follows:

a) There shall be three classes of membership in the corporation:

(1) Life membership—eligibility for this class of membership is predicated on the donation of a minimum of one acre of land or an equivalent amount of money as determined from time to time in the bylaws. Life members shall be exempt from the annual dues charged regular members and shall have the right to attend and vote at all meetings of the members of the corporation.

(2) Charter membership—is an honorary membership to be applied to all persons who contribute $50. to the corporation within the first year of its existence and includes the rights of regular membership during the first two fiscal years of the corporation's existence.

(3) Regular membership—shall include all those persons who shall have paid their annual dues as set forth by the bylaws, for each current calendar year.

b) Each member in good standing shall be entitled to one vote on any matter that may properly come before a regular or special meeting of the membership. No member may vote by proxy or otherwise delegate his right to vote.

SIXTH: The affairs of the corporation shall be managed by a Board of Trustees consisting of at least nine residents of the Town of Redding. The Trustees shall be elected by a majority vote of the membership in good standing at an organizational meeting called for such purpose. The Trustees shall elect from their number officers in accordance with the bylaws. Thereafter, the Trustees shall be elected, replaced, or added to, in accordance with the bylaws of the corporation.

SEVENTH: No part of the activities of the corporation shall consist of carrying on propaganda or otherwise attempting to influence legislation.

EIGHTH: Upon the dissolution of the corporation, no member, officer, or director thereof shall receive any profit from or share in any property of the corporation, but all of its property and assets shall, by a majority vote of the full Board of Trustees, be conveyed all or in part as the Board shall see fit, to the Nature Conservancy, Washington, D.C., or the Audubon Society, Connecticut Avenue, Fairfield, Connecticut, or a nonprofit organization having purposes similar to this Trust or the Town of Redding, Connecticut. Should the Board of Trustees be unable for any reason to arrive at a majority vote in favor of one or more of the above organizations, then all of the trust property and assets shall be conveyed to the Town of Redding, Connecticut.

Dated at Redding, Connecticut, this 23rd day of November 1965.

Mary Anne Guitar	of Redding, Connecticut
Helene Noble O'Neill	of Redding, Connecticut
William Miller	of Redding, Connecticut

J. M. Polseno   of Redding, Connecticut
June G. Gorton   of Redding, Connecticut
(THE INCORPORATORS)

TOWN OF REDDING

WETLANDS AND WATER COURSES ORDINANCE

An ordinance regulating the use of wetlands and water courses including, but not by way of limitation: the deposition, filling, or removal of materials; the diversion or obstruction of water flow; the placement of structures and other uses within the Town of Redding and providing for the requirement of permits therefor.

Upon the advice and recommendation of the Conservation Commission of the Town of Redding, and in order to implement regulations to be adopted by said Commission in accordance with the authority granted to it by the General Statutes to develop, conserve, supervise and regulate natural resources, including water resources, within the territorial limits of the Town, BE IT ENACTED by the Town of Redding, Connecticut as follows:

Section i—Legislative Intent

1.0 The legislative body of the Town of Redding (hereinafter called the "Town") finds that rapid growth, the spread of development and increasing demands upon natural resources are encroaching upon, despoiling, polluting or eliminating many of its wetlands and water courses, WHEREFORE,

It is the intent of the legislative body to protect the citizens of the Town by providing for the protection, preservation, proper maintenance and use of its wetlands and water courses, in order to minimize their disturbance, maintain and improve water quality in accordance with the highest standards set by state or local authority, prevent damage from erosion, turbidity or siltation, loss of fish or other beneficial aquatic organisms, aquatic wildlife and vegetation and the destruction of the natural habitats thereof, the danger of flood damage and pollution, and to otherwise protect the quality of wetlands and water courses for their conservation, economic, aesthetic, recreation and other public and private uses and values and further to protect the Town's potable fresh water supplies from the dangers of drought, overdraft, pollution, misuse and mismanagement. Therefore, the legislative body declares that regulation of the wetlands and water courses of the Town is essential to the health, safety, economic and general welfare of the people of the Town and for their interest.

Section 2—Title

2.0 This ordinance may be known and may be cited as The Wetlands and Water Courses Ordinance of the Town of Redding.

Section 3—Definitions

3.0 The following words and phrases, as used in these regulations, shall have the following meanings:

(a) *Wetlands:* Land, including submerged land, which consists of any of the following soil types as defined by the Soil Conservation Service of the U. S. Department of Agriculture: ⚥43-M, Soils of the Leicester, Ridgebury, Whiteman

Association; ☖58, Mixed Alluvium; ☖91, Muck, Shallow; ☖92, & 93, Peat and Muck; ☖158-D, Sandy Terrace Breaks; ☖463, Raynham Silt Loam Soils; and ☖823, Saco Silt Loam Soils, all as generally delineated on that certain map entitled "Soil Survey Map Redding, Connecticut" and referring to soil survey report by U. S. Department of Agriculture Soil Conservation Service, Sept. 1969 (hereafter called "Map") on file in the office of the Redding Town Clerk and/or land upon which typically may grow in a natural state some, but not necessarily all, of the following:

red maple (*Acer rubrum*); black gum (*Nyssa sylvatica*); high bush blueberry (*Vaccinium corymbosum*); sweet pepperbush (*Clethra alnifolia*); winterberry (*Ilex verticillata*); swamp azalea (*Rhododendron viscosum*); spicebush (*Lindera benzoin*); button bush (*Cephalanthus occidentalis*); alders (*Alnus spp.*); willows (*Salix spp.*); cattails (*Typha latifolia*); pickerelweed (*Pontederia cordata*); water lilies (*Nuphar avena* and *Nymphaea odorata*); water plantain (*Alisma plantago acquatica*); bur-reed (*Sparganium spp.*); rushes (*Juncus spp.*); grasses (*Glyceria spp.*); sedges (*Carex stricta* and other *Carex spp.*); pondweeds (*Potamogeton spp.*); duckweed (*Lemna spp.*); bladderwort (*Ultricularia spp.*); arrowhead (*Sagittaria spp.*); bulrushes (*Scirpus spp.*); silver maple (*Acer saccharinum*); black willow (*Salix nigra*); cotton wood (*Populus deltoides*).

(b) *Water Courses:* Streams (including intermittent streams), marshes, swamps, bogs, ponds (including vernal or intermittent ponds) and lakes.

(c) *Waste Disposal System:* Any system for the disposal of human excretions, liquid domestic wastes and/or such liquid, agricultural, commercial, manufacturing or other wastes which may pollute or tend to pollute, the wetlands and water courses of the town, or as may tend to the detriment of the public health.

(d) *Material:* Shall include, but not by way of limitation, soil, land, gravel, clay, bog, mud, debris, refuse or any other substance, solid or liquid, organic or inorganic.

(e) *Commission:* Redding Conservation Commission.

(f) *Person:* Any person, firm, partnership, association, corporation, company, organization or legal entity of any kind including municipal corporations, governmental agencies or subdivisions thereof.

(g) *Remove:* Shall include, but not by way of limitation, dig, dredge, suck, bulldoze, dragline, or blast.

(h) *Deposit:* Shall include, but not by way of limitation, place, discharge, or emit.

(j) *Operation:* Any use or activity, including, but not by way of limitation, removal, deposition or construction, or all of these.

SECTION 4—PROHIBITED ACTS

4.0 Except as hereinafter provided it shall be unlawful for any person, without obtaining a written permit therefore to:

(a) Deposit, or permit to be placed or deposited, (directly or indirectly) and material and/or conduct any operation within or upon any wetlands or water courses.

(b) Alter any wetland or water course or remove, or permit to be altered or removed, (directly or indirectly) any material therefrom.

(c) Locate within one hundred (100) feet of the mean high water mark of the Norwalk, Saugatuck, Aspetuck and Little rivers; Great, Umpawaug, Steichens', Factory, Sterrett's, South, Falls, Hedmond's and Putnam Park ponds and

Mirror Lake and Saugatuck Reservoir and within twenty five (25) feet of all other water courses and wetlands any portion of any waste disposal system.

Section 5—Permitted Acts

5.0 The acts defined in 4.0 are permissible if done pursuant to terms and conditions of a permit approved by the Commission and obtained from the Town Clerk.

5.1 The following operations are permitted in the wetlands and water courses of the Town as a matter of right and without permit unless any such operation is subject to the provisions of Section 4.0:

(a) Conservation of soil, vegetation, water, fish, and wildlife.

(b) Outdoor recreation including play and sporting areas, field trials, nature study, horseback riding, swimming, skin diving, camping, boating, waterskiing, trapping, hunting and fishing where otherwise legally permitted or regulated.

(c) Operation of dams and other water control devices including temporary alteration or diversion of water levels or circulation for emergency, maintenance or aquaculture purposes.

(d) Grazing, forestry, farming, nurseries, gardening and harvesting of crops.

(e) Uses accessory to residental or other permitted primary uses of adjoining lands or waters provided they are consistent with the intent and objectives of this ordinance.

5.2 A special permit may be issued for an exception to Section 4.0, subject to such special conditions or safeguards as the Commission may deem necessary, for the following operations:

(a) Docks, bulkheads, boat launching or landing sites.

(b) Temporary storage of materials.

(c) Appropriate municipal use such as parks, recreation, wildlife sanctuaries, and accessory uses such as concessions where permitted under the zoning regulations of the Town of Redding.

(d) Commercial or private recreation facilities consistent with this ordinance as determined by the Commission, provided the same are permitted uses under the zoning regulations of the Town.

(e) Dams and other water control devices, dredging or diversion of water levels or circulation or changes in water courses for the improvement of fish or wildlife habitat, recreation facilities or drainage improvements deemed to be consistent with the intent and objectives of this ordinance by the Commission.

(f) Driveways and roads where alternative means of access are proven to be impractical in the considered judgment of the Commission.

5.3 All uses and operations permitted or approved by special permit shall be conducted in such manner as will cause the least possible damage and encroachment upon or interference with natural resources and natural processes within the wetlands and water courses.

Section 6—Permit Procedure

6.0 All applicants for a permit to do any of the acts prohibited or permitted by Sections 4 and 5 shall present an original and six copies of the permit application together with such other information as is required herein to the Town Clerk. All applications and copies thereof must be accompanied by or include the following information:

(a) Name and address of applicant and applicant's agent if any and whether applicant is owner, lessee, licensee, etc. If applicant is not owner, the written consent of the owner, duly acknowledged, must be attached.

(b) Purpose of proposed removal or deposition operations, use or activity.

(c) Amount and kind of material proposed to be removed or deposited or type of use.

(d) Description of the area in which removal, deposition or use is proposed. The description shall be by bearing distance and based upon a monumented survey on file in the office of the Town Clerk.

(e) Depth to which removal or deposition operations are proposed and angle of repose of all slopes including deposited materials and sides of channels or excavations resulting from removal operations.

(f) Manner in which material will be removed or deposited and/or in which any structure will be erected, and/or use carried out, including a detailed description of the nature of the use proposed.

6.1 Except as hereinafter provided, each permit application shall be accompanied by:

(a) A survey and topographical map, with contours shown at two foot intervals and the area of removal, deposition, use or construction indicated.

(b) All maps shall be certified by a registered land surveyor or professional engineer licensed by the State of Connecticut.

(c) Survey and topographical map shall show soundings, depth or height of proposed removal and deposition area. The horizontal control of survey shall be based upon a monumented survey on file in the office of the Town Clerk. The vertical control for elevation and sounding shall be based upon U. S. Geological Survey datum and the Connecticut coordinate system.

(d) The names and addresses of all owners of lands contiguous to lands and waters where proposed operations will take place.

(e) A filing fee in the amount of $50 (Fifty) dollars.

6.2 This ordinance does not obviate the necessity for the applicant to obtain any assent or permit required by any other agency of the Town of Redding or State of Connecticut before proceeding with operations under an approved Commission permit. The obtaining of such approvals or permits, including notices and applications with respect thereto, are solely the responsibility of the applicant.

No operations shall be initiated by the applicant until such other permits as may be required are issued.

6.3 All applications for building permits, subdivision plans or any other development within the wetlands and water courses, shall be reviewed by the Commission and shall receive its approval before the permit or approval of the agency to which the application was made may be issued. Whenever feasible, in its discretion, the Commission will seek the advice of appropriate town and state agencies in developing its recommendation concerning any such application.

6.4 If the act for which the permit is sought involves an area not in excess of 1,000 (one thousand) square feet and the material sought to be deposited, altered or removed does not exceed 100 (one hundred) cubic yards and/or the structure sought to be erected does not exceed 500 (five hundred) square feet and such act, or structure shall be completed within 6 (six) months, an administrative permit may be issued by the Sanitary

Inspector. Such permit shall be subject to all the considerations and requirements set forth herein except that:

(a) A survey and topographical map (Sec. 6.1 (a)–(c)) shall not be required;

(b) the filing fee shall be in the amount of $25 (Twenty-five) dollars;

(c) study by the Commission and other town officers, boards and Commissions (Sec. 7.0) shall not be required;

(d) A public hearing (Sec. 7.1) shall not be required; and

(e) A performance bond (Sec. 8.0) shall not be required.

Section 7—Administration of Permit Application

7.0 The Town Clerk shall retain the original permit application for his files and distribute one copy each to the Board of Selectmen, Redding Planning Commission, Redding Zoning Commission, and forward the remaining copies of the application to the Conservation Commission. Each of those agencies shall study the permit application and forward a report and recommendation thereon to the Commission within thirty (30) days, indicating approval, disapproval or approval with conditions. Recommended conditions or reasons for disapproval shall be itemized and explained in writing.

7.1 The Commission shall review all comments and recommendations of such agencies pertaining to the permit application and upon prior reasonable public notice published in a newspaper of general circulation in the Town, the Commission shall hold a public hearing on the permit application. The Commission shall thereafter render a decision to deny, approve or approve with conditions the permit application. In rendering a decision of approval, approval with conditions or denial of a permit, the Commission shall state in writing its findings of fact and conclusions. Such decision shall be transmitted to the Town Clerk who will advise the applicant of such decision by transmitting a copy of the permit application and the decision with conditions, if any, to the applicant.

7.2 If any decision of the Commission, or of the Sanitary Inspector, regarding a permit application shall be held by a court of competent jurisdiction to be judicially reviewable and if, on review, it is held by such court that the denial of an application, or approval with unacceptable conditions, constitutes a taking of private property for public use requiring the exercise of eminent domain, the Commission shall within the time specified by the Court:

(a) institute condemnation proceedings on behalf of the Town to acquire the applicant's land in fee by purchase at fair market value without further vote of the legislative body, in accordance with the authority granted by the General Statutes, as amended, and the procedure set forth therein. In such event the Town shall appropriate the requisite funds, borrow such sums as may be deemed necessary for the financing thereof and make such applications to state and federal agencies for grants-in-aid thereof as may be deemed advisable.

(b) approve the application with lesser restrictions or conditions acceptable to the applicant; or

(c) invalidate all conditions and the application of this ordinance to the applicant's land and grant a permit without conditions.

7.3 The permit applicant or his agent proceeding with operations approved shall carry on his person or have readily available the approved permit and show same to any agency or agent of the Town of Redding whenever requested.

7.4 Operations conducted under permit shall be open to inspection at any time by any agency or agent of the Town of Redding.

SECTION 8—COMPLIANCE WITH CONDITIONS

8.0 The applicant, upon approval of the permit, shall file with the Town Clerk a performance bond in an amount and with sureties and in a form approved by the Commission:

(a) The bond and sureties shall be conditioned on compliance with all provisions of this ordinance and conditions imposed on permit approval.

(b) Applicant shall certify that he has public liability insurance against liability which might result from proposed operation or use covering any and all damage which might occur within three years of completion of such operations, in an amount to be determined by the Commission commensurate with the projected operation.

SECTION 9—PENALTIES AND CORRECTIVE ACTION

9.0 Any person who shall commit, take part or assist in any violation of any provision of this ordinance or conditions imposed by the Commission upon an approved permit shall be served with a written notice at the direction of the Commission stating the nature of the violation and providing a specified time within which the violation shall cease and satisfactory corrective action taken by the violator:

(a) Such person may, upon conviction for such violation be fined a sum not to exceed $100 (One Hundred) dollars for each offense.

(b) Any person who shall continue such violation beyond

the time limit specified by the Commission, shall be guilty of another offense and upon conviction therefor, may be fined in a sum not to exceed $100 (One Hundred) dollars for each offense.

(c) Each violation shall be a separate and distinct offense and, in the case of a continuing violation, each day's continuance thereof shall be determined to be a separate and distinct offense.

(d) In the event any person shall continue any violation beyond the time limit specified by the Commission, the Commission shall apply to the Superior Court for an order directing the violation be corrected or removed, and that all costs and expenses incurred by the Town in connection with such proceedings, including the actual costs of correction or removal, shall be assessed against the offender.

(e) Any person violating the provisions of this ordinance shall become liable to the Town for any expense or loss or damage occasioned the Town by reason of such violation.

Section 10—Existing or Prior Acts

10.0 Any act or acts regulated by this ordinance but legally existing prior to the effective date of this ordinance shall be exempt from this ordinance and permitted to continue provided that:

(a) No new or additional act or acts will be permitted after the effective date of this ordinance, except by permit as provided herein.

(b) Where damage or hazardous conditions exist, the landowner may be required by the Commission to repair such damage or remedy such hazardous conditions as the Commission may direct.

Section 11—Validity

11.0 All ordinances or parts of ordinances in conflict herewith are repealed; however, in the event that any ordinance prescribes more stringent standards, such standards shall be applicable.

11.1 The invalidity of any word, clause, sentence, section, part or provision of this ordinance shall not affect the validity of any other part of this ordinance which can be given effect without such invalid part or parts.

11.2 This ordinance shall not limit the authority of the Commission to promulgate rules and regulations pursuant to the General Statutes for the development, conservation, supervision and regulation of natural resources, including water resources, within the territorial limits of the Town and the passage of this ordinance shall be deemed to be an approval of such action on the part of the Commission. In the event that this ordinance be judicially declared an illegal exercise of legislative power, then, from the time of such decision, it shall, with the exception of Sections 4 (a), (b) and (c) be deemed regulations promulgated by the Commission with the approval of the legislative body of the Town in accordance with said General Statutes.

Section 12—Valuation of Wetlands and Water Courses

12.0 The valuation placed on wetlands and water courses for purposes of real estate taxation shall take into account and be limited by the limitation of future use of such land, provided; the landowner grants to the Town or the Redding Land Trust a permanent easement to run with the land. Such easement shall not necessarily include public access, but shall give to the Town or Redding Land Trust all development and management rights upon the land subject to the easement.

SECTION 13—EFFECTIVE DATE

13.0 This ordinance shall become effective fifteen (15) days after publication thereof in a newspaper having a circulation in the Town.

A Sample Easement

AGREEMENT GRANTING EASEMENT

AND

ESTABLISHING RESTRICTIONS

THIS AGREEMENT made this 21st day of June, 1969, by and between H. K. and P., INC., a Connecticut corporation having its principal place of business in Ridgefield, Connecticut, (the "Developer"), acting herein by H. Kennedy Miller, its President, duly authorized, and REDDING LAND TRUST, INC., a Connecticut non-stock corporation having its principal place of business in Redding, Connecticut (the "Trust"), acting herein by Mary Anne Guitar, its President, duly authorized.

WITNESSETH:

Whereas, the Developer has applied to the Redding Planning Commission for the approval of a proposed subdivision of certain property owned by the Developer in the Town of Redding, County of Fairfield and State of Connecticut, shown and described on a map entitled "Subdivision Map Prepared for H. K. and P., Inc., Redding, Connecticut, Total Area=19.269 Acres, Residential and Farming District 'A'", dated May 27, 1969, certified "substantially correct" by Robert M. Henrici, L.S., hereinafter referred to as "the Map"; and

Whereas, there are brooks and streams which presently flow through the premises, as more particularly shown on the Map, which the Redding Planning Commission and the Redding

Conservation Commission desire to preserve and maintain in order to protect and enhance the natural beauty, vegetation, wildlife and other natural and scenic resources of the area adjacent to such streams and brooks; and

Whereas, Article VII, paragraph H, of the Town of Redding Subdivision Regulations, as amended, provides that the Redding Planning Commission may require that not more than ten per cent of the total area of a subdivision be set aside as Open Space; and

Whereas, said Planning Commission is willing to waive the open space requirement in the case of the present subdivision if the Developer will make suitable provision for the preservation, maintenance and protection of the aforementioned streams and brooks, by entering into this Agreement with the Trust;

Now, therefore, in consideration of One Dollar ($1.00) and other good and valuable consideration paid by the Trust to the Developer, the receipt of which is hereby acknowledged, the Developer hereby irrevocably grants to the Trust, its successors and assigns forever, all rights which the Developer may now have or which the Developer or its successors or assigns may hereafter require by operation of law or otherwise, to alter the boundary lines of Parcels 1 through 7 as shown on the Map hereinabove described, or to divide said Parcels into lots having lesser acreage, or in any way to increase the number of dwellings which may be placed upon said Parcels; and

The Developer does hereby give, grant, bargain, sell and confirm unto the Trust, its successors and assigns forever, the right, privilege and authority to enforce the following scenic and conservation easement with respect to a strip of land along the streams and brooks and around the ponds shown on the Map, said strip of land being comprised of all land located within the lines designated "Brook Easement Line" on the Map. Such strip of land shall henceforth be subject to the restrictions set forth below, which shall run with the land forever and which are hereby imposed upon the premises for the exclusive benefit of the Trust, and its successors in interest:

1. Said strip of land will forever be kept open and free of all buildings or other structures; no sewage or other objectionable or offensive material or refuse shall be permitted to be discharged into any brook, stream or pond, nor shall any portion of said strip of land be used for a leeching or other sewage disposal field, nor shall any dumping or burning of refuse be permitted there.

2. No dams shall be constructed in any part of any stream or brook, nor shall ponds other than those shown on the Map be constructed without the prior written approval of the Trust.

3. No topsoil, sand, gravel, rock or minerals shall be excavated or removed, except as needed for construction of the ponds shown on the Map and necessary access roads and driveways, without the prior written consent of the Trust, nor shall anything be permitted to occur which would contribute to the erosion of the land, nor shall any trees be cut or removed or plants or vegetation be destroyed or removed, except for the removal of such dead, diseased or decayed trees or vegetation as may be required for conservation or scenic purposes or for the construction of the ponds shown on the Map and necessary access roads and driveways.

4. No diversion of any stream or brook shall be permitted without the prior written approval of the Trust.

5. No hunting, trapping or picnicking shall be allowed, and no fishing shall be allowed by persons other than the owners of the property upon which the stream or pond is located and their invitees.

This deed is only for the development rights to and the above described scenic and conservation easement over the premises to the extent indicated herein, and the Developer shall retain the fee title to said premises and all incidents of ownership therein except those rights specifically prohibited herein, it being the intent of the parties hereto that the Developer shall have full rights to construct houses upon the lots set forth on said map and to sell the individual lots with the houses thereon to purchasers, who, however, shall acquire title to such lots subject to the restrictions herein set forth.

To have and to hold the above-granted rights, privilege and authority unto the said Grantee, its successors and assigns forever, to its and their own proper use and behoof.

In witness whereof, the parties hereto have caused their corporate names to be affixed with their respective seals by their respective duly authorized officers the day and year first above written.

In the Presence of:

John E. Dowling	H. K. AND P., INC.
Craig D. Spafford	By *H. Kennedy Miller*
John B. Tyler	Its President
Herbert Brinckerhoff	REDDING LAND TRUST, INC.
	By *Mary Anne Guitar*
	Its President

STATE OF CONNECTICUT } ss: *Ridgefield*
COUNTY OF FAIRFIELD

CERTIFICATE OF INCORPORATION

OF

REDDING OPEN LANDS, INC.

We, the incorporators, certify that we hereby associate ourselves as a body politic and corporate under the Non-Stock Corporation Act of the State of Connecticut.

FIRST: The name of the Corporation is REDDING OPEN LANDS, INC.

SECOND: The nature of the activities to be conducted, and the purposes to be promoted or carried out by the Corporation, are as follows:

(a) To promote and carry on responsible development of real estate in the Town of Redding, Connecticut, so as to preserve and enhance its natural beauty and rural aspects and to provide suitable areas for housing, recreation and open space in the Town.

(b) To operate exclusively for religious, charitable, scientific, literary, or educational purposes.

(c) To make contributions to any organization described in Section 501(c)(3) of the Internal Revenue Code of 1954, with the exception of organizations testing for public safety.

(d) To engage in any and all lawful activities incidental to the foregoing purposes, except as restricted herein.

THIRD: No part of the net earnings of the Corporation shall inure to the benefit of any member, officer or Director of the Corporation or to the benefit of any other private individual, except that the Corporation may pay reasonable compensation for services rendered and make payments and distributions in furtherance of the purposes set forth in Article SECOND hereof. No substantial part of the activities of the Corporation shall consist of carrying on propaganda, or otherwise attempting, to influence legislation, nor shall it participate in, or intervene in (including the publishing or distributing of statements), any political campaign on behalf of any candidate for public office. Notwithstanding any other provision of these articles, the Corporation shall not carry on any activities not permitted to be carried on (1) by a corporation exempt from Federal income taxation under Section 501(c)(3) of the Internal Revenue Code of 1954, as amended, or (2) by a corporation, contributions to which are deductible under Section 170(c)(2) of the Internal Revenue Code of 1954, as amended.

FOURTH: The Corporation is nonprofit and the Corporation shall not have or issue shares of stock or pay dividends.

FIFTH: The Corporation shall be managed by a Board of Directors consisting of eleven persons. The initial Board of Directors shall include:

John Behan	Samuel E. Hill	Alvin Ruml
Harry Boyd	Alfred Winslow Jones	Axel Bruzelius
William Karraker	Saul Poliak	Stuart Chase

The rights, powers, duties, privileges and responsibilities, and manner of selection or election, of Directors shall be set forth in the by-laws.

SIXTH: The Corporation shall have one class of members, whose rights, powers, duties, privileges and responsibilities, and manner of selection or election, shall be set forth in the by-laws. Each member shall have one vote in the election of Directors.

SEVENTH: The private property of the members, officers or Directors of the Corporation shall not be subject to the payment of corporate debts except to the extent of specific guarantees signed by such member, officer or Director.

EIGHTH: The Board of Directors may by majority vote adopt and from time to time amend by-laws for the management of the Corporation's affairs.

NINTH: Upon the dissolution of the Corporation, the Board of Directors shall, after paying or making provision for the payment of all of the liabilities of the Corporation, distribute all assets of the Corporation exclusively to (1) such organization or organizations organized and operated exclusively for charitable, educational, religious, scientific or literary purposes as shall at the time qualify as an exempt organization or organizations under Section 501(c)(3) of the Internal Revenue Code of 1954, as amended, or (2) to the Town of Redding, as the Board of Directors shall determine.

Dated at Redding, Connecticut, this 19th day of July, 1969.

/s/ *Samuel E. Hill*

/s/ *Stuart Chase*

BIBLIOGRAPHY

BOOKS THAT CAN HELP

Alexander B. Adams, *Eleventh Hour*, New York: G. P. Putnam's Sons, 1970.
> *An insider's view of the conservation establishment. Frank, knowledgeable assessment of what's right and wrong with the movement.*

Peter L. Johnson, *Wetlands Preservation*, New York: Open Space Institute, 1969.
> *Good resource material on drafting regulations to protect coastal and inland wetlands.*

Norman J. Landau and Paul D. Rheingold, *The Environmental Law Handbook*, New York: A Friends of the Earth/Ballantine Book, 1971.
> *Legal action simplified for the environmentalist. Some landmark cases used for illustration.*

George Laycock, *The Diligent Destroyers*, Garden City, N.Y.: Doubleday & Company, Inc., 1970.
> *Good exposé of the engineering mentality as exhibited in well-publicized environmental battles of the decade.*

Helen Leavitt, *Superhighway—Super Hoax*, Garden City, N.Y.: Doubleday & Company, Inc., 1970.
> *A thoroughgoing account of the disasters wrought by the Interstate Highway System. Good ammunition here for any antiroad group.*

Charles E. Little, *Challenge of the Land*, New York: Open Space Institute, 1968.
> *Addressed to civic leaders and government officials, this string of success stories should inspire officials to use the land-save techniques at their disposal.*

Charles E. Little, *Stewardship,* New York: Open Space Institute, 1965.

Should be in the hands of anyone who could give land to local or national groups. An inspiring, yet practical, account of how land philanthropy benefits both the donor and his community.

Ian McHarg, *Design With Nature,* Garden City, N.Y.: Doubleday & Company, Inc., 1969.

Many of the ideas expressed here have formed the foundation for a philosophy of land use, one where planners allow nature to dictate the design. A classic.

Joseph L. Sax, *Defending the Environment,* New York: Alfred A. Knopf, Inc., 1970.

The author believes citizens' environmental rights should be established in the courtroom. Michigan's model law, described here by its initiator, gives citizens legal leverage. Sax is also worth reading for his attack on the environmental bureaucrats.

William H. Whyte, *The Last Landscape,* Garden City, N.Y.: Anchor Books, Doubleday & Company, Inc., 1970.

A most readable history of the evolving techniques being used to save the land by a participant observer of the environmental scene.

PEOPLE WHO CAN HELP*

National Audubon Society, 950 Third Avenue, New York, N.Y. 10022

Conservation Foundation, 1250 Connecticut Avenue, Washington, D.C., 20036

Environmental Defense Fund (Roderick A. Cameron, Executive Director) 162 Old Town Road, E. Setauket, N.Y. 11733

* Described in Chapter 8.

Friends of the Earth, 30 E. 42 Street, New York, N.Y. 10017
The Nature Conservancy, 1800 N. Kent Street, Suite 800,
    Arlington, Va. 22209
Open Space Institute, 145 E. 52 Street, New York, N.Y. 10022
Richard H. Pough, 145 E. 52 Street, New York, N.Y. 10022
Sierra Club, 250 W. 57 Street, New York, N.Y. 10019
David Sive, 445 Park Avenue, New York, N.Y. 10022
Victor J. Yannacone, Jr., 39 Baker Street, Patchogue, N.Y.
    11772

PUBLICATIONS THAT CAN HELP

*Someone once described the crusading conservation journalists
as "conscience-builders." Certainly they have had a profound effect on the success of the movement. These publications
regularly carry news of environmental battles. They are worth
following, as are* The New York Times, Newsweek, Time, Life,
Sports Illustrated, *and* Reader's Digest, *which also cover conservation news and events.*

Audubon, 1130 Fifth Avenue, New York, N.Y. 10028 (6 issues
a year: $8.50)
    *Exhaustive coverage of environmental abuse and reform in
    the back-of-the-book section, plus in-depth articles on cur-
    rent crises.*

Clear Creek, 617 Mission Street, San Francisco, Calif. 94105
(1 year: $5)
    Young, intransigent monthly, with a western point of view.

Cry California, Monadnock Building, 681 Market Street, San
Francisco, Calif. 94105 (1 year: $9)
    *Established quarterly which popularizes technical planning
    jargon so that Californians may understand what their of-*

ficials are doing to the landscape. Anyone, anywhere can profit by the lessons taught here.

Maine Times, 13 Main Street, Topsham, Maine (1 year: $7)
The text is Maine and how to save it but this weekly is worth reading because Maine's crisis is the one we all face.

National Wildlife, 534 N. Broadway, Milwaukee, Wis. 53202 (1 year: $5)
An old-timer (monthly) which covers conservation in a bouncy style.

Natural History, Central Park West at 79 Street, New York, N.Y. 10024 (1 year: $7)
Dignified, high-quality scientific reporting. Frequent pieces on environmental problems. Monthly.

Index

Absentee homeowners, 15–17, 100–1, 214–15

ACUTE (Active Citizens Urging Transmission Ecology), Conn., 7, 154, 155, 156

Adams, Alexander B., 220, 248–49

Agencies, government. *See* Government agencies; specific agencies

Aircraft (airplanes), 91. *See also* Airports (jetports)

Air pollution, 91. *See also* Pollution

Airports (jetports), 4, 9, 28–29, 91, 174, 177, 273–74

Amherst, Mass., 205–11

Anderson, George, 229

Army Corps of Engineers, U. S., 9, 179

"Arts of Crafts, The" (*New London Day* editorial), 53

Aspen, Colo., 207–8

Assessments, land values and, 115–16, 117, 119–20

Atkinson, Brooks, 180

Atlantic City Electric Company, 45, 46

Atomic Energy Commission, 250–51

Atomic energy power plants, 175, 250–52, 269

Audubon Bird Guide, 217

Audubon Magazine, 226, 312

Aububon Society, 10, 35, 111, 141, 216, 217, 226–29, 231, 233, 311

Babcock, Richard, 103–4

Badillo, Herman, 253

BASF (German chemical company), 33–36

Bastian, Mrs. Robert, 178–79

Bates, Robert H., 38

Beamish, Richard, 209–10

Becker, Loren, 70–71

Bergeron, Tom, 86

Berkshires, 154, 214

Berman, Jules, 41, 42

Bethel, Conn., 152, 153

Bickley, Ervin, Jr., 265

Big Sky project, Mont., 109

Blacks: and conservation movement, 274, 281–82; and zoning, 261–63

BLEC (Berkshire Litchfield Environ-mental Council), Conn., 154

Blue Hill development, 106–7

Blumenthal, Albert H., 19–20

Boise Cascade, 98, 102, 107–9

Borge, Victor, 202

Bradley, Dorothy, 109–10

Bragdon, Henry, 38–39

Bragg, Charles, 269–70

Brandywine Creek, 231

Brandywine Valley, 233

Branford (Conn.) Land Trust, 131–32

Breezy Point, Rockaway, N.Y., 8

Brenneman, Russell, 156

Bridgewater, Conn., 153–54

Brooks, Joanne, 160

Brooks, Paul, 143–44

Brower, Dave, 224, 225–26

Browne, Willie, 113–14

Building, 33–36, 88, 102–3, 104–7, 126, 136–37, 149ff. *See also* Development; Growth; specific aspects, kinds, locations

Bulldozers, 2, 4, 10, 23, 31, 60, 90, 208–9

C & O Canal Association, 179

California, 11, 116–17, 135, 178, 224, 241 (*see also* specific locations); freeways, 2; open land programs, 135, 140; population growth and zoning, 28; property tax revision, 134; San Jose and growth, 29–30; zoning and subdividers, 41–43

Cameron, Roderick A., 235, 251

Camp, Herbert V., 71, 72, 73

Cape May, N.J., 50

Carbon dioxide pollution, 91

Carpenter, Richard, 74

Casco Bay, Maine, 99–100

Catskills, proposed power line on, 180

Chaney, Ed, 254–55

Charleston, S.C., bridge at, 31

Chasan, Daniel Jack, 229–30

Chase, Stuart, 61, 75, 138

Chesapeake & Ohio Canal National Historical Park, 176, 179

Chester County (Pa.) Water Resources Authority, 231

Chicago, Ill., 136, 137

Ciampi, Frank, 167, 168, 170

Citizen activists (citizen groups), 7, 8, 18, 23, 31, 33–36, 38, 111–47, 242–45, 246–68, 269–82 (*see also* Preservationists; specific aspects, groups, locations); help for, 214–45; and local safeguards, 181–213; and protest and threat to environment, 148–80
Civil rights, 38, 104–5, 264
Clear Creek (monthly), 312
Clemens, Fred, 164
Clement, Roland C., 141, 142
Cluster zoning, 145–46, 195–99
Coal industry, 253–54
Cockenoe Island, 238–39
Cole, James, 8–9
Cole, John, 255–57
Cole, Lamont C., 91
Collins, Francis J., 167
Commoner, Barry, 230
Community planning boards, New York City, 23–24
"Comprehensive Development Plan for 1985" (Long Island), 199
Concerned Citizens' groups, 7–8
Connecticut, 23, 117, 128 (*see also* specific locations); and conservation zoning, 140–41; historic site preservation, 50–52; Land Trusts, 128–34, 139; Power Line, 149–74; Public Act 490, 117, 118, 141; Redding and Route Seven ("designed enterprise") development, 59–86
Connecticut Light and Power Company, 2, 25, 149–74
Connecticut River Watershed Council, 101
Conservation commissions, 181, 183–95ff.; and "beautification," 191–95; and development, 195ff.; and land inventory, 188–91; powers of, 187–88
"Conservation Commissions in New England" (Scheffey), 184–86, 188
Conservation Foundation, 233, 311
Conservation zoning, 140–43. *See also* Zoning
Cooper, Diana Starr, 228
Corona, Queens, New York City, 36
Cottrell, Annette, 127
Courts, and conservation, 5, 8, 9, 22, 99–100, 235–37. *See also* Litigation (lawsuits)

Crafts, George, 53
Cry California (quarterly), 140, 312

D'Amato, Anthony A., 235
Dams, 175–76, 179, 249–50
Danbury (Conn.) Airport, 80, 84
Daniel, James, 163–64
Defending the Environment (Sax), 233
Delaware, 27
Delaware River, 175–76
Del Belle, Alfred B., 263
Delogu, Orlando E., 100
Dempsey, John, 72
Dennis (Mass.) Conservation Commission, 190
Design With Nature (McHarg), 232–33
Development, 4, 6–31 (*see also* Building; Growth; specific aspects, locations); guiding growth and proper development, 139–47; local safeguards and, 195ff., 201–13, 214ff., 246–68; no-growth concept and, 246–68 (*see also* Progress); and saving of land, 111–47
Diamond, William J., 24
Dingall, John D., 10–11
Douglas, William O., 176–77
Dowling, Sylvia, 238
Dredging, 141, 147. *See also* Wetlands

Earth Day celebrations, 27, 107
Earth Times, 107–8
Easements, 118–20, 126; negative, 119–20; sample, 303–6
Easton, Conn., 159
Eberle, W. D., 102–3
Eckbo, Dean, Austin and Williams (land development consultants), 135–36
Ecology, 91ff., 111ff.; building local safeguards and, 181–213; durability of environmentalists and, 269–82 (*see also* Preservationists); economic growth and, 246–68, 269ff.; environmental threats and positive protest, 181–213; outside help and, 214–15
Economic Development Departments, state, 27
Edson, Lake, 107–9
Edmondson, W. T., 229–30

Education of the public, conservation
and, 187, 232, 250
Edwards, Jim, 79
Ehrlich, Paul, 230
El Capitan Ranch, 41–42
Electric power, 149–74, 180, 238–39,
250–55, 269–70
Ellis, James, 230
Emerson, Ralph Waldo, 166
Employment (jobs), conservation and,
28–29, 246, 255–257, 264
English, the, land ethic of compared to
Americans, 280–81
Environment (environmentalists). *See*
Ecology; Preservationists (en-
vironmentalists); specific aspects,
e.g., Land; Pollution
Environmental Consciousness I, II,
and III, 31
Environmental Defense Fund, 10, 311
Environmental Law Handbook, 235
Erb, Lillian, 52, 53
Erlanger, Mary, 77–78
Erosion, 90, 184, 187, 193
Ewing, Gay, 183
Exeter, N.H., preservation of Rocking-
ham National Bank and Dudley
House in, 38–39
Exploiters, land. *See under* Land

Fairfield, County, Conn., 159. *See also*
specific locations
Farb, Peter, 207–8
Farmlands, 136, 141, 199
Federal Power Commission (F.P.C.),
252–53
Federal Trade Commission (F.T.C.),
253–54
Fell, George, 219
First National City Bank, N.Y., 105–6
Fischer, John, 278–79
FLEC (Fairfield Litchfield Environ-
mental Council), Conn., 153–72,
236
Flewellyn, Laura, 39–41
Florida, 27–28, 114
FOE, 7, 10, 35, 224–25, 312
Ford Foundation, 231, 232–34
Forest Hills, N.Y., public housing
controversy in, 261–63
Forger, Daniel R., 158–59
Foster, Charles H. W., 188
Foundations, and conservation, 230–

34, 242–43. *See also* individual or-
ganizations
Fowles, John, 280–81
Frady, Marshall, 34–36
Friends of Earth (FOE), 7, 10, 35,
224–25, 312
Frisk, Alfred G., 161–62
Funding, and conservation, 121–22,
138, 143–44, 188, 190, 218, 230–34

Galantowicz, Richard, 234
Garrett, Elmer, 155
Gerlach, Luther P., 271–75
Gifts, and conservation: land, 111, 112,
113ff., 119–20, 123–25ff., 183, 222,
223; money (*see* Funding)
Glendinning Corporation, 126
Glick, Frank, 156
Goodman, Bob, 20
Goose Lake Prairie, 137
Government, federal, 88, 121–22, 127,
138, 182, 190, 237–42, 250–54. *See
also* Government agencies; Politi-
cians (public officials)
Government, state and local, 34, 88,
237–42, 250–54. *See also* Politi-
cians (public officials)
Government agencies, 127, 138, 182,
239–42, 252–54. *See also* individual
agencies
Grand Canyon, 9, 224
Grasso, Ella P., 163
Gravel mining, 3, 6, 31, 60, 81–82, 90,
92–93, 184, 189, 191, 193
Great Barrington, 214–15
Great Lakes, 256
Great Swamp National Wildlife Ref-
uge Wilderness, N.J., 177
Green Acres bond issue (N.J., 1971),
10
Greenwich, Conn., 228
Greenwich, N.J., 44–50; Emergency
Committee, 46–50; "Historic Vil-
lage" (Main Street; "Ye Greate
Streete"), 44–50
Growth, and conservation, 140–47,
269ff. (*see also* Building; Develop-
ment; Progress); no-growth con-
cept, 246–68
Guilford (Conn.) Land Conservation
Trust, 129–30
Gunther, George, 167, 170
Gunther, Jack, 133–34
Gussow, Alan, 281–82

Hancock, Mary Louise, 98
Harper's, 34
Harrison, Gordon, 232
Harroff, Robert E., 203–4
Hawaii, 117
Hawkins, Joseph P., 22
Heritage Village, Southbury, Conn., 202–6, 208–9
Highway construction, 2–3, 4, 9, 10, 33, 36, 37, 50–54, 59ff., 87, 90, 163–64, 179–80, 192. *See also* Bulldozers; specific aspects, locations
Hill, Samuel, 64
Hilton Head, S.C., 33–36
Hine, Virginia H., 271, 274–75
Historic site preservation, 38, 44–52, 178–79. *See also* individual locations
Homeowners groups. 215. *See also* Property owners
Housatonic River, 23
House & Home, 103
Housing, 22, 24, 41–43, 62ff., 88ff., 104–7, 145ff., 196–99, 201–13, 258–68, 279 (*see also* Building); zoning and, 260–68 (*see also* Zoning)
Hudson River, 14, 37, 174–75
Hudson River Expressway, 9, 11
Hull, Clark, 68–69
Huntington, Long Island, 38
Huntley, Chet, 109
Huxtable, Ada Louise, 31, 49–50
Hydroelectric plants, 174–75

IBM, 80–81
Illinois, Open Lands Project in, 136–37
Incline Village (Lake Tahoe) development, 107–9
Industry (industrialization), 14, 27, 33–36, 37–39, 59ff., 80–86, 88, 99–100, 102ff., 127, 135–36, 185 (*see also* specific aspects, companies, industries, locations); and economic growth and development and environment, 185, 246–68, 269–70ff.; protest and conservation and, 149ff., 238–39, 269ff.; and real estate development, 102–3, 104ff., 185
International Paper Co., 102

Jetports. *See* Airports (jetports)
Jobs. *See* Employment (jobs)

Johnson, Haynes, 156
Johnson, Lady Bird, 191
Joyce Kilmer-Slick Rock forest, 179–80

Kaufman, Gertrude, 74
Kaunitz, Dr. Rita, 270
Keirstead, Donald N., 55, 56, 57
Kenney, William F., 33–35
Kent School (Conn.), Sierra Club and Nature Conservancy joint conference (1971) at, 269–70
King Resources, Inc., 99–100
Kinney Shores Association (Maine), 16
Knapp, Bob, 71
Koppleman, Lee, 199–200
Kreuger, Alfred P., 202
Kusko, Dr. Alexander, 156

Land (land preservation), 93; buying in competition with developers, 120–22ff., 135ff., 143–47, 190–91, 199–200, 219ff.; conservation commissions and, 181, 183–95ff. (*see also* Conservation commissions); developers, speculators, and exploiters, 4, 6–31, 90ff., 111ff., 266–68; dwindling resources, 93; economic growth and development and, 140–47, 246–68 (*see also* Development; Growth; Progress); gifts and, 111, 112, 113ff., 11''–20, 123–25ff., 183, 222, 223; local safeguards and, 112ff., 182–213; major ways of saving, 112ff.; saying, 111–47, 276ff. (*see also* Preservationists; specific aspects, locations); trusts (*see* Land trusts)
Landau, Norman J., 235
Land ethic, 30–31, 276–82
Landis, J. Meade, 46, 47
Landmarks Society, 179
Land resources, 93–94
Land trusts, 111–12, 120, 123–34, 181, 183, 212, 223; certificate of incorporation, 285–88; easement (sample), 303–6; funding, 134, 143; help for, 133–34; mailings and brochures, 129–34; organizing, 127–30
Lautenschlager, Dr., 36
Law(s), environmental. *See* Legislation (laws, ordinances)

Lawsuits (litigation), 5–6, 22, 49, 99–100, 235–37
Lazzarro, Victor, 65
League of Women Voters, 215
Legal aid, environmental threat and, 155, 156, 161, 234–37
Legislation (laws, ordinances), 6, 8, 27, 52–54, 90, 167–68, 170–71, 173–74, 176, 182, 183, 187–88, 192, 234–37, 239–40; enforcement of, 209; wetlands and, 189, 289–302
Legislators, 8, 163, 164, 166–69, 170–71, 173–74, 179–80, 237–39, 240, 252, 253. *See also* Government entries in index; Politicians (elected officials)
Lemire, Bob, 144–45
Lenz, Elinor, 243–44
Leopold, Aldo, 276
Like, Irving, 250
Lillinonah, Lake (Conn.), 150
Lincoln, Mass., Rural Land Foundation of, 143–45
Litigation. *See* Courts; Lawsuits (litigation)
Little, Charles (Chuck), 133, 195–96, 233, 234, 260–61
Lloyd Harbor (Long Island) Study Group, 250
Lobbying, 238
Long Island, Maine, 99–100
Long Island, N.Y., 199–200, 281. *See also* specific locations
Loughlin, Eugene S., 166
Luce, Charles, 254
Ludewig, Joseph E., 22
Lunenberg, Mass., 135
Lyme, Conn., application of land use value concept in, 117

McCall, Tom, 27, 240
McCarthy, Lynn, 57
McCollum, Charles, 152
McGeorge, Bill, 155
McHarg, Ian, 232–33
McKinney, Stewart, 163, 238–39
McLeod, William, 190
Mailings, landsaving and, 90, 129–34
Maine, 8–9, 15–17; ecology and employment in, 255–57; Environmental Improvement Commission, 240; oil industry in, 99–100; Site Law, 99–100

Maine Times (weekly), 8, 16–17, 255, 313
Maps (mapping), and conservation, 87, 172, 183, 188–89, 190, 200, 233
Marshland. *See* Salt marshes; Wetlands
Maryland, 117
Massachusetts, 187–99. *See also* specific locations
Massachusetts Trustees of the Reservation, 54
Meskill, Thomas J., 171
Metcalf, Lee, 164
Michigan, Lake, 137
Miller, Arthur, 14–15, 25–26, 165–66
Mining. *See* Coal industry; Gravel mining; Strip mining
"Monograph on Land Trusts," 133
Montana, 109–10
Morrissey, William, 192
Mount Kisco, N.Y., 39–41
"Movement Dynamics in Action," 271–74
Murray, Linda A., 133
Myers, Anna Laura, 41–43
Mystic, Conn., 50–54; Allyn Street Connector project, 51–54

Nader, Ralph, 10, 241, 277
Nassau-Suffolk (Long Island) Regional Planning Board, 199–200
National Wildlife (monthly), 313
Natural History (monthly), 313
Nature Conservancy, 40, 111, 114, 150, 151, 216, 219–23, 231, 312
Negroes. *See* Blacks
Nevada, 11
Newburgh, N.Y., proposed jetport in, 28–29
New Canaan, Conn.: Land Trust, 133–34; RCA and housing in, 264–66
"New Canaan Experience," 133–34
Newell, Harmon F., Jr., 197–99
New England (*see also* specific locations): conservation commissions in, 83, 184–86ff.; land acquisition in, 123ff., 138, 146
New Hampshire, 98, 100–2, 127, 134; Enabling Act, 187
"New Hampshire Tomorrow," 134
New Jersey, 117; Farm Land Assessment Act, 46; Great Swamp National Wildlife Refuge Wilderness, 177; Green Acres bond issue, 10;

historic site preservation in, 44–50; Open State Policy Commission, 10
New Milford, Conn., 153–54
Newsweek (magazine), 29
Newtown, Conn.: Conservation Commission, 192–93; Forest Association, 123
New York City: community planning boards, 23–24; Corona school plan, 36; Crotona Park housing, 21; Forest Hills public housing controversy, 261–62; Planning Commission, 23, 24; West Side Drive and Riverside Park, 18–20
New Yorker (magazine), 2
New York Magazine, 21, 24
New York State (*see also* specific locations): Hudson River Expressway, 9; I-684 Highway, 36; landsaving organizations, 129; Newburgh jetport, 28–29; transportation bond issue, 9–10; Urban Development Corporation (UDC), 88
New York Times, 20, 28, 31, 98, 101, 102–3, 105–6, 179–80
Nisqually River Delta project, 227–28
Nissitissit River Land Trust, 127
Nixon, Richard M., "Message on Energy" speech by, 251
North Andover, Mass., Stevens-Coolidge Place preservation in, 54–57, 175
Northeast Utilities, 149–74, 269–70; Grid System, 157
Northwestern Connecticut Linear Park, 74, 82
Nuclear energy power plants, 175, 250–52, 269

O'Beirne, Kathleen, 52–54
Oil industry, 3, 8, 14, 99–100, 253, 255–56, 269
Open Lands Project (Ill.), 136–37
Open Space Action Committee, 231
Open Space Institute, 119, 133, 233–34, 312
Open-space programs, 121–22ff., 139–47, 181ff. (*see also* Land); economic growth and development and, 140–47, 246–68; planning and, 121–22ff., 139–47, 181ff., 199–213, 246–68
Oregon, 27, 240
Organizations, environmental, 7, 111–

47 *passim*, 214–34; help from, 214–34, 311–13
Ottinger, Richard L., 252
Overland Realty, 45–46
Oyster Bay, N.Y., 177–78

Page, Gordon, 130–31
Paparazzo Brothers, 202–11
Paper industry, 102
Parks (parkland), 1, 18–20, 21–22, 74, 176–77, 179
Pauling, Linus, 251
Pennsylvania, 116–17
Percy, Christopher, 101–2
Pesticides, 184, 193–94
Peterson, Russell W., 27
Peterson, Walter, 101
Petitions, use of, 172–73
Pitts, Carolyn, 50
Planning, open space programs and, 121–22ff., 139–47, 181ff., 199–213, 246–68
Planning and zoning commissions, 6, 183, 184, 186, 189, 194, 196, 199–213
Politicians (public officials), 5, 6, 7–8, 16–23 *passim*, 33, 34, 39–42, 44, 47, 52–58, 67, 68–69, 71, 72, 179, 237–42 (*see also* Government entries; Legislators); and landsaving, 112–13, 115ff., 182, 183, 194–95, 201ff.
Politics, conservation commissions and, 87–88, 212–13
Pollution, 2, 11, 23, 27, 33, 35, 91, 98, 101–2, 105, 139, 143, 149, 163, 184, 187, 189, 192, 193–95, 229–30, 277, 281
Pomperaug River, 23
Population growth, 27–28, 62–63, 93–94, 98, 136
Post, Herschel, 21
Potomac Park, 176–77, 179
Pough, Richard H., 216–23, 242
Pound Ridge, N.Y., 196–99; Indian Hill conservation in, 197–99
Power (power plants), 250–55, 269–70. *See also* Electric power; Nuclear energy power plants
Power (utility) line construction, 3, 10, 12, 14–15, 54, 149–74, 180
Preferential tax treatment. *See* Tax breaks

Preservationists (environmentalists), 6–18ff., 32–58, 59ff., 87–110, 111–47, 246–68 (*see also* Citizen activists; specific aspects, groups, locations); and building of local safeguards, 181–213; and development, 195ff., 246–68 (*see also* Development); organizations of (*see* Organizations, environmental); outside help for, 214–45, 311–12; and positive protest, 148–80; staying power of, 269–82

President's Council on Environmental Quality, 9

Price, Irving, 95–96

Private property concept, 278–82

Progress (*see also* Development; Growth): local safeguards and, 186ff.; preservationists against, 32ff.; price of, 4ff., 31; property values and environmental equity and, 25–31

Property owners, 15–16, 88ff., 100–1 (*see also* Property values; Taxes); absentee, 15–17, 100–1, 214–15; environmental threat and positive protest, 148–80; homeowners groups, 215; local safeguards for, 181–213; outside help for, 214ff.; spoilers and exploiters and, 88ff., 111–47, 246–68

Property power, meaning and uses of term, 4–31, 32ff.

Property values (land values), environmental protection and, 25–27, 88ff., 111–47, 246–68 (*see also* Property owners); local safeguards and, 181–213

Protest (protest movement), and environmental threat, 38, 74ff., 148–80; outside help for, 214–15; staying power of, 269–82

Protestant Protective Society for the Preservation of Old St. Hilary's Church, 178

Publications, conservation, 312–13. *See also* specific publications

Public hearings, 172–73

Public officials. *See* Politicians (public officials)

Public opinion, and conservation, 34–36, 90, 146–47, 188; positive protest and, 148ff., 154ff.; education of public and, 182, 232, 250

Public Rights (public interest), 181–213, 246ff.; and local safeguards, 181–213, 246ff.; and positive protest to environmental threat, 148–80

Public Utilities Environmental Standards Act (Conn.), 167–68

PUC (Public Utilities Commission), 54, 151–70

Quay, Mrs. Charles, 174

Racism, zoning and, 260–63

Ramsey, Robert W., 259

Ratchford, William, 171

RCA, 264–66

Real estate development, 102–3, 104–10. *See also* Development

Recreation, land resources and use and, 93, 100–2, 103, 107ff., 136, 142, 183. *See also* Parks (parkland)

Redding, Conn.: Citizens Action Council, 66ff., 82–86; Conservation Commission, 64, 75, 77; and land acquisition programs, 122, 130–31, 133, 135, 285–88; and land tax breaks, 117–18; Land Trust, 130–31, 133, 135, 285–88; Land Trust easement, 303–6; Land Trust incorporation certificate, 307–9; Planning Commission, 64ff., 84–86; and power line construction, 12–15, 153; and Route 7 highway development, 60–86

Redwoods, preservation of, 9, 224, 231

Regional Plan Association, 122, 264

Remsenberg (Long Island) Civic Association, 174

Resort developers, 88, 107ff.

Reston, James, 7

Rheingold, Paul D., 235

Richards, Thomas, 220

Richardson Paul, 108–9

Rickerby, Arthur and Wanda, 152, 153, 154, 155, 160, 167, 168, 169–70, 171

Ridgefield, Conn., 67, 68, 70, 72, 73, 80; Conservation Commission, 193–95

Rimer, Edward S., 167

Rivers (streams), 89–90, 98, 101–2, 127, 184, 248. *See also* Water resources; Wetlands

Riverside Park (New York City), 18-20
Rockefeller, Avery, 219
Rockefeller, Nelson, 9–10, 18, 28–29, 36
Roemer, Roberts, 47, 49, 50
Rogala, Dietrich, 36
Rogers, Henrietta, 265–66
ROLI (Redding Open Lands, Inc.), 79–80; certificate of incorporation of, 307–9
Roll, Barbara, 77–78
Roper, Elmer, 61, 63
Rosenthal, Benjamin, 262
Roxbury, Conn., 153–54, 155, 165
Rubin, Selma, 42–43
Rural Land Foundation (Lincoln, Mass.), 143–45
Russell, Lewis, 143

Sacco, Humbert, 67, 68
Saco, Maine, 15–17
St. Joseph, Mo., 1
Salt marshes, 140–43. *See also* Wetlands
San Francisco, Calif., 178–79
San Jose, Calif., 28, 29–30; *Mercury News,* 28
Santa Barbara, Calif., 41–43; Master Plan, 41–43
Santa Clara County, Calif., 140
Satterthwaite, Sheafe, 267
Saugatuck Reservoir (Conn.), 150
Savannah, Ga., 36
Save-the-Redwoods League, 231
Sax, Joseph L., 5–6, 233, 236–37, 241, 248
Scenic Hudson Preservation Conference, 174–75
Scheffey, Andrew J. W., 184–86, 188
Scientists, and conservation, 229–30, 251
Self-interest, enlightened, as key to landsaving, 113ff., 133ff.
Sevin (pesticide), 184, 193–94
Sewage, 23, 107, 128, 192
Shelford, Victor E., 219
Shilstone, Arthur, 131
Sierra Club, 10, 215–16, 223–26, 269, 312; chapters and representatives, 225
Silent Spring, 32
Simon, Robert E., 196–99

Sive, David, 156, 166, 215, 234, 236, 312
Smith, Ned, 119, 233–34
Soil(s), 13, 136, 183, 188–89
Southbury, Conn.: Clean Water Task Force, 23; Heritage Village development, 202–6, 208–9
Southeast Open Spaces, Inc. (SOS), 129
"Special 12-Page Report on Raw Land: How to Find, Finance & Develop It" (Prentice-Hall), 94–95
Sports Illustrated, 280
Springfield (Mass.) Conservation Commission, 187–88
Stahr, Elvis, 228–29, 246, 249–50
Staten Island, N.Y., Annual Greenbelt Hikes in, 175
Steichen, Edward, 61; sale of property of, 74–80
Stern, Peter, 150
Sternlief, George, 263
Stewardship (Little), 133, 234
Storm King Mountain, 217
Stratton, Vt., 97
Streams. See Rivers (streams)
Strip mining, 14, 254–55
Subdividers, 41–43
Suburban Action Institute, 264–66
Suburbs, 26–27, 62, 138, 210, 246–68, 279; industry and development of, 104–7 (*see also* Development)
Suffolk County, Long Island, 37–38, 174, 199–200; Defenders of the Environment, 37; zoning, 37–38

Tahoe (Lake) region, 107–10
Tax breaks (preferential tax treatment), and landsaving, 81, 113, 114ff., 123, 199
Taxes (taxpayers), and land conservation, 5–31, 41–43, 115–17, 119–20, 123, 137, 138–40, 141, 142, 204, 257–59, 264, 265. *See also* Property owners; Tax breaks
Tax Reform Act of 1969, 134
Taylor, Patsy and Gray, 228
Time Magazine, 26–27
Tocks Island, 9, 175–76
TREE (Toward Restoring Earth's Environment), 7
TREES (To Reassess Ecology-Environment Safety), 52–54

"Use value" concept of land, 117, 118

Vahur, Lembit, 68, 70, 73
Vermont, 96, 97, 100–2, 108; Environmental Board, 239–40
Village Voice, 261, 262–63
Voting (elections), 5, 6, 42, 212–13, 237–39; and land acquisition, 138–39

Wallace, Anthony E., 168–69
Washington, Lake (Seattle), 229–30
Water pollution, 23. *See also* Pollution
Water resources, 88, 89, 101–2, 107, 138–39, 182, 189, 229–30, 248, 256 (*see also* Rivers; Wetlands); local ordinances and, 289–302
Watershed associations, 181, 212
Wayland, Mass., land conservation in, 138–39, 142–43
Webster, Sally, 56
Weston, Conn., 153, 159, 161–62, 163

Westport, Conn., 126; Cockenoe Island, 175, 238–39; Design Development District zoning law, 126; Save Cockenoe Island Committee, 175
Wetlands, 88–89, 132, 177–78, 182, 183, 189, 194; local ordinances and, 189, 192, 289–302; zoning and, 140–43
White, William T., 11
Whyte, William H. ("Holly"), 118, 195, 210
Woodcock, Mortimer J., 194

Yannacone, Victor J., Jr., 37, 235, 312

Zoar, Lake, 23
Zoning, 16–17, 22, 37–38, 41–43, 45–50, 60, 64, 65, 80–86, 90, 96–97, 104–5, 126, 140–43, 183, 181, 183, 201, 202–11; cluster, 145–46, 195–99; and housing, 260–68